Front cover: Ben Revell and others, wearing the 1890s uniform of 1st Battalion (57th) Middlesex Regiment, in a re-enactment at Kenilworth Castle.

Designed by Collins & Brown Limited
Reproduction by Dot Gradations, Chelmsford, Essex
Printed by Jarrolds, Norwich
ISBN 1 85074 624 9

Foreword

As the leading conservation organisation in England, we care for an extraordinary range of historic properties. We are only able to do this by working together with Government and local authorities, private owners and charitable institutions, churches and local communities and, of course, the public. We never forget that the heritage is yours and it is our job to look after it.

English Heritage's primary concern is with the continuity of the heritage that our predecessors built. We are, in effect, custodians for future generations, safeguarding the best of the past so that it has a place in the future.

Last year almost 10 million people visited our properties and we are constantly trying to make our historic sites more visitor-friendly and to increase the number of visitors who are able to enjoy them. As a member of English Heritage you can visit all of our properties free and provide us with the vital income necessary to conserve the nation's heritage. Last year our membership increased to 340,000 and we earned £17 million, without which we could not operate.

1996 promises to be an exciting year for members and visitors alike. We are continuing to expand our hugely popular special events. As well as our musical concerts and historical re-enactments, we are putting on a festival of living history at Kirby Hall, a Regency fair at Wrest Park and just under 300 mini-events during the summer holidays. In addition we have acquired a number of new responsibilites in the last year, including the management and conservation of the Albert Memorial, where there is now a Visitor Centre, and Eltham Palace.

This year's handbook provides detailed information on all of the over 400 properties in our care – from ancient monuments and historic houses to Roman villas and romantic ruins. It also includes over 20 special features on some of our more important and interesting sites, such as Battle Abbey, Brodsworth Hall, Dover Castle, Hadrian's Wall and, of course, Stonehenge, the most remarkable of them all.

I hope this will encourage you to visit as many of the properties as you can and enjoy the fascinating glimpse that they offer into England's past.

SIR JOCELYN STEVENS
Chairman

Introduction

This handbook provides you with the information you need to visit all the English Heritage sites around the country. To make it easier for you, we have divided England into six regions – South West, South East, Greater London, Eastern Counties, Central England and North – and listed the sites alphabetically within the region. Each region is colour-coded, as shown on the key map on page 209, which, with the maps on following pages, shows the area each region covers. Map references appear at the beginning of every entry.

Dan Revell in the 1890s uniform of Ist Battalion (57th) Middlesex Regiment, at Kenilworth Castle

The diversity of historic properties makes it important to check the key on the inside front cover so that you have a fairly clear idea about what you are going to see. We have retained the classification of sites introduced last year to make it easier for you to choose those of particular interest. Most are self-explanatory. Of the others, 'Humps and Bumps' are archaeological remains – many still remarkably intact – 'Pot Luck' can be anything from a medieval shrine to a tiny Norman priory, and 'Far From the Crowd' are remote sites that are mostly free but tend to be less easily accessible.

The level of facilities also varies from restaurants, shops, car parks and toilets at the larger properties to nothing at all at free sites in more remote parts of the country. Please check the symbols for a site before visiting.

Red coats of 1746 at Kenilworth (right) and family fun at Teddy Bears Picnic, Bayham Old Abbey (below)

Planning your visit

Opening times

- Full details of opening arrangements are shown under each entry.
- Many properties are open daily but this varies in the winter months.
- Where you can visit a property only by prior arrangement, contact details are provided.
- Where an entry states that a property is open 'Any reasonable time', we ask that you visit only during daylight hours for reasons of safety and to avoid disturbance to adjoining properties. We suggest these hours might be 1 April–31 Oct: daily, 10am–6pm (6pm/dusk – whichever is earlier – in Oct). 1 Nov–31 March: daily, 10am–4pm.
- For reasons of safety, many sites close at 6pm or dusk (whichever is earlier) in October. We define dusk as when the levels of light prevent a safe and enjoyable visit. You may wish to contact the site you intend to visit for further advice.
- Properties which are opened and locked by a 'keykeeper' have specific opening times. When this is so please contact the keykeeper.
- If anything is unclear please contact the custodian of the property, the appropriate regional office or our Customer Services department (see inside back cover).

Children enjoying a visit to the Medieval Merchant's House, Southampton (below)

Admission charges

- All admission prices in this handbook are valid from 1 April 1996 to 31 March 1997.
- Admission to all properties is free to English Heritage members unless otherwise stated. Most special events are also free to members.
- Admission charges for non-members are set out as in follows: *£1.20/90p/60p*.
    - The first figure is the charge for adults.
    - The second for concessions (senior citizens, unemployed people – on production of UB40 – and students – on production of student union card).
    - The third for children (under fives are admitted free).
- Group discounts are available at most English Heritage properties – a 15% discount for groups of 11 or more, with an accompanying group leader being admitted free (at Stonehenge the discount is 10%). An extra person is admitted free for every 20 people in the group. Contact our Customer Services department (see inside back cover) for a free copy of our Group Visits Guide.
- Student groups and school parties are admitted free to English Heritage properties provided they book in advance through the relevant English Heritage regional office (see inside back cover).

Travelling by road, train or bus

- The entry for each property includes brief directions on how to get there by road, rail or bus, where a suitable service exists.
- We are grateful to Barry S Doe for providing the public transport information. He will welcome letters from anyone who finds an error in the directions or can suggest an easier route (please write to 25 Newmorton Road, Moordown, Bournemouth, Dorset BH9 3NU or telephone 01202 528707).

Discover great days out for kids

When you visit

- We warmly welcome families with children of all ages to our properties. However, inside some of our grander properties we regret that babies cannot be carried in back carriers as this increases the risk of damage to house contents. Alternative means of carrying babies are provided free of charge at these sites.
- Photography is welcomed in the grounds of all our properties provided it is not for commercial use. We regret that, for conservation reasons, photography is not permitted inside certain properties. Please enquire on arrival.
- Smoking is not permitted inside any of the historic houses listed in this guide.
- We aim to welcome dogs at as many sites as possible. Where there are restrictions on dogs there will be symbols (see inside front cover) in the individual entry indicating that dogs are either only allowed in certain areas, that they have to be on leads, or, that they are not allowed. Guide dogs and hearing dogs for the deaf are welcome at all our properties.
- Unforeseen closures of our sites are extremely rare. However, to avoid possible disappointment we do advise ringing the site before your visit.

Lively medieval musical at Kenilworth

Special features and facilities

Visitors with disabilities

- English Heritage aims, wherever possible, to make our properties open to everyone who wishes to enjoy them. Over 100 of the properties in this guide are marked as suitable for people with disabilities, indicating that much of the site is easily accessible.
- At many properties there are personal stereo guided tours specifically for wheelchair users or visitors with a visual impairment. At some, there are personal stereo tours in basic language for visitors with learning difficulties.
- At our properties, staff will be pleased to assist visitors with special needs, if at all possible. We recommend you contact the custodian at the site in advance so that preparations can be made to ensure a more rewarding visit.
- Admission is free for the assisting companion of a visitor with disabilities.
- Our Guide for Visitors with Disabilities (also available in braille, large print and on tape) gives full details. For a free copy please contact our Customer Services department (see inside back cover).

The personal stereo tour at Hailes Abbey (left), and visitors with a guidebook at Stokesay (below)

Guidebooks, tape tours and interactive audio tours

- Guidebooks, often illustrated in colour, are on sale at almost all the properties where an entrance fee is charged. If you prefer, you can buy guidebooks in advance of your visit through our postal sales service (telephone 01604 781163 for a catalogue of publications and order form).
- Personal stereo guides, which combine history with drama and music to add an extra touch of realism to your visit, are now available at nearly 40 sites.
- Interactive audio tours at Battle Abbey, Stonehenge, Framlingham Castle and Dover Castle's Secret Wartime Tunnels allow you to control the information you hear as you move around the site.

Families and children

- We welcome families and children to our properties, and at many sites there are special features, exhibitions, or educational facilities to make the visits particularly interesting for children. Look out for the family friendly symbol (●) and free activity sheets.
- From April to October, special events take place at our sites, most of which are especially suitable for children.

Shops and restaurants

- Many of our properties have a shop offering an attractive range of souvenirs, gifts and books. No two English Heritage shops are the same, as our merchandise is carefully selected to suit each individual property.
- Snacks are available at many sites, while at others you can enjoy a sit-down meal in one of our restaurants or tea rooms, which are often located within the historic buildings. See individual entries for details.

Displays and exhibitions

- At most properties, display panels explain how the site would have appeared in the past, often with the help of reconstruction drawings or interactive displays.
- There are special exhibitions at many sites highlighting particular aspects of the site's history.
- Other properties host temporary exhibitions of paintings and sculpture.

Special events and concerts

- Our special events programme runs from April to October and ranges from military displays and re-enactments of famous battles to family entertainments and re-creations of life in days gone by. Among this year's highlights are

Avebury museum (left) which houses one of the most important prehistoric archaeological collections in Britain

'History in action', a festival of living history at Kirby Hall, 15–16 June; a Regency fair at Wrest Park, 10–11 August; and 'Dover Castle on the eve of D-day', 25–26 August.

- We have a summer open-air concert series, combining world-class performances with superb surroundings. This year's highlights will be the celebration of Edward Heath's 80th birthday at Kenwood and two fabulous operas – *The Pearl Fishers* and Gershwin's *Porgy and Bess*, not forgetting our firework displays which accompany many of the concerts.
- For full details please ask for our free Events and Concert Diaries, available from sites, or contact our Customer Services department (see inside back cover).

A concert (above) and fireworks (left) at Marble Hill

Elizabethan Living History (above)

If you have any queries about the information in this handbook, or any other aspect of English Heritage work, please contact our Customer Services department (PO Box 9019, London, W1A 0JA. Tel 0171 973 3434). We aim to provide information, answer your questions and to investigate on your behalf the service we provide if it does not reach the very high standards we have set for ourselves. In the meantime we do hope you enjoy visiting our various sites and share our pride in England's rich history.

Membership

- English Heritage plays a central role in the conservation of all England's historic buildings and archaeological sites through the grants and advice it offers.
- By becoming a member you will be making a personal commitment to the protection of our heritage.
- Members can visit over 400 English Heritage properties free of charge.
- Members are also entitled to reduced admission to a number of other historic attractions in England (see pp.198–99) and to free or half-price admission to more than 100 properties in Scotland, Wales and on the Isle of Man (see pp 200–208).
- Members can enjoy our special events and concerts free or at a reduced price.
- There is a range of exclusive activities – open days, weekend breaks and cruises for members.
- Members receive *Heritage Today*, an exclusive, full-colour quarterly magazine.

To join, please contact our Customer Services department on 0171 973 3434.

BRODSWORTH HALL

One of England's most beautiful Victorian country houses, Brodsworth Hall has survived almost completely intact since the 1860s – an extraordinary time warp of richly marbled walls, Axminster carpets, sculpture, family portraits and even a billiard room scorebook. Opened for the first time last year, Brodsworth Hall and gardens offer visitors a breathtaking journey through the intriguing passage of time, from the rich and luxurious life of England's landed gentry more than a century ago to the late 1980s. When the hall was bequeathed to English Heritage, conservation policy was aimed at preserving the faded grandeur rather than the strict restoration to its past condition.

In the long-abandoned kitchen, visitors can readily picture how meals were really made in the age of Mrs Beeton. And deep in the cluttered remains of the servants' wing, it is all too easy to imagine how the working class fared below stairs, with all the intrigues, privileges, benefits and drawbacks that such an insular Victorian existence brought.

Looking east towards the house from the flower garden with the central fountain in the foreground

Brodsworth's history has certainly been fraught. Rather like Jarndyce and Jarndyce in Charles Dickens' *Bleak House*, the celebrated action contesting the 1797 will of Peter Thellusson 'dragged its dreary length through the Court' in the first half of the 19th century. Unlike Dickens's fictional case, the outcome was not 'perennially hopeless'. By tying his wealth up until the death of his last grandson, hoping to create a monumental fortune and rich dynasty, Thellusson only produced generations of anguish and work for a succession of lawyers. The matter was finally resolved by Parliament in 1859, by which time the estate had been considerably reduced. Two descendants were entitled to share it, and as part of his inheritance Charles Sabine Thellusson

Watercolour of the south front of Brodsworth showing only minor differences from the house as it was built

One of the marble greyhounds that flank each set of steps down from the south front of the house. Greyhounds also feature in the family crest.

acquired the old Yorkshire property of Brodsworth Hall with its rich estate.

The new house that Charles Sabine built gives away little to suggest that it had such a contested origin. The exterior is formal, Italianate, four-square, and lacks fanciful detail, but was built to impress. The architect, Chevalier Casentini, had met Thellusson in Italy.

His designs were executed under the supervision of a little-known English architect, Philip Wilkinson.

Marble statues (left) feature in the gardens as well as inside the house

It is said that Casentini never came to Yorkshire to view what he had designed, fearing the cold, and a setting wholly different from the pastoral landscape and blue skies he had drawn.

At the same time, a new garden incorporating both formal and informal features was created, all contained within magnificent parkland.

Statues in the woodland (above)

The flower garden (right) with its symmetrical beds cut into the turf

If the exterior seems a little pompous, the interior is Brodsworth's chief glory. The entrance hall, with its gold, red and marbled walls, is a prelude to the splendours of the inner halls and reception rooms.

The colours provide a dramatic background to another of the house's remarkable features, the succession of white marble statues with typically Victorian themes. Casentini created a grand processional route through the house from the entrance hall, via the soaring height of the top-lit staircase, to the pillared south hall. The ceremonial feel is emphasized by the poise of the statues.

Nymph going to Bathe **(left) by Giuseppe Lazzarini, a statue in the South Hall (below)**

While some sculptures are by known, principally Italian, artists, pieces by little-known artists were chosen for their sentimentality or charm. Of all the sculptures, Argenti's 'Sleeping Venus' is particularly memorable, lying beneath the

The Doncaster Cup, won by Rataplan at the St Leger in 1855. The silver trophy depicts an episode from Walter Scott's *Ivanhoe*

Charles Sabine Thellusson, the builder of Brodsworth Hall, as Captain of the 12th Royal Lancers, by Alfred Courbould, 1848

The drawing room (left) with many of the original furnishings from Lapworths

huge painted-glass internal window at the end of the hall. The window was inserted by Wilkinson in order to lighten what would otherwise have been the impenetrable gloom of Casentini's original design. With its colourful garlands and playful cherubs, it provides a busy foil to the statue's lines.

Rich decorative schemes appear everywhere in the house: in the grand reception rooms, bedrooms and private quarters. The drawing room, with a dividing screen of Corinthian columns, red silk damask on the walls, sparkling chandeliers and gilding, is a grand monument that would not have disappointed the Thellussons' ambitious ancestor. The dining room, intended as much for show as for eating, contains some of the finest paintings in the house. Away from the finery of reception rooms are the more intimate spaces of the library and morning room. Each has original wallpaper, a hand-painted pattern of flowers, roses and trellises resembling leather wallcoverings. Looking less aged, but older than most objects in the house, is a stunning, 1725 portrait of Peter Thellusson's mother.

Library with the 1725 portrait of Peter Thellusson's mother

The dining room (right) with many family portraits including one of Charles Sabine's father and grandmother, Charles and Sabine, painted in 1807 (above)

The inner staircase hall with its marbled walls, white marble statues and crimson carpets

Walton **(below) by James Ward in 1821, one of the group of equestrian paintings that hang in the billiard room.**

When Brodsworth was first built and occupied, it amply fulfilled its role as a grand residence. Weekend parties or shoots on the estate were conducted in sumptuous style; and in the evenings the gentlemen would relax in the billiard room, which, since then, has survived remarkably untouched.

By the mid-19th century a billiard room was considered an essential part of a country house, and the one at Brodsworth retains its original massive table, supplied by Cox and Yemen of London, together with its wooden scoreboard and leather-bound book in which scores have been recorded since the 1880s. Two large ventilation hatches in the billiard room doubtless helped to disperse the gentlemen's cigar smoke, and the furnishings are completed by a remarkable collection of 19th-century equestrian paintings, which were assembled by the Theobald family and came to Brodsworth through a marriage settlement in 1850.

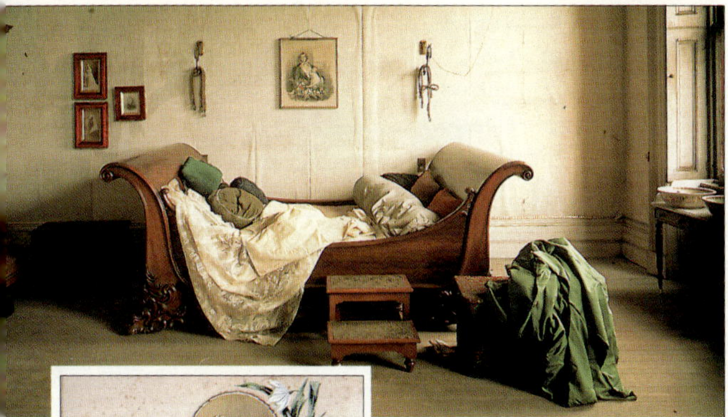

Bedroom 8 (above)with its boat-shaped bed or lit en bateau

Charles Sabine Thellusson's children (left) from a family album in about 1870

Some of the few remaining Victorian toys that are on display in Bedroom 5

The billiard room (left) with the scoreboard (above) and the leather-bound volume (far left) in which scores have been recorded since the 1880s

The bedrooms at Brodsworth have always been identified by a simple numbering system. Although much of their original decoration has been lost through frequent refurbishment, many pieces of mahogany furniture provided by Lapworths remain, including four half-tester (canopied) beds, marble-topped washstands, chests of drawers and armchairs.

Other intriguing features of the bedrooms include a magnificent bed – or *lit en bateau* – a selection of Victorian toys in the bedroom traditionally belonging to the head of the household, and the original furniture, including dressing table, washstand, low clothes press and fine central table in what was used for much of its history as a dressing room.

The servants were housed in a wing abutting the main block of the house. From the 1860s until about 1918 there would have been about ten female servants and several male.

The servant's bedrooms were originally quite comfortably decorated with furniture and carpets from Lapworths, and the housekeeper's bedroom had even better-quality furnishings. It was gradually turned over to storage, just as the original housemaids' sitting room became the laundry room, with the decline in the number of servants after World War I. The rooms are now presented largely in the state of disuse in which they were found.

The Victorian kitchen is one of the most delightful features. Its 'Eagle Range' by Farr and Sons of Doncaster and its grained dressers containing a vast range of cooking utensils, show the sheer space and equipment needed to cater for a well-to-do Victorian family and its staff. After the war, it too was used for storage and was gradually abandoned, although many of its original contents can still be seen today.

The butler had easy access to the front door and main part of the house, and the butler's pantry was where silver plate, cutlery and glasses were cleaned and stored, in a massive cupboard with sliding doors, originally installed for the sum of £10.

Both house and estate flourished, bolstered by the profits from coal mining, until World War I. Those days of style were numbered, however, not only because it was so costly to maintain, but also because of the vagaries of inheritance.

Pewter and copper moulds for jellies, patties and ices, and other utensils in the kitchen

The kitchen (top), abandoned since 1919, with the 'Eagle Range', made by Farr and Sons of Doncaster, with two ovens to each side of the central fire (above)

Each of Charles Sabine's sons inherited the house. On the last brother's death in 1931, Brodsworth passed to his nephew, Charles Grant-Dalton. The Grant-Daltons struggled valiantly to keep Brodsworth going. Gradually, they shut away parts of the house, and, almost inadvertently, preserved house and contents for the future. Sylvia Grant-Dalton, widow of

Part of the large collection of pots and pans in the kitchen

Gas mask, a reminder of World War II

Charles and subsequently of his cousin Eustace, lived in the immense house largely alone between 1970 and her death in 1988. She became something of a national treasure by featuring in one of Lucinda Lambton's sparky television essays, when the splendours of the house were revealed, as well as the efforts to maintain them. Her daughter, Pamela Williams, bequeathed Brodsworth to English Heritage, although sadly she did not live to see it open to the public in 1995.

Brodsworth's history is written everywhere in its decoration: in the carpets in the library, laid one upon the other as each wore out; the model yacht propped on a towel rail in Bedroom 7; the High Victorian taste, marbling and painted decorative effects; the sculptures adorning the house; and the grandeur of the ground floor. The gardens are now being coaxed from their very overgrown state. They include croquet lawns and a large formal flower garden to the west of the house; a quarry garden, 'The Grove', set among tall sheltering trees; and a formal rose garden, with clipped box hedges and a central iron pergola. The house itself has emerged from its slumber. Brodsworth, the grand Victorian sleeping beauty, has now awakened.

Exhibitions at Brodsworth include 'Family Life and Brodsworth', 'Serving the House' and 'The Gardens'.
Free Children's Activity Sheet available.
Open *30 March–27 Oct: Tues–Sun & Bank Holidays, 1pm–6pm (6pm/dusk in Oct). Gardens open 12 noon. Guided tours are available from 10am for pre-booked parties.*
Entry *£4.20/£3.20/£2.10.*
01302 722598
(colour) ('Brodsworth Hall Tearoom') (house and formal gardens)
In Brodsworth, 6m NW of Doncaster. W of A1 between A635 & A638.
(OS Map 111; ref SE 507071.)
Yorkshire Traction 211 Doncaster–Barnsley; Yorkshire Rider 497/8 Doncaster–Wakefield (Tel 0114 276 8688).
South Elmsall 4m; Moorthorpe 4½m; Doncaster 5½m.

Abbotsbury Abbey Remains

DORSET (211, 3G)

The remains of a cloister building of this Benedictine abbey, founded in 1044.

Open *Any reasonable time.*
Entry *Free.*
In Abbotsbury, off B3157, near churchyard. (OS Map 194; ref SY 578852.)
Upwey 7½m.

Avebury Museum (above and left)

Avebury

WILTSHIRE

See also Silbury Hill, The Sanctuary, West Kennet Avenue, West Kennet Long Barrow and Windmill Hill.

Avebury Museum

WILTSHIRE (211/212, 5J)

The investigation of Avebury Stone Circles was largely the work of Alexander Keiller in the 1930s. He put together one of the most important prehistoric archaeological collections in Britain, and this can be seen in the Avebury Museum.

Open *1 April–31 Oct: daily, 10am–6pm. 1 Nov–31 March: daily, 10am–4pm (closed 24–26 Dec, 1 Jan).*
Entry *£1.50/80p. (Collection on loan to the National Trust.)*
01672 539250
(in village)
In Avebury 7m W of Marlborough. (OS Map173; ref SU 100700.)
Thamesdown 49A Swindon–Devizes/Marlborough; Wilts & Dorset 5/6 Salisbury–Swindon (Tel: 01345 090 899). All pass close to BR Swindon.
Pewsey 10m, Swindon 11m.

Avebury Stone circles

Avebury Stone Circles

WILTSHIRE (211/212, 5J)

Complex, gigantic and mysterious, the Circles were constructed 4,000 years ago and originally comprising more than 180 stones. The remains of the Circles still surround the later village of Avebury.

Open *Any reasonable time.*
(Site owned and managed by the National Trust.)
Entry *Free.*
🚻 *(in village)* P ♿ ⊛
➲ *In Avebury 7m W of Marlborough.*
(OS Map173; ref SU 103700.)
🚌 *Thamesdown 49A Swindon–Devizes/Marlborough; Wilts & Dorset 5/6 Salisbury–Swindon (Tel: 01345 090 899). All pass close to BR Swindon.*
🚆 *Pewsey 10m, Swindon 11m.*

Bant's Carn burial chamber

Ballowall Barrow

St Just, CORNWALL
(210, 1A)

In a spectacular position, this is an unusual Bronze Age chambered tomb with a complex layout.

Open *Any reasonable time.*
(Site managed by the National Trust.)
Entry *Free.*
⊛
➲ *1m W of St Just, near Carn Gloose.*
(OS Map 203; ref SW 354313.)
🚌 *Western National 10/A/B, 11/A BR Penzance–St Just, thence 1m (Tel: 01209 719988).*
🚆 *Penzance 8m.*

Bant's Carn Burial Chamber and Halangy Down Ancient Village

St Mary's, ISLES OF SCILLY
(210, 4A)

In a wonderful scenic location, on a hillside above the site of the ancient Iron Age village, you will find this Bronze Age burial mound with entrance passage and chamber.

Open *Any reasonable time.*
Entry *Free.*
⊛
➲ *1m N of Hugh Town.*
(OS Map 203; ref SV 911124.)

Bayard's Cove Fort

Dartmouth, DEVON (211, 2E)

A small artillery fort built 1509–10 to defend the harbour entrance.

Open *Any reasonable time.*
Entry *Free.*
⊛
➲ *In Dartmouth, on riverfront.*
(OS Map 202; ref SX 879510.)
🚌 *Bayline 200 BR Paignton–Kingswear, 22 Brixham–Kingswear (connections from BR Paignton), thence ferry to Dartmouth (Tel: 01803 613226); Western National/Tally Ho! 89, 91, X93 from Totnes (passes BR Totnes) (Tel: 01392 382800).*
🚆 *Paignton 7m via vehicle ferry.*

Belas Knap Long Barrow

GLOUCESTERSHIRE
(212/217, 7H)

A good example of a Neolithic long barrow, with the mound still intact and surrounded by a stone wall. The chamber tombs, where the remains of 31 people were found, have been opened up so that visitors can see inside.

Open *Any reasonable time.*
Entry *Free.*
⊛
➲ *2m S of Winchcombe, near Charlton Abbots, ½ mile on Cotswold Way.*
(OS Map 163; ref SP 021254.)
🚌 *Castleways from Cheltenham to within 1¾m (Tel: 01242 602949).*
🚆 *Cheltenham 9m.*

Berry Pomeroy Castle (above) and the castle gatehouse (left)

Berry Pomeroy Castle

DEVON (211, 2E)

A romantic late-medieval castle, unusual in combining the remains of a large castle with a flamboyant courtier's mansion. It is reputed to be haunted.

Picnic spot of exceptional beauty.

Open *1 April–31 Oct: daily, 10am–6pm (6pm/dusk in Oct).*

Entry *£2.00/£1.50/£1.00.*

01803 866618

(grounds & ground floor only) *(not managed by English Heritage)*

2½m E of Totnes off A385. (OS Map 202; ref SX 839623.)

Western National 149 BR Torquay–Totnes (passes close to BR Totnes) (Tel: 01392 382800).

Totnes 3½m.

Blackbury Camp

DEVON (211, 3F)

An Iron Age hillfort, defended by a bank and ditch.

Open *Any reasonable time.*

Entry *Free.*

1½m SW of Southleigh off B3174/A3052. (OS Map 192; ref SY 188924.)

Honiton 6½m.

Blackfriars

Gloucester, GLOUCESTERSHIRE (212/217, 7H)

A small Dominican priory church. Most of the original 13th-century church remains, including a rare scissor-braced roof.

Open *Please contact Regional Office for further information (Tel: 0117 975 0700).*

Entry *Free.*

In Ladybellegate St off Southgate St and Blackfriars Walk. (OS Map 162; ref SO 830186.)

From surrounding areas (Tel: 01452 425543).

Gloucester ½ m.

Bowhill

Exeter, DEVON (211, 3E)

A mansion of considerable status built *c.*1500 by a member of the Holland family. The impressive Great Hall has been carefully restored by English Heritage craftsmen using traditional materials and techniques.

Open *By guided tour only, please contact Regional Office (Tel: 0117 975 0700), or Exeter Tourist Information Centre (Tel: 01392 265700).*
Entry *Free.*

1½m SW of Exeter on B3212. (OS Map 192; ref SX 906916.)
Exeter Mini-Bus C, P from City Centre (Tel: 01392 56231).
Exeter, St Thomas ¾m.

Bowhill

Bradford-on-Avon Tithe Barn

WILTSHIRE (211/212, 5H)
A medieval stone-built barn with slate roof and wooden beamed interior.

Open *Daily, 10.30am–4pm (closed 25 Dec). Keykeeper.*
Entry *Free.*

¼m S of town centre, off B3109. (OS Map 173; ref ST 824604.)
Badgerline X4 Bath–Salisbury, Badgerline 265 Bath–Frome (Tel: 01345 090 899).
Bradford-on-Avon ¼m.

Blackfriars

Bratton Camp and White Horse

WILTSHIRE (211/212, 5H)
A large Iron Age hill fort.

Open *Any reasonable time.*
Entry *Free.*

2m E of Westbury off B3098, 1m SW of Bratton. (OS Map 184; ref ST 900516.)
Westbury 3m.

Butter Cross

Dunster, SOMERSET (211, 4E)
A medieval stone cross.

Open *Any reasonable time.*
Entry *Free.*

Beside minor road to Alcombe, 350m (400 yds) NW of Dunster parish church. (OS Map 181; ref SS 988439.)
Southern National 28 BR Taunton–Minehead, also 38/9 from Minehead to within ½m (Tel: 01823 272033).
Dunster (W Somerset Rly) 1m.

Carn Euny Ancient Village

CORNWALL (210, 1A)

The remains of an Iron Age settlement, with foundations of stone huts and an intriguing curved underground passage, or *fogou*.

Open *Any reasonable time.*
Entry *Free.*

1¼m SW of Sancreed off A30. (OS Map 203; ref SW 402289.)
Western National 10/A/B, BR Penzance–St Just, to within 2m (Tel: 01209 719988).
Penzance 6m.

Chisbury Chapel

WILTSHIRE (211/212, 5J)

A thatched 13th-century chapel rescued from use as a farm building.

Open *Any reasonable time.*
Entry *Free.*

On classified road ¼m E of Chisbury off A4 6m E of Marlborough. (OS Map 174; ref SU 280658.)
Bedwyn 1m.

Chisbury Chapel

Christchurch Castle and Norman House

DORSET (211/212, 3J)

Early 12th-century Norman keep, and Constable's house, built c.1160.

Open *Any reasonable time.*
Entry *Free.*

In Christchurch, near Priory. (OS Map 195; ref SZ 160927.)
From surrounding areas (Tel: 01202 673555).
Christchurch ¾m.

Chysauster Ancient Village

CORNWALL (210, 1A)

A deserted Romano-Cornish village with a 'street' of eight

Chysauster Ancient Village with a temporary roof over one of the houses

well-preserved houses, each comprising a number of rooms around an open court.

***Open** 1 April–31 Oct: daily, 10am–6pm (6pm/dusk in Oct). Tel: 01326 212044 for details.*
***Entry** £1.50/£1.10/80p.*

2½m NW of Gulval off B3311. (OS Map 203; ref SW 473350.)
Western National 16 BR Penzance-St Ives to within 1½m (not Sundays) (Tel: 01209 719988).
Penzance 3½m.

Cirencester Amphitheatre

GLOUCESTERSHIRE (211/212/217, 6H)

A large well-preserved Roman amphitheatre.

***Open** Any reasonable time.*
***Entry** Free.*

Next to bypass W of town – access from town or along Chesterton Lane from W end of bypass onto Cotswold Ave. Park next to obelisk. (OS Map 163; ref SP 020014.)
Alex Cars/James rail-link from BR Kemble (Tel: 01452 425543).
Kemble 4m.

Cleeve Abbey

SOMERSET (211, 4F)

One of the few 13th-century monastic sites where you will see such a complete set of cloister buildings, including the refectory with its magnificent timber roof.

***Open** 1 April–31 Oct: daily, 10am–6pm (6pm/dusk in Oct). 1 Nov–31 March: Wed–Sun, 10am–4pm (closed 24-26 Dec, 1 Jan). Closed 1–2pm in winter.*
***Entry** £2.20/£1.70/£1.10.*
01984 640377
(grounds & ground floor only)
In Washford, ¼m S of A39. (OS Map 181; ref ST 047407.)
Southern National 28 BR Taunton–Minehead, also 38 from Minehead (Tel: 01823 27033).
Washford (W Somerset Rly) ½m.

Cleeve Abbey dormitory buildings (above) with detail of the carved timber ceiling in the refectory (left)

Cromwell's Castle

Cromwell's Castle

Tresco, ISLES OF SCILLY (210, 5A)

Standing on a promontory guarding the lovely anchorage between Bryher and Tresco, this 17th-century round tower was built to command the haven of New Grimsby.

***Open** Any reasonable time.*
***Entry** Free.*

On shoreline, ¾m NW of New Grimsby. (OS Map 203; ref SV 882159.)

Dartmouth Castle

DEVON (211, 2E)

This brilliantly positioned defensive castle juts out into the narrow entrance to the Dart estuary, with the sea lapping at its foot. It was one of the first castles constructed with artillery in mind and has seen 450 years of fortification and preparation for war.

Picnic spot of exceptional beauty.

Dartmouth Castle

Open *1 April–31 Oct: daily, 10am–6pm (6pm/dusk in Oct). 1 Nov–31 March: Wed–Sun, 10am–4pm (closed 24–26 Dec, 1 Jan). Closed 1–2pm in winter.*
Entry *£2.20/£1.70/£1.10.*
01803 833588
(limited)
1m SE of Dartmouth off B3205, narrow approach road. (OS Map 202; ref SX 887503.)
Bayline 200 BR Paignton–Kingswear, 22 Brixham–Kingswear (connections from BR Paignton), thence ferry to Dartmouth; Western National/ Tally Ho! 89, 91, X93 from Totnes (passes close to BR Totnes) (Tel: 01932 382800). In all cases 1m walk from Dartmouth or local ferry from Dartmouth to Castle.
Paignton 8m via vehicle ferry.

Daws Castle

SOMERSET (211, 5F)

The site where the people of the Saxon town of Watchet sought refuge against the threat of Viking attack.

Open *Any reasonable time.*
Entry *Free.*
(layby 200m)
3m W of Watchet near Blue Anchor off B3191 on cliff top. (OS Map 181; ref ST 062432.)
Southern National 28 BR Taunton–Minehead (Tel: 01823 272033).
Watchet (West Somerset Rly) ¾m.

Dupath Well

Callington, CORNWALL (210, 2D)

A charming granite-built well house set over a holy well of *c.*1500 and still almost complete.

Open *Any reasonable time. (Site managed by the Cornwall Heritage Trust.)*
Entry *Free.*
1m E of Callington off A388.

Farleigh Hungerford Castle

(OS Map 201; ref SX 374693.)
Western National 76 Plymouth–Callington (passes close to BR Plymouth), thence 1m (Tel: 01752 222666).
Gunnislake 4½m.

Farleigh Hungerford Castle

SOMERSET (211/212, 5H)

Ruins of a 14th-century castle with a chapel containing wall paintings, stained glass and the fine tomb of Sir Thomas Hungerford, builder of the castle.

Open *1 April–31 Oct: daily, 10am–6pm (6pm/dusk in Oct). 1 Nov–31 March: Wed–Sun, 10am–4pm (closed 24–26 Dec, 1 Jan). Closed 1–2pm in winter.*
Entry *£1.50/£1.10/80p.*
P *(exterior only).*
01225 754026.
In Farleigh Hungerford 3½m W of Trowbridge on A366.
(OS Map 173; ref ST 801577.)
Badgerline X3 Bristol-Frome (passes BR Bath Spa & close to BR Frome) to within 1m (Tel: 0117 955 3231).
Avoncliff 2m; Trowbridge 3½m.

Fiddleford Manor

DORSET (211/212, 4H)

Part of a medieval manor house, with a remarkable interior. The splendid roof structures in the hall and upper living room are the best in Dorset.

Open *1 April–30 Sept: daily, 10am–6pm. 1 Oct–31 March: daily, 10am–4pm (closed 24–26 Dec, 1 Jan). Keykeeper.*
Entry *Free.*

Fiddleford Manor

P *(ground floor only – 1 step)*
1m E of Sturminster Newton off A357.
(OS Map 194; ref ST 801136.)
Damory 310 from Blandford (Tel: 01258 452545).

Gallox Bridge

Dunster, SOMERSET (211, 4E)

A stone packhorse bridge with two ribbed arches which spans the old mill stream.

Open *Any reasonable time.*
Entry *Free.*
Off A396 at S end of Dunster.
(OS Map 181; ref SS 990432.)
Southern National 28 BR Taunton–Minehead, also 38/9 from Minehead to within ⅛m (Tel: 01823 272033).
Dunster (W Somerset Rly) ¾m.

Garrison Walls

St Mary's, ISLES OF SCILLY (210, 4A)

You can take a pleasant walk along the ramparts of these well-preserved walls and earthworks, built as part of the island's defences.

Open *Any reasonable time.*
Entry *Free.*
Around the headland W of Hugh Town.
(OS Map 203; ref SV 898104.)

Glastonbury Tribunal

SOMERSET (211, 4G)

A well-preserved medieval town house, reputedly once used as the courthouse of Glastonbury Abbey.

Open *5 April–30 Sept: Sun–Thurs, 10am–5pm (Fri & Sat 5.30pm). 1 Oct–27 March: Sun–Thurs, 10am–4pm. (Fri & Sat 4.30pm). (Site managed by Glastonbury Tribunal Ltd.)*

Entry *Tourist Information Centre free. Display areas £1.50/£1.00/75p.*

01458 832954

(ground floor only – 2 steps)

In Glastonbury High St. (OS Map 182; ref ST 499390.)

Badgerline 376, 676, Southern National 29A BR Bristol Temple Meads–Street (Tel: 0117 955 3231).

Great Witcombe Roman Villa

GLOUCESTERSHIRE (211/212/217, 6H)

The remains of a large villa. Built around three sides of a courtyard, it had a luxurious bath-house complex.

Open *Exterior any reasonable time. Guided tours 27 May, 23 June, 18 Aug, 15 Sept only. Please contact Regional Office for details (Tel 0117 975 0700).*

Entry *Free.*

5m SE of Gloucester, off A417, ½m S of reservoir in Witcombe Park. (OS Map 163; ref SO 899144.)

Stagecoach City of Gloucester 50 BR Gloucester–Cheltenham to within 1½m (Tel: 01452 527516).

Gloucester 6m.

Greyfriars

Gloucester, GLOUCESTERSHIRE (217, 7H)

Remains of a late 15th- early 16th-century Franciscan friary church.

Open *Any reasonable time.*

Entry *Free.*

On Greyfriars Walk, behind Eastgate Market off Southgate St. (OS Map 162; ref SO 830186.)

From surrounding areas (Tel: 01452 425543).

Gloucester ½m.

Grimspound

Dartmoor, DEVON (210, 3E)

This late Bronze Age settlement displays the remains of 24 huts in an area of four acres enclosed by a stone wall.

Open *Any reasonable time. (Site managed by Dartmoor National Park Authority.)*

Entry *Free.*

6m SW of Moretonhampstead off B3212. (OS Map 191; ref SX 701809.)

Western National 82 Plymouth–Exeter, to within 2m (Tel: 01392 382800).

Hailes Abbey (above) with Christ/Sampson boss (left) and a manuscript and seal (above right)

Hailes Abbey

GLOUCESTERSHIRE (212/217, 7H)

13th-century Cistercian abbey, set in wooded pastureland, with examples of high quality sculpture in the site museum.

Open *1 April–31 Oct: daily, 10am–6pm (6pm/dusk in Oct). 1 Nov–31 March: Wed–Sun, 10am–4pm (closed 24–26 Dec, 1 Jan). Closed 1–2pm in winter.*

Entry *£2.20/£1.70/ £1.10. National Trust members*

admitted free. (Site maintained and managed by English Heritage, and owned by the National Trust.)

01242 602398

(also available for the partially sighted and those with learning difficulties) (general access, 1 step to museum)

2m NE of Winchcombe off B4632. (OS Map 150; ref SP 050300.)

Castleways from Cheltenham to within 1½m (Tel: 01242 602949).

Cheltenham 10m.

Halliggye Fogou

CORNWALL (210, 1B)

One of several strange underground tunnels, associated with Iron Age villages, which are unique to Cornwall.

***Open** Any reasonable time but completely blocked between 31 Oct and 31 March. A torch is advisable.*

***Entry** Free.*

5m SE of Helston off B3293 E of Garras on Trelowarren estate. (OS Map 203; ref SW 714239.)

Truronian 326 from Helston (Tel: 01872 73453); Western National 2/A links Helston with BR Penzance (Tel: 01209 719988).

Penryn 10m.

Harry's Walls

St Mary's, ISLES OF SCILLY (210, 4B)

An uncompleted 16th-century fort intended to command the harbour of St Mary's Pool.

***Open** Any reasonable time.*

***Entry** Free.*

¼m NE of Hugh Town. (OS Map 203; ref SV 910110.)

Hatfield Earthworks

WILTSHIRE (211/212, 5J)

Part of a Neolithic enclosure complex 3,500 years old, formerly with a Bronze Age barrow in its centre.

***Open** Any reasonable time.*

***Entry** Free.*

5½m SE of Devizes off A342 NE of village of Marden. (OS Map 173; ref SU 091583) or SU 092583).

Hound Tor Deserted Medieval Village

Dartmoor, DEVON (210, 3E)

Remains of three or four medieval farmsteads, first occupied in the Bronze Age.

***Open** Any reasonable time. (Site managed by Dartmoor National Park Authority.)*

***Entry** Free.*

1½m S of Manaton off Ashburton road. Park in Hound Tor car park, ½ m walk. (OS Map 191; ref SX 746788.)

Western National 170/1 Newton Abbot–Tavistock, Summer Suns only (Tel: 01392 382800).

Harry's Walls

Hurlers Stone Circles

CORNWALL (210, 2C)

These three Bronze Age stone circles in a line are some of the best examples of ceremonial standing stones in the South West.

Open *Any reasonable time. (Site managed by the Cornwall Heritage Trust.)*
Entry *Free.*

½m NW of Minions off B3254. (OS Map 201; ref SX 258714.)
Caradon Riviera BR Liskeard–Higher Tremar, thence 1½m (Tel: 01579 62226).
Liskeard 7m.

Innisidgen Lower And Upper Burial Chambers

St Mary's, ISLES OF SCILLY (210, 4B)

Two Bronze Age cairns, about 30 metres (200 feet) apart, with stunning views towards St Martins.

Open *Any reasonable time.*
Entry *Free.*

1¾m NE of Hugh Town. (OS Map 203; ref SV 921127.)

Jordan Hill Roman Temple

Weymouth, DORSET (211/212, 3H)

Foundations of a Romano-Celtic temple enclosing an area of about 22 square metres (240 square feet).

Open *Any reasonable time.*
Entry *Free.*

2m NE of Weymouth off A353. (OS Map 194; ref SY 698821.)
Southern National A from Weymouth (Tel: 01305 783645).
Upwey or Weymouth, both 2m.

King Charles's Castle

Tresco, ISLES OF SCILLY (210, 5A)

At the end of a bracing coastal walk to the northern end of Tresco you will find the remains of this castle built for coastal defence.

Open *Any reasonable time.*
Entry *Free.*

¾m NW of New Grimsby. (OS Map 203; ref SV 882161.)

King Doniert's Stone

St Cleer, CORNWALL (210, 2C)

Two decorated pieces of a 9th-century cross with an inscription believed to commemorate Durngarth, King of Cornwall, who drowned *c.*875.

Open *Any reasonable time. (Site managed by the Cornwall Heritage Trust.)*

King Charles's Castle

***Entry** Free.*

(lay-by)

1m NW of St Cleer off B3254. (OS Map 201; ref SX 236688.)

Caradon Riviera BR Liskeard–St Cleer, thence ½m (Tel: 01579 62226).

Liskeard 4m.

Kingston Russell Stone Circle

DORSET (211, 3G)

A Bronze Age stone circle of 18 stones.

***Open** Any reasonable time.*

***Entry** Free.*

(on verge near entrance to Gorwell Farm)

2m N of Abbotsbury, 1m along footpath off minor road to Hardy Monument. (OS Map 194; ref SY 577878.)

Dorchester West or South, both 8m.

Kingswood Abbey Gatehouse

GLOUCESTERSHIRE (211/212/217, 6H)

The 16th-century gatehouse, with a richly carved mullioned window, is all that remains of the Cistercian abbey.

***Open** Exterior any reasonable time. Key for interior obtainable from shop nearby during opening hours.*

***Entry** Free.*

(adjacent to monument)

In Kingswood off B4060 1m SW of Wotton-under-Edge. (OS Map 162; ref ST 748919.)

Badgerline 309 Bristol–Dursley (Tel: 0117 955 3231).

Yate 8m.

Kirkham House

Paignton, DEVON (211, 2E)

A well preserved, medieval stone house, much restored and repaired, which gives a fascinating insight into life in a town residence in the 15th century.

***Open** 17 April, 15 May, 12 June, 17 July, 14 Aug, 18 Sept only, 10am–5pm.*

***Entry** Free.*

01803 522775

In Kirkham St, off Cecil Rd, Paignton. (OS Map 202; ref SX 885610.)

From surrounding areas (Tel: 01803 613226).

Paignton ½m.

Kingswood Abbey Gatehouse

Knowlton Church and Earthworks

DORSET (211/212, 4J)

The ruins of this Norman church stand in the middle of Neolithic earthworks, symbolizing the transition from pagan to Christian worship.

Open *Any reasonable time.*
Entry *Free.*

3m SW of Cranborne on B3078.
(OS Map 195; ref SU 024100.)

Launceston Castle

Launceston Castle

CORNWALL (210, 3D)

Set on the motte of the original Norman castle and commanding the town and surrounding countryside, this medieval castle controlled the main route into Cornwall. The shell keep and tower survive.

Open *1 April–31 Oct: daily, 10am–6pm (6pm/dusk in Oct).*
Entry *£1.50/£1.10/80p.*
01566 772365
(outer bailey)
In Launceston.
(OS Map 201; ref SX 330846.)
Western National 76 Plymouth–Launceston; Tilleys from Exeter (Tel: 01392 382800).

Leigh Barton

DEVON (210, 2E)

A small late-medieval domestic complex with a fine gatehouse and three ranges around a galleried courtyard. Access is limited to certain days.

Open *By guided tour only. Contact Regional Office for details (Tel: 0117 975 0700).*
Entry *Free.*
(limited)
(grounds & ground floor only)
2m NW of Kingsbridge at Leigh on unclassified road off B3194.
(OS Map 202; ref SX 721467.)
Western National 93 Plymouth–Dartmouth to within ¾m (passes close to BR Plymouth, with connections from BR Totnes at Kingsbridge) (Tel: 01392 382800).
Ivybridge 10m.

Ludgershall Castle and Cross

WILTSHIRE (211/212, 5J)

Ruins of an early 12th-century royal hunting palace and a late-medieval cross.

Open *Any reasonable time.*
Entry *Free.*
(limited) *(part of site only & village cross)*
On N side of Ludgershall off A342.
(OS Map 184; ref SU 264513.)
Stagecoach Hampshire Bus/Wilts & Dorset 7–9 BR Andover–Salisbury (Tel: 01345 090899).
Andover 7m.

Lulworth Castle

DORSET (211/212, 3H)

Built in the early 16th century as a romantic hunting lodge, Lulworth Castle was changed into a fashionable country house set in beautiful parkland during the 18th century. Gutted by fire in 1929, the exterior is now being restored by English Heritage.

Open *1 April–30 Sept: daily, 10am–6pm. 1 Oct–22 Dec: daily, 10am–4pm.*
Entry *£1.50/£1.20/75p.*
Members may be charged for certain special events held in the park. (Site managed by the Weld Estate.)
01929 400510
(by ramp)

Lulworth Castle

In east Lulworth off B3070, 3 miles NE of Lulworth Cove. (OS Map 194; ref SY 853822.)
Garrison Cars 225/7 BR Wool–Lulworth Cove (Tel: 01929 462467); Dorset Queen 220 Dorchester–Lulworth (Tel: 01305 852829).
Wool 4m.

Lydford Castle

Lydford Castles And Saxon Town

DEVON (210, 3D)

Standing above the gorge of the River Lyd, this 12th-century tower was notorious as a prison. The earthworks of the original Norman fort are to the south.

Open *Any reasonable time. (Site managed by the National Trust.)*
Entry *Free.*

In Lydford off A386 8m S of Okehampton. (OS Map 191; Castle ref SX 510848, Fort ref SX 509847.)
Western National 183 Plymouth–Okehampton (passes close to BR Plymouth); Devon Bus 187 BR Gunnislake– Okehampton (Tel: 01392 382800).

Maiden Castle

DORSET (211, 3G)

This is the finest Iron Age hill fort in Britain. The earthworks are enormous, with a series of ramparts and complicated entrances, but they could not prevent the castle's capture by the Romans *c.*AD 43.

Open *Any reasonable time.*

Maiden Castle

Entry *Free.*

2m S of Dorchester. Access off A354, N of bypass. (OS Map 194; ref SY 670885.)
Dorchester South or West, both 2m.

Meare Fish House

SOMERSET (211, 4G)

A simple, well-preserved stone dwelling.

Open *Any reasonable time. Key from Manor House farm.*
Entry *Free.*

In Meare village on B3151. (OS Map 182; ref ST 458418.)

Odda's Chapel

Deerhurst,
GLOUCESTERSHIRE
(212/217, 7H)

A rare Anglo-Saxon chapel attached, unusually, to a half-timbered farmhouse.

Open *1 April–30 Sept: daily, 10am–6pm. 1 Oct–31 March: daily, 10am–4pm (closed 24–26 Dec, 1 Jan). Keykeeper.*
Entry *Free.*

In Deerhurst (off B4213) at Abbots Court SW of parish church. (OS Map 150; ref SO 869298.)
Swanbrook Coaches BR Gloucester–Tewkesbury (Tel: 01452 425543).
Cheltenham 8m.

Offa's Dyke

GLOUCESTERSHIRE
(211/217, 6G)

Three-mile section of the great earthwork built by Offa, King of Mercia 757–96, from the Severn estuary to the Welsh coast as a defensive boundary to his kingdom.

Open *Any reasonable time.*
Entry *Free.*

3m NE of Chepstow off B4228. Access via Forestry Commission Tidenham car park. 1m walk (way marked) down to Devil's Pulpit on Offa's Dyke. (Access suitable only for those wearing proper walking shoes; not suitable for very young, old or infirm). (OS Map 162; ref SO 545005–549977.)
Stagecoach Red & White 69 Chepstow–Monmouth to within ½m (Tel: 01633 266366).
Chepstow 7m.

Okehampton Castle

DEVON (210, 3D)

The ruins of the largest castle in Devon include the Norman motte and the jagged remains of the keep. There is a picnic area and lovely woodland walks.

Picnic spot of exceptional beauty.
Open *1 April–31 Oct: daily, 10am–6pm (6pm/dusk in Oct).*
Entry *£2.20/£1.70/£1.10.*
01837 52844
(picnic tables available)

1m SW of Okehampton town centre.

Okehampton Castle motte and keep (left) and Okehampton from the bluebell wood (below)

Old Wardour Castle from the south (below) and the stairway to Grand Hall (below right)

(OS Map 191; ref SX 584942.)
Devon General 51, Bow Belle 628, Jennings 629, Western National 187, Tilleys from Exeter (some pass BR Exeter St David's) to within 1m (Tel: 01392 382800).

Old Blockhouse

Tresco, ISLES OF SCILLY (210, 5A)

The remains of a small 16th-century gun tower overlooking the white sandy bay at Old Grimsby.

Open *Any reasonable time.*
Entry *Free.*

On Blockhouse Point, at S end of Old Grimsby harbour. (OS Map 203; ref SV 898155.)

Old Sarum

WILTSHIRE (211/212, 4J)

See pp 34–5 for full details.

Old Wardour Castle

WILTSHIRE (211/212, 4H)

The unusual hexagonal ruins of this 14th-century castle are on the edge of a beautiful lake, surrounded by landscaped grounds, which include an elaborate rockwork grotto.

Open *1 April–31 Oct: daily, 10am–6pm (6pm/dusk in Oct). 1 Nov–31 March: Wed–Sun, 10am–4pm (closed 24–26 Dec, 1 Jan). Closed 1–2pm in winter.*
Entry *£1.50/£1.10/80p.*
01747 870487
(grounds only)
Off A30 2m SW of Tisbury. (OS Map 184; ref ST 939263.)
Wilts & Dorset 26 Salisbury–Shaftesbury (passes BR Tisbury) (Tel: 01722 336855).
Tisbury 2½m.

Over Bridge

GLOUCESTERSHIRE (212/217, 7H)

A single-arch masonry bridge spanning the River Severn, built by Thomas Telford 1825–27.

Open *Any reasonable time.*
Entry *Free.*
(in layby)
1m NW of Gloucester city centre at junction of A40 (Ross) & A419 (Ledbury). (OS Map 162; ref SO 817196.)
Frequent services from BR Gloucester (Tel: 01452 425543).
Gloucester 2m.

OLD SARUM

This great earthwork lies near Salisbury, on the edge of the Wiltshire chalk plains. It was built by Iron Age peoples around 500 BC and was overtaken by succeeding settlers and conquerors.

Romans, Saxons and, most importantly, the Normans have all occupied what is now known as Old Sarum. The Normans made it into one of their major strongholds, with a royal castle and a great cathedral. But when the new city we know as Salisbury was founded in the early 13th century, the settlement faded away. Despite its virtual abandonment, a handful of electors still returned a member of Parliament to Westminster until 1832, when a wave of anti-corruption electoral reform swept through Britain.

Stone carving from Old Sarum cathedral

Today the remains – of the prehistoric fortress, of the Norman palace, castle and cathedral – evoke powerful memories of the people who have ruled England over the millenia. In addition, the chalk downland, with its many wild flowers, makes it a magical spot.

Romano-British brooch found at Old Sarum

The great earth banks and ditches, a mile round, of the Iron Age hill fort at Old Sarum were used by successive invaders. It was here, in 1070, that William the Conqueror paid off his army and, in 1085, demanded loyalty from his nobles. A castle, a sumptuous palace and a great cathedral were built within the earthwork. Yet disputes between soldiers and priests, and inadequate water supplies, were huge hindrances. In 1226 cathedral and town moved. New Sarum, modern Salisbury with its magnificent cathedral, was built in the valley with plentiful water. The cathedral at Old Sarum was abandoned, although the castle remained in use until Tudor times.

Carved heads from Old Sarum cathedral

Open 1 April–31 Oct: daily, 10am–6pm (6pm/dusk in Oct). 1 Nov–31 March: daily, 10am–4pm.

The foundations of the cathdral marked out in the grass

Entry £1.70/£1.30/90p
✆ 01722 335398
(outer bailey & grounds only)
2m N of Salisbury off A345. (OS Map 184; ref SU 138327.)
Wilts & Dorset/Hampshire Bus 3, 5–9 from Salisbury (Tel: 01722 336855).
Salisbury 2m.

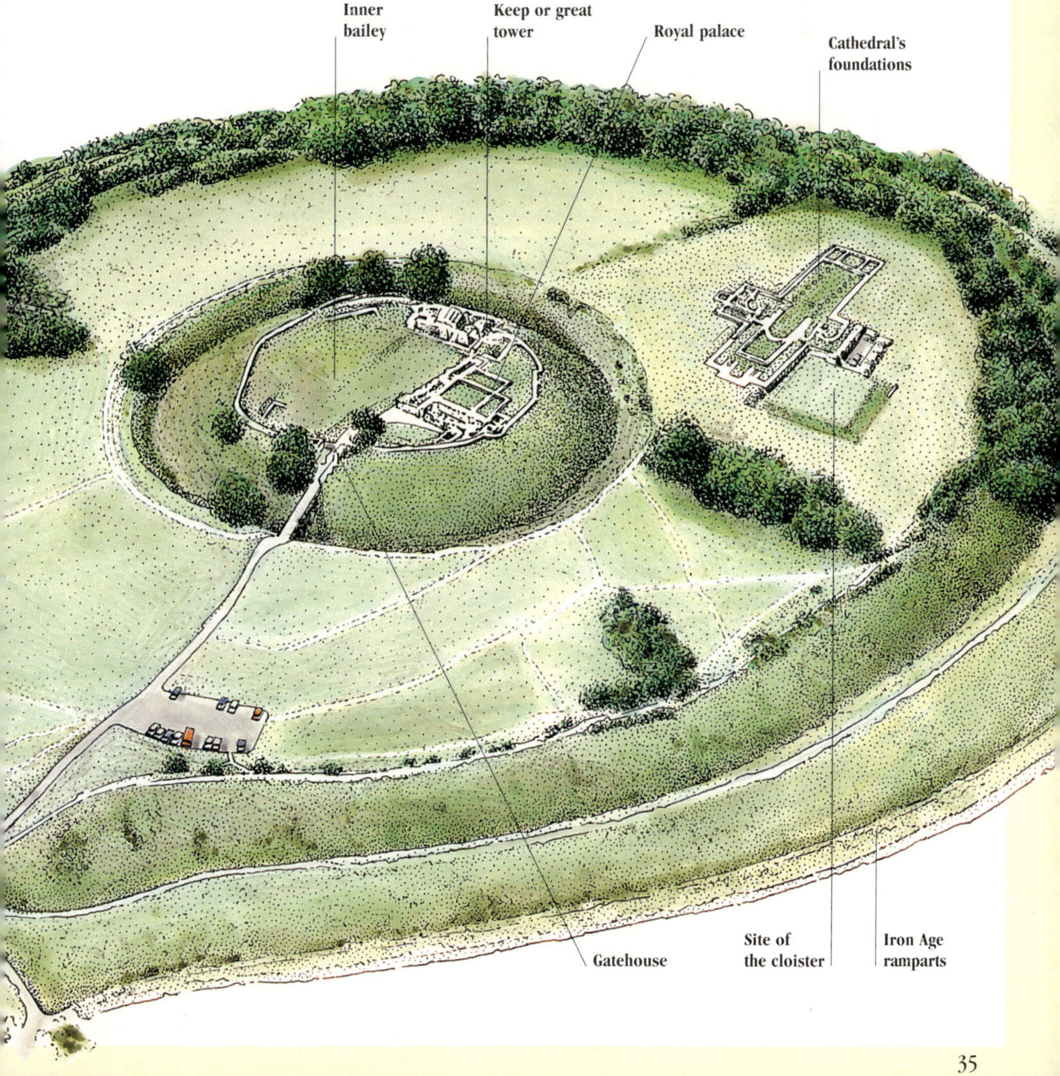

Portland Castle

Pendennis Castle
CORNWALL (210, 1B)
See pp 38–9 for full details.

Penhallam
CORNWALL (210, 3C)
Ruins of a medieval manor house surrounded by a protective moat.

Open *Any reasonable time.*
Entry *Free.*
(limited)
1m NW of Week St Mary, off minor road off A39 from Treskinnick Cross (10 minute walk from car park).
(OS Map 190; ref SX 224974.)

Porth Hellick Down Burial Chamber
St Mary's, ISLES OF SCILLY (210, 4B)
Probably the best-preserved Bronze Age burial mound on the Islands, with an entrance passage and chamber.

Open *Any reasonable time.*
Entry *Free.*
1 ½m E of Hugh Town.
(OS Map 203; ref SV 929108.)

Portland Castle
DORSET (211/212, 3H)
One of the best preserved of Henry VIII's coastal forts, built of white Portland stone. It was originally intended to thwart attack by the Spanish and French, and changed hands several times during the Civil War.

Open *1 April–31 Oct: daily, 10am–6pm (6pm/dusk in Oct).*
Entry *£2.00/£1.50/£1.00.*
01305 820539
(ground floor only – 1 deep step)
Overlooking Portland harbour adjacent to RN helicopter base.
(OS Map 194; ref SY 684743.)
Southern National 1/A, 10, Smith's Coaches Weymouth–Portland (Tel: 01305 783645). Water bus from Brewers Quay in Weymouth.
Weymouth 4 ½m.

Ratfyn Barrows
WILTSHIRE (211/212, 4J)
Part of Bronze Age cemetery containing burial mounds of different styles.

Open *Access by consent of owner only. Contact Regional Office (Tel: 0117 975 0700).*
Entry *Free.*
1 ½m E of Amesbury on both sides of A303. Barrows can be seen from A303 (no stopping).
(OS Map 184; ref SU 180417.)

Wilts & Dorset 5–6 Salisbury–Swindon, 6–9 Salisbury–Andover, to within 1m (passes close to BR Salisbury) (Tel: 01722 336855).
Salisbury 10m

Restormel Castle

CORNWALL (210, 2C)

Perched on a high mound, surrounded by a deep moat, the huge circular keep of this splendid Norman castle survives in remarkably good condition. It offers splendid views over the surrounding countryside.

Open *1 April–31 Oct: daily, 10am–6pm (6pm/dusk in Oct).*
Entry *£1.50/£1.10/80p.*
01208 872687

1½m N of Lostwithiel off A390. (OS Map 200; ref SX 104614).
Lostwithiel 1½m.

Restormel Castle

Royal Citadel

Plymouth, DEVON (210, 2D)

A large, dramatic 17th-century fortress, with walls up to 21 metres (70 feet) high, built to defend the coastline from the Dutch, and still in use today.

Open *By guided tour only (1¼ hours) 1 May–30 Sept: 2pm and 3.30pm. Tickets from Plymouth Dome below Smeaton's Tower on Hoe. For security reasons tours may be suspended at short notice.*
Entry *£2.50/£2.00/£1.50.*
01752 775841

At E end of Plymouth Hoe. (OS Map 201; ref SX 480538.)
From surrounding areas (Tel: 01752 222666).
Plymouth 1¼m.

St Breock Downs Monolith

CORNWALL (210, 2C)

A prehistoric standing stone, originally about 5 metres (16 feet) high, set in beautiful countryside.

Open *Any reasonable time. (Site managed by the Cornwall Heritage Trust.)*
Entry *Free.*

On St Breock Downs, 3¾m SW of Wadebridge off unclassified road to Rosenannon. (OS Map 200; ref SW 968683.)
Roche 5½m.

St Briavel's Castle

GLOUCESTERSHIRE (211/217, 6G)

A splendid 12th-century castle now used as a youth hostel, which is appropriate for a building set in such marvellous walking country.

St Breock Downs Monolith

Open *Exterior any reasonable time. Bailey 1 April–30 Sept: daily 1pm–4pm.*
Entry *Free.*

In St Briavel's, 7m NE of Chepstow off B4228. (OS Map 162; ref SO 559046.)
Chepstow 8m.

Pendennis Castle

Pendennis and its neighbour St Mawes Castle face each other across the mouth of the estuary of the River Fal. They are the Cornish end of a chain of castles built by Henry VIII along England's south coast from 1539–1545 as protection against the threat of attack and invasion from France. Many of these castles are in the care of English Heritage. Few of them have ever seen active service, but many, especially Pendennis, were extended or adapted to meet the changing threats to national security. These came from the French and then the Spanish in the 16th century, and continued right through to World War II. Pendennis today stands as a landmark, with fine sea views and excellent site facilities, including an introductory exhibition, museum display and the Guardhouse, which has been returned to its World War I appearance.

One of the grotesque water spouts

Sir Walter Raleigh, who ordered the refortification of Pendennis

The land on which Pendennis stands was originally owned by the Killigrew family, governors of Pendennis for many years. The proud lodging fronting the keep was built around 1550 to provide them with more comfortable accommodation. In the later years of Elizabeth I's reign, a new type of defensive wall with bastions was added around the original fort. Strengthened again prior to the Civil War, Pendennis was host to the future Charles II in 1646, who sailed from there to the Isles of Scilly. It withstood five months of siege before becoming the penultimate Royalist Garrison to surrender on the mainland. Pendennis was heavily rearmed in the late 19th and early 20th centuries, culminating in the installation of huge 6-inch guns during World War II.

The Governor's lodging (below), built in the mid-16th century

The Battery observation post

'The Seige of Pendennis, 1646', a Sealed Knot event on the weekend of 17/18 August commemorates the 350th anniversary of the five month siege in the Civil War.

Vivid re-creation of the gun defences (nearly 40 historic guns on display).

Free Children's Activity sheet available.

An exciting CD Rom unit with information on English castles' function and purpose.

Open *1 April–31 Oct: daily, 10am– 6pm (6pm/dusk in Oct). 1 Nov–31 March: daily, 10am–4pm (closed 24–26 Dec, 1 Jan).*

Entry *£2.50/£1.90/£1.30.*

☎ 01326 316594

(grounds, parts of keep) ('Pendennis Castle Coffee Shop'; normally open summer season only)

On Pendennis Head 1m SE of Falmouth. (OS Map 204; ref SW 824318.)

Falmouth Docks ½m.

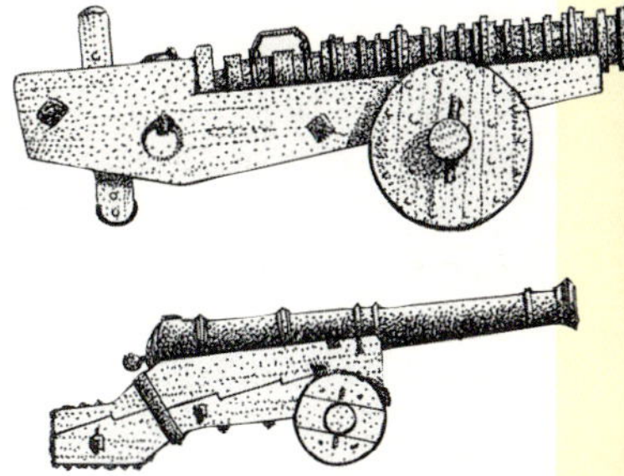

Wrought-iron, breech-loading gun of the 1540s (top) and late 17th-century gun on a carriage designed for fortress use (above)

Aerial view of Pendennis from the south east (above)

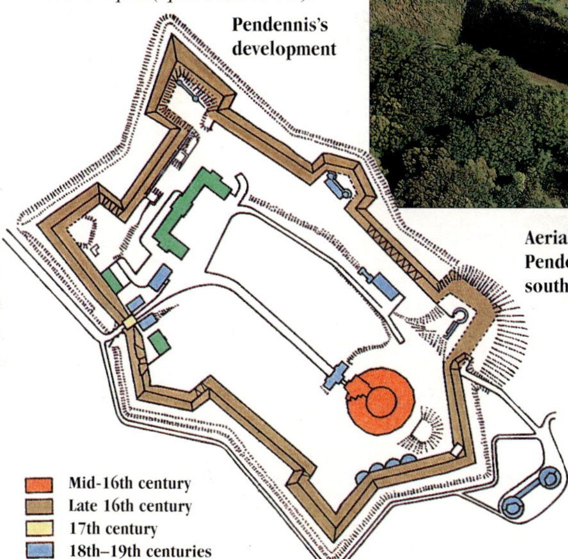

Pendennis's development

The deeply modelled facade of the granite building (above)

St Catherine's Castle

Fowey, CORNWALL
(210, 2C)

A small fort built by Henry VIII to defend Fowey Harbour.

Open *Any reasonable time.*
Entry *Free.*
P in Fowey – ½m walk.
¾m SW of Fowey along footpath off A3082.
(OS Map 200; ref SX 118508.)
Western National 24 St Austell– Fowey, thence ¾m (Tel: 01209 719988).
Par 4m.

St Catherine's Chapel

Abbotsbury, DORSET
(211, 3G)

A small stone chapel, set on a hilltop, with an unusual roof and small turret used as a lighthouse.

Open *Any reasonable time.*
Entry *Free.*
½m S of Abbotsbury by pedestrian track from village off B3157.
(OS Map 194; ref SY 572848.)
Upwey 7½m.

St Mary's Church

Kempley, GLOUCESTERSHIRE (217, 7G)

A Norman church with superb wall paintings from the 12th–14th centuries.

Open *1 April–30 Sept: daily, 10am–6pm. 1 Oct–31 March: daily, 10am–4pm (closed 24–26 Dec, 1 Jan). Keykeeper.*
Entry *Free.*
1m N of Kempley off B4024, 6m NE of Ross-on-Wye.
(OS Map 149; ref SO 670313.)
Ledbury 8m.

St Mawes Castle

CORNWALL (210, 1B)

Together with Pendennis, St Mawes Castle was built by Henry VIII to guard the entrance to safe anchorage in the Carrick Roads. Its three huge circular bastions with gun ports were formidable defences indeed. Today the castle stands in delightful sub-tropical gardens featuring plants from around the world. Some of the finest views of the surrounding coastline can be enjoyed from here.

Free Children's Activity Sheet available.
Open *1 April–31 Oct: daily, 10am–6pm (6pm/dusk in Oct). 1 Nov–31 March: Wed–Sun, 10am–4pm (closed 24–26 Dec, 1 Jan). Closed 1–2pm in winter.*

St Mawes Castle

Entry *£2.00/£1.50/£1.00.*
☎ 01326 270526

➲ In St Mawes on A3078. (OS Map 204; ref SW 842328.)
Western National 51 Truro–St Mawes (Tel: 01209 719988).
Foot Ferry: St Mawes Ferry Co. from Falmouth, Prince of Wales Pier (Tel: 01326 313234). Car via King Harry Ferry at Feock on B3289 (Tel: 01872 72463).
Penmere, via Prince of Wales Pier.

Sherborne Old Castle

DORSET (211/212, 4G)

The ruins of this early 12th-century castle are a testament to the 16 days Cromwell took to capture it during the Civil War. It was then abandoned.

Open *1 April–31 Oct: daily, 10am–6pm (6pm/dusk in Oct). 1 Nov–31 March: Wed–Sun, 10am–4pm (closed 24–26 Dec, 1 Jan). Closed 1–2pm in winter.*

An aerial view of Sherborne Old Castle

Entry *£1.50/£1.10/80p.*
☎ 01935 812730

➲ ½m E of Sherborne off B3145. (OS Map 183; ref ST 647167.)
Sherborne ¾m.

Silbury Hill

WILTSHIRE (211/212, 5J)

An extraordinary artificial prehistoric mound, the largest Neolithic construction of its type in Europe.

Silbury Hill

Open *Any reasonable time (no access to hill itself). (Site managed by the National Trust.)*
Entry *Free.*
(viewing area)
➲ 1m W of West Kennet on A4. (OS Map 173; ref SU 100685.)
Thamesdown 49/A Swindon– Devizes/ Marlborough; Wilts & Dorset 5/6 Salisbury–Swindon (Tel: 01345 090 899). All pass within ¾m and pass close to BR Swindon .
Pewsey 9m, Swindon 13m.

Sir Bevil Grenville's Monument

Lansdown, AVON (211, 5H)

Sir Bevil Grenville's Monument

Commemorates the heroism of a Royalist commander and his Cornish pikemen at the Battle of Lansdown.

Open *Any reasonable time.*
Entry *Free.*
(in layby)
➲ 4m NW of Bath, on N edge of Lansdown Hill, near road to Wick. (OS Map 172; ref ST 721703.)
Badgerline 2, 702 BR Bath Spa–Ensleigh, thence 2½m (Tel: 01225 464446).
Bath Spa 4½m.

Stanton Drew Circles and Cove

AVON (211, 5G)

A fascinating assembly of three stone circles, two avenues and a burial chamber makes this one of the finest Neolithic religious sites in the country.

Open *Cove any reasonable time. Two main stone circles access at discretion of owner who may levy a charge. Tel: 0117 975 0700 for details.*
Entry *Free but see above.*

Circles: E of Stanton Drew village; Cove: in garden of Druid's Arms. (OS Map 172; Circles ref ST 601634, Cove ref ST 598633.)
Badgerline 376 Bristol–Yeovil (passes BR Bristol Temple Meads), alight Pensford, 1½m (Tel: 0117 955 3231).
Bristol Temple Meads 7m.

Stonehenge

WILTSHIRE (211/212, 5J)

See pp 44–9 for full details.

Stoney Littleton Long Barrow

AVON (211/212, 5H)

This Neolithic burial mound is about 30 metres (100 feet) long and has chambers where human remains once lay.

Open *Exterior any reasonable time.*
Entry *Free.*
(limited)

1m S of Wellow off A367. (OS Map 172; ref ST 735573.)
Bath Spa 6m.

Temple Church

Bristol, AVON (211, 5G)

The handsome tower and walls of this 15th-century church defied the bombs of World War II. The graveyard is now a pleasant public garden.

Open *Exterior any reasonable time. Access to interior during shop hours (key from local florist).*
Entry *Free.*

In Temple St off Victoria St. (OS Map 172; ref ST 593727.)
From surrounding areas (Tel: 0117 955 3231).
Bristol Temple Meads ¼m.

The Nine Stones

Winterbourne Abbas, DORSET (211, 3G)

Remains of a prehistoric circle of nine standing stones constructed about 4,000 years ago.

Open *Any reasonable time.*
Entry *Free.*
(small layby opposite, next to barn; cross road with care)
½m W of Winterbourne Abbas, on A35. (OS Map 194; ref SY 611904.)
Southern National 31, X31 Weymouth–Taunton (pass BR Dorchester South and Axminster) (Tel: 01305 783645).
Dorchester West or South, both 5m.

The Sanctuary

The Sanctuary

WILTSHIRE (211/212, 5J)

A prehistoric monument, possibly 5,000 years old, consisting of two concentric circles of stones and six of timber uprights indicated by concrete posts. The Sanctuary is connected to Avebury by the West Kennet Avenue of standing stones.

Open *Any reasonable time. (Site managed by the National Trust.)*
Entry *Free.*

⊛ P *(in layby)*
➲ *Beside A4, ½m E of West Kennet.*
(OS Map 173; ref SU 118679.)
Wilts & Dorset 5/6 Salisbury–Swindon (passes close to BR Swindon) (Tel: 01345 090 899).
Pewsey 9m, Bedwyn 12m.

Tintagel Castle

CORNWALL (210, 3C)
See pp 52–3 for full details.

Totnes Castle

DEVON (210, 2E)
A superb motte and bailey castle, with splendid views across the roof tops and down to the River Dart – a fine example of Norman fortification.

Family Discovery Pack available.

Open *1 April–31 Oct: daily, 10am–6pm (6pm/dusk in Oct). 1 Nov–31 March: Wed–Sun, 10am–4pm (closed 24–26 Dec, 1 Jan). Closed 1–2pm in winter.*
Entry *£1.50/£1.10/80p.*
01803 864406
P *(64 metres [210 feet], small charge)* ⊛
➲ *In Totnes, on hill overlooking the town.*
(OS Map 202; ref SX 800605.)
Totnes ¼m.

Tregiffian Burial Chamber

St Buryan, CORNWALL (210, 1A)
A Neolithic or early Bronze Age chambered tomb by the side of a country road.

Open *Any reasonable time. (Site managed by the Cornwall Heritage Trust.)*
Entry *Free.*
⊛
➲ *2m SE of St Buryan on B3315.*
(OS Map 203; ref SW 430245.)
Penzance 5½m.

Trethevy Quoit

St Cleer, CORNWALL (210, 2D)
An ancient Neolithic burial chamber, standing 2.7 metres (9 feet) high and consisting of five standing stones surmounted by a huge capstone.

Open *Any reasonable time. (Site managed by the Cornwall Heritage Trust.)*
Entry *Free.*
⊛
➲ *1m NE of St Cleer near Darite off B3254.*
(OS Map 201; ref SX 259688.)
Caradon Riviera BR Liskeard–Tremar (Tel: 01579 62226)
Liskeard 3½m.

Totnes Castle

Stonehenge

The great and ancient stone circle of Stonehenge is one of the wonders of the world, as old as many of the great temples and pyramids of Egypt, as old as Troy. Stonehenge is not an isolated monument, however. Although visitors over the centuries have tended to focus on the massive stones, these stand at the centre of an extensive landscape filled with the remains of ceremonial and domestic structures. Some are older than the great monument itself. Many of these features – earthworks, burial mounds, and other circular 'henge' monuments – are accessible by road or public footpath.

Bronze dagger (left) and gold-plated ornaments from Stonehenge

Now a World Heritage Site, Stonehenge and its surroundings remain powerful witnesses to the once-great civilization of the Stone and Bronze Ages, between 5000 and 3000 years ago.

What the visitor sees today are the substantial remnants of the last in a sequence of monuments erected between *c*. 3000 and 1000 BC. Each was a circular structure, aligned along the rising of the sun at the midsummer solstice and the setting of the sun at the midwinter solstice.

The first 'Stonehenge' consisted of circular banks and ditches enclosing a structure made of wooden posts, with an earthwork avenue along the line of the rising midsummer sun. Later monuments all used (and re-used) the great stones we see today, which were brought from some distance away.

The best-surviving portion of the circle of sarsen stones

The final phase of Stonehenge's construction

Fallen stones show the method of mortice-and-tenon fixing

The final phase comprised a circle of huge standing stones – super-hard sarsens, from the Marlborough Downs – and topped by lintel stones making a continuous ring. Inside this stood a horseshoe of still larger stones, five pairs of uprights with a lintel stone across each pair. All stones were connected using mortice and tenon joints, possibly copying the construction techniques of the previous wooden henge. Smaller 'blue' stones, from the Preseli Mountains in south Wales, were arranged in a circle and a horseshoe within the great sarsen stone circle and horseshoe. (In an earlier phase these bluestones had been erected in a different pattern.)

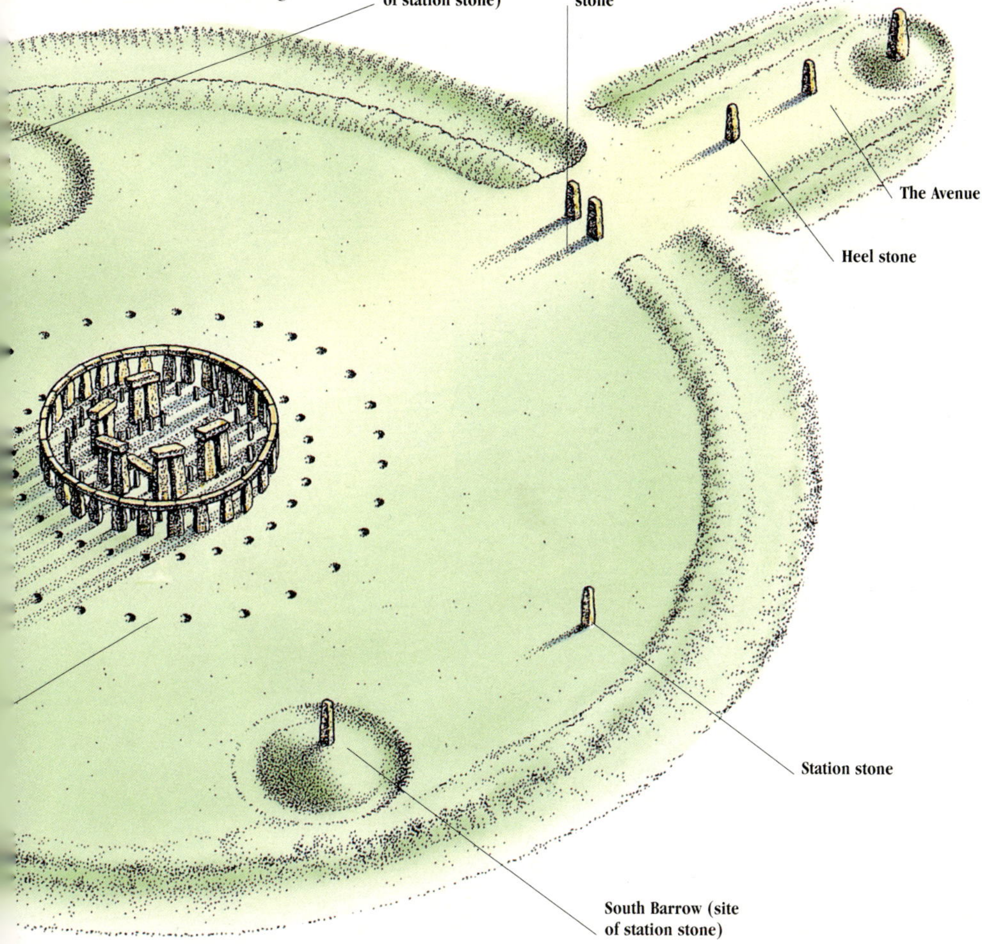

The likely method of raising the sarsen stones into an upright setting

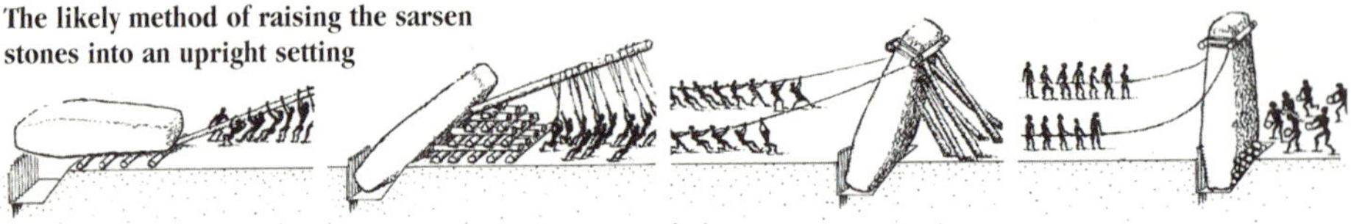

There has always been intense debate over quite what purpose Stonehenge served. Certainly it was the focal point for thousands of years within a ceremonial landscape. It also represented a huge investment of labour and time. The stones were carried dozens, sometimes hundreds, of miles by land and water. Huge efforts were needed to transport the stones, and then to shape and raise them. It must have been a sophisticated society to command the amount of labour, and to design and construct this and the many other surrounding monuments.

The monument complete with sarsen and bluestone circles enclosing the great central trilithon

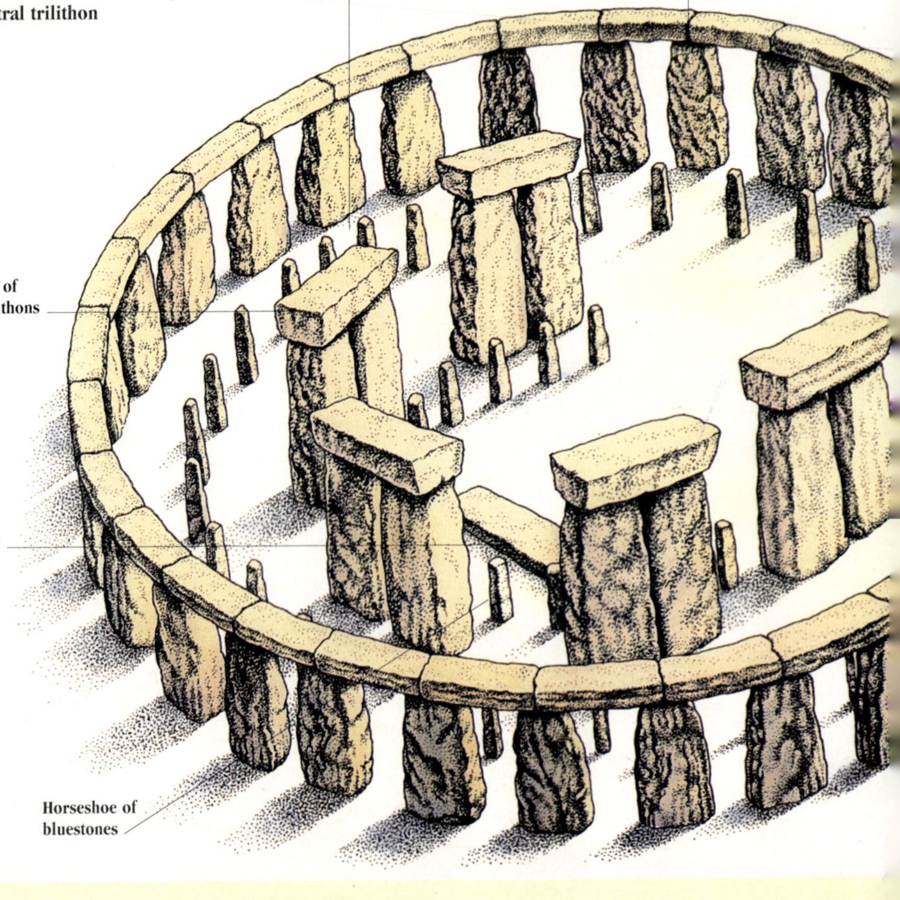

The likely method of raising a lintel to the top of two sarsens

Stonehenge's orientation on the rising and setting sun has always been one of its most remarkable features. Whether this was simply because the builders came from a sun-worshipping culture, or because – as some scholars believe – the circle and its banks were part of a huge astronomical calendar, remains a mystery.

What cannot be denied is the ingenuity of the builders of Stonehenge. With just very basic tools at their disposal, they shaped the stones and formed the mortices and tenons (holes and projecting stumps) that linked uprights and lintels. Using antlers, they dug the pits to hold the stones and made the banks and ditches that enclosed them.

Digging tools of the type used at Stonehenge

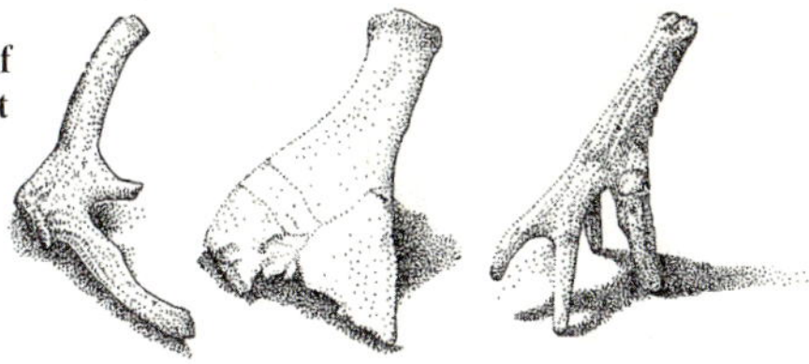

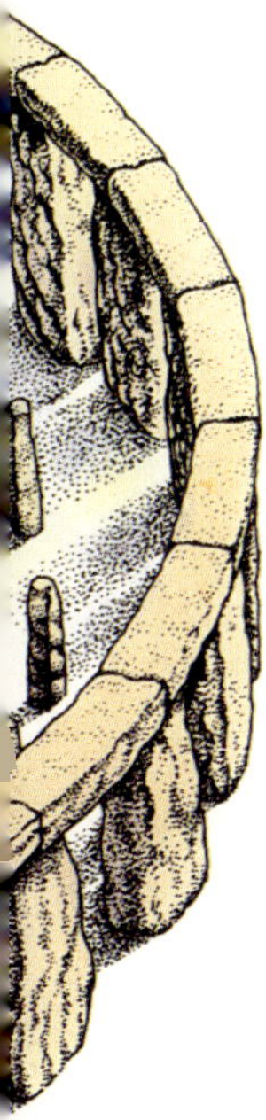

Grooved bluestone, forming part of bluestone horseshoe

Stonehenge from the air in winter

A man buried *c*.2000 BC, holding a pottery drinking vessel

Stone axe hammers and arrow heads

The long barrows of the New Stone Age, and the various types of circular barrows that came after, are still visible, as are other earthworks and monuments. Some, such as the long oval earthwork to the north, the Cursus, once thought to be a chariot race course, remain enigmatic. The Cursus and other parts of the Stonehenge landscape may be visited.

There are direct links with the people who built Stonehenge in their artefacts: tools, pottery and even the contents of graves. Some of these are displayed in the museums at Salisbury and Devizes.

Burial mounds, which possibly contained the bodies of ruling families, are also integral to the landscape.

Pottery funerary vessels of the early Bronze Age

Map with the barrows and monuments in the Stonehenge area

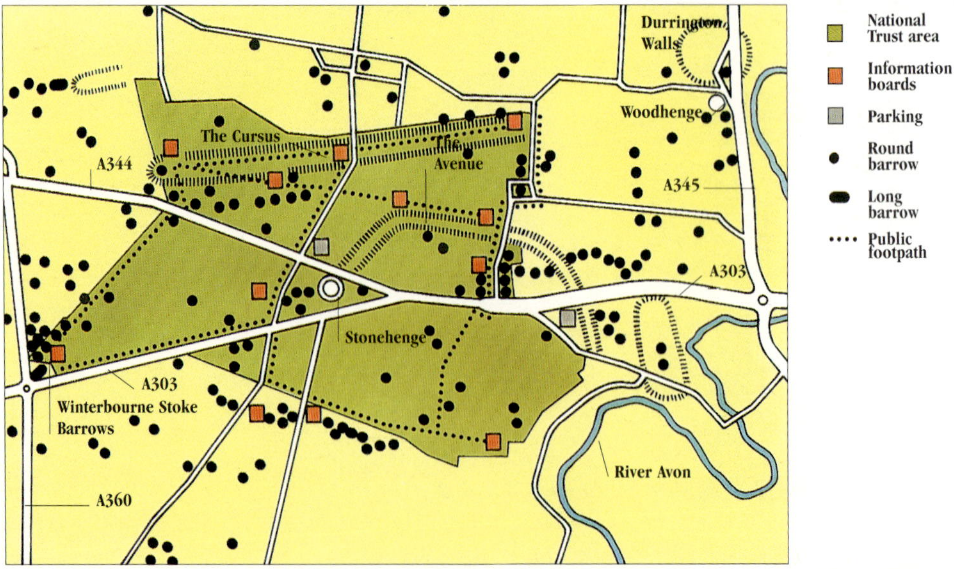

The chalk and grass Stonehenge landscape, with the Cursus, the Stonehenge circle, and clusters of barrow burials

An artist's impression (right) of a possible reconstruction of Woodhenge, 2 miles to the north-east of Stonehenge

William Cunnington (below), one in the great line of antiquarians, who studied Stonehenge around 1800

Woodhenge, to the east, was a wooden version of Stonehenge: a circular post structure aligned with the solstice sun. Stonehenge and its surrounding monuments have been an object of fascination and appeal since well before the dawn of recorded history.

Interactive audio tour of the facts and legends of Stonehenge, available in six languages.

Superb gift shop.

Open *16 March–31 May: daily, 9.30am–6.00pm. 1 June–31 Aug: daily, 9am–7pm. 1 Sept–15 Oct: daily, 9.30am–6pm. 16 Oct–15 March (1997): daily, 9.30am–4pm (closed 24–26 Dec, 1 Jan).*

Entry *£3.50/£2.60/£1.80. National Trust members admitted free. (Maintained and managed by English Heritage, site surrounded by nearly 1,500 acres of land owned by the National Trust.)*

☎ 01980 624715

('Stonehenge Kitchen')

*(also available in French, German and Japanese) (braille guides) * (available in six languages).*

2m W of Amesbury on junction A303 and A344/A360. (OS Map 184; ref SU 123422.)

Wilts & Dorset 3 BR Salisbury–Stonehenge (Tel: 01722 336855).

Salisbury 9½m.

Midsummer sunrise

Uley Long Barrow (Hetty Pegler's Tump)

GLOUCESTERSHIRE
(211/212/217, 6H)

Dating from around 3000 BC, this 55 metre- (180 foot-) long Neolithic chambered burial mound is unusual in that its mound is still intact.

Open *Any reasonable time.*
Entry *Free.*

3½m NE of Dursley on B4066. (OS Map 162; ref SO 790000.)
Stagecoach Stroud Valleys 15, Churchdown Coaches Stroud–Dursley (passes close to BR Stroud) (Tel: 01452 425543).
Stroud 6m.

Upper Plym Valley

Dartmoor, DEVON (210, 2D)

Scores of prehistoric and medieval sites covering six square miles of ancient landscape.

Open *Any reasonable time. (Sites managed by the National Trust.)*
Entry *Free.*

4m E of Yelverton. (OS Map 202.)
Western National 82, 98A Plymouth–Exeter (Tel: 01392 382800).

West Kennet Avenue

Avebury, WILTSHIRE
(211/212, 5J)

An avenue of standing stones, which ran in a curve from Avebury Stone Circles to The Sanctuary, probably dating from the late Neolithic Age.

Open *Any reasonable time. (Site owned and managed by the National Trust.)*
Entry *Free.*
(on roadway)
Runs alongside B4003. (OS Map 173; ref SU 105695.)
Thamesdown 49A Swindon–Marlborough; Wilts & Dorset 5/6 Salisbury–Swindon (Tel: 01345 090 899). All pass close to BR Swindon.
Pewsey 9m, Swindon 12m.

West Kennet Long Barrow

WILTSHIRE (211/212, 5J)

A Neolithic chambered tomb, consisting of a long earthen mound containing a passage with side chambers, and with the entrance guarded by a large stone.

Open *Any reasonable time. (Site managed by the National Trust.)*
Entry *Free.*
(in layby)
¾m SW of West Kennet along footpath off A4. (OS Map 173; ref SU 104677.)

West Kennet Long Barrow

Windmill Hill

Thamesdown 49A Swindon–Devizes/Marlborough; Wilts & Dorset 5/6 Salisbury–Swindon (Tel: 01345 090 899). All to within 1m. All pass close to BR Swindon.

Pewsey 9m, Swindon 13m.

Windmill Hill

WILTSHIRE (211/212, 5J)

Neolithic remains of three concentric rings of ditches, enclosing an area of 21 acres.

Open *Any reasonable time. (Site owned and managed by the National Trust.)*
Entry *Free.*

1½m NW of Avebury. (OS Map 173; ref SU 086714.)

Thamesdown 49A Swindon–Devizes/Marlborough; Wilts & Dorset 5/6 Salisbury–Swindon. All to within 1m. All pass close to BR Swindon (Tel: 0345 090 899).

Swindon 11m.

Winterbourne Poor Lot Barrows

DORSET (211, 3G)

Part of an extensive 4,000-year-old Bronze Age cemetery.

Open *Any reasonable time.*
Entry *Free.*

2m W of Winterbourne Abbas, S of junction of A35 with minor road to Compton Valence. Access via Wellbottom Lodge – 180 metres (200 yards) E along A35 from junction. (OS Map 194; ref SY 590906.)

Southern National 31, X31 Weymouth–Taunton (passes BR Dorchester South and Axminster) (Tel: 01305 783645).

Dorchester West or South, both 7m.

Woodhenge

WILTSHIRE (211/212, 5J)

Neolithic ceremonial monument of *c.*2300 BC, consisting of six concentric rings of timber posts, now marked by concrete piles. The long axis of the rings, which are oval, points to the rising sun on Midsummer Day. *See p. 49 for more details.*

Open *Any reasonable time.*
Entry *Free.*

1½m N of Amesbury, off A345 just S of Durrington. (OS Map 184; ref SU 151434.)

Wilts & Dorset 5/6 Salisbury–Swindon (passes close to BR Salisbury & Swindon), 16 from Amesbury (Tel: 01722 336855).

Salisbury 9m.

Yarn Market

Dunster, SOMERSET (211, 4E)

A 17th-century octagonal market hall.

Open *Any reasonable time.*
Entry *Free.*

In Dunster High St. (OS Map 181; ref SS 992437.)

Southern National 28 BR Taunton–Minehead to within ¼m, also 39 from Minehead (Tel: 01823 272033).

Dunster (W Somerset Rly) ½m.

TINTAGEL CASTLE

With its specacular location on one of England's most dramatic coastlines, Tintagel Castle is a place of legends. Joined to the mainland by a narrow neck of land, Tintagel Island faces the full force of the Atlantic. On the mainland itself, the gaunt remains of the medieval castle, thought to date from the second quarter of the 13th century, represent only one phase in a long history of occupation. Even before Richard, Earl of Cornwall, built his castle there, Tintagel had come to be associated with King Arthur, as the great warrior leader's birthplace. The legend, depicted in Geoffrey of Monmouth's fabulous History (written *c.* 1139), has lived on. Today, fact and fiction lie inextricably intertwined. We know for sure, however, that with the surf thundering against the cliffs and the waves breaking over the threshold of Merlin's cave, Tintagel remains one of the most awe-inspiring and romantic spots in Britain.

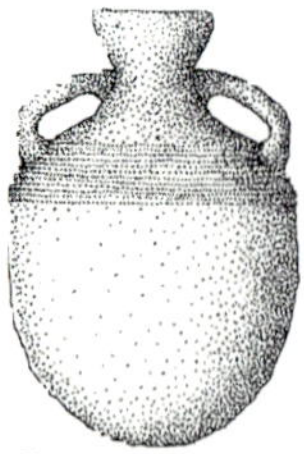

A Mediterranean wine jar

After a period as a Roman settlement and military outpost, Tintagel is thought to have been the stronghold of a Celtic king during the fifth and sixth centuries. An early Christian church stands on the site of what may have been a cemetery for important men. Here legend and archaeology come together. Whether one of those men was King Mark, whose nephew Tristan fell in love with Isolt (or Isolde), history cannot tell.

King Arthur receives his sword Excalibur from the Lady in the Lake

Their doomed romance is part of Tintagel's story, as are Geoffrey of Monmouth's tales, in which Uther Pendragon, aided by Merlin, seduced Queen Igerna at Tintagel. Tintagel's Arthurian connection was later renewed by Alfred, Lord Tennyson in his *Idylls of the King*.

The island of Tintagel

The so-called Merlin's cave (left) and the Tennysonian vision of Merlin and baby Arthur (below)

Thomas Hardy's fanciful reconstruction of Tintagel

The remains of the 13th-century castle are breathtaking. Steep stone steps, stout walls and rugged windswept cliff edges encircle the Great Hall, where Richard, Earl of Cornwall may once have feasted. The emphasis at Tintagel is always on the word 'may' as it has so many legends and unanswered questions.

Family Discovery Pack and free Children's Activity Sheet available.

Open *1 April–31 Oct: daily, 10am–6pm (6pm/dusk in Oct). 1 Nov–31 March: daily, 10am–4pm (closed 24–26 Dec, 1 Jan).*

Entry *£2.50/£1.90/£1.30*

01840 770328

(in Tintagel village)

(Please note steep climb up steps to reach castle.)

On Tintagel Head, ½ mile along uneven track from Tintagel, no vehicles. (OS Map 200; ref SX 048891.)

Western National 122,125 from Wadebridge (with some from BR Bodmin Parkway) (Tel: 01209 719988); Fry's service from Plymouth (except Suns and Bank Holidays) (Tel: 01840 770256).

Tintagel castle ruins

Appuldurcombe House

ISLE OF WIGHT (212, 3K)

Although now mainly a shell, Appuldurcombe was once the grandest house on the Isle of Wight. The fine 18th-century baroque-style house retains its elegant east front and stands in its own ornamental grounds, designed by 'Capability' Brown. The rolling green landscape beyond makes this an idyllic setting. An exhibition of prints and photographs depicts the house and its history.

Open *1 April–31 Oct: daily, 10am–6pm (6pm/dusk in Oct).*
Entry *£1.50/£1.10/80p.*
01983 852484
(¼m walk uphill from car park)
½m W of Wroxall off B3327. (OS Map 196; ref SZ 543800.)
Southern Vectis 2A Newport–Ventnor, 16B Ryde–Ventnor (Tel: 01983 562264).
Shanklin 3½m.
Ryde (Wightlink) 11m (Tel: 01705 827744).

Bayham Abbey

Battle Abbey and Battlefield

SUSSEX (213, 4N)

See pp 56–61 for full details.

Bayham Old Abbey

SUSSEX (213, 4N)

Ruins of a house of 'white' canons, founded in *c.*1208, in an 18th-century landscaped setting. The Georgian House (Dower House) is also open to the public.

Open *1 April–31 Oct: daily, 10am–6pm (6pm/dusk in Oct).*
Entry *£2.00/£1.50/£1.00.*
01892 890381
1¾ m W of Lamberhurst off B2169. (OS Map 188; ref TQ 651366.)
Autopoint/Wealden 256 BR Tunbridge Wells–Wadhurst (Tel: 0800 696 996).
Frant 4m.

Appuldurcombe House

Bishop's Waltham Palace

HAMPSHIRE (212, 4K)

This medieval seat of the Bishops of Winchester once stood in an enormous park. There are still wooded grounds surrounding the mainly 12th- and 14th-century remains we can see today. They include the Great Hall and three-storey tower, as well as the moat which once surrounded the palace.

Bishop's Waltham Palace shield

The ground floor of the Dower House is furnished as a 19th century farmhouse, with an exhibition on the powerful Winchester Bishops on the first floor.

Open *1 April–31 Oct: daily, 10am–6pm (6pm/dusk in Oct). Keykeeper in winter, please telephone 01732 778030.*
Entry *£2.00/£1.50/£1.00.*
01489 892460
(opposite car park on other side of main road)
(grounds only)
In Bishop's Waltham 5m from junction 8 of M27. (OS Map 185; ref SU 552173.)
Stagecoach Hampshire Bus 69/A Winchester-Southsea (passes close to BR Winchester) (Tel: 01256 464501); Solent Blue Line/Provincial 48A/C Eastleigh–Fareham (passes close to BR Eastleigh) (Tel: 01703 226235). All pass close to BR Fareham.
Botley 3½ m.

Boxgrove Priory

SUSSEX (212, 4L)

Remains of the Guest House, Chapter House and church of a 12th century priory.

Open *Any reasonable time.*
Entry *Free.*
N of Boxgrove, 4m E of Chichester on minor road off A27. (OS Map 197; ref SU 909076.)
Stagecoach Coastline 58 BR Chichester–Littlehampton (passes BR Barnham) (Tel: 01243 783251).
Chichester 4m.

Bramber Castle

SUSSEX (212, 4M)

The remains of a Norman castle gatehouse, walls and earthworks.

Open *Any reasonable time.*
Entry *Free.*
(limited)
On W side of Bramber village off A283 (OS Map 198; ref TQ 187107.)
Brighton & Hove 20 BR Shoreham-by-Sea-Steyning (Tel: 01273 886200).
Shoreham-by-Sea 4½ m.

Bishop's Waltham Palace (below)

BATTLE ABBEY & BATTLEFIELD

The one date in English history that everyone can remember is 1066: the Battle of Hastings, when the conquering Normans vanquished the Anglo-Saxons on 14 October. There is just as much myth surrounding the conflict as known fact. The two armies did not even fight at Hastings, but at the place which became the town of Battle, 6 miles inland. There, on the valley slopes, it is possible to retrace the lines of conflict. In the ruins of the abbey that King William built to atone for the blood spilt, you may stand on the very spot where the vanquished King Harold fell. A visit to the battlefield itself provides an unparalleled chance to absorb the reality of conquest and its aftermath. Battle Abbey stands at one of the turning points of English history.

Harold

The old name given to the site of the conflict, Senlac, is taken to mean 'field of blood'. The Battle of Hastings is etched deep into the self-image of the English, and the Bayeux Tapestry depicting it is so familiar that the reality and consequences of what happened at Battle are often misunderstood.

It was never a foregone conclusion that Harold would lose at Battle and William win. Only days before, Harold had won a famous victory in the north at Stamford Bridge against Harold Hardraada, King of Norway.

A bird's eye view of the abbey and school buildings as they are today

The great abbey gatehouse from the south

William *did* win, but only after a tremendous struggle. Today an audio tape tour re-creates the sounds of the battle, as you stand exactly where the English were, watching the Normans advance towards them. The English occupied the high ground, ranged along the ridge, and so the Normans were forced to fight uphill. The latter overcame this disadvantage by fighting both on foot and horseback, while the English dismounted to fight, using swords or the huge two-handed axes which were their most vicious and successful weapon. The course of the battle was reversed when the Normans pretended to flee, but then turned back to cut down the English who had broken ranks in pursuit.

The south end of the dorter (Monastic dormitory)

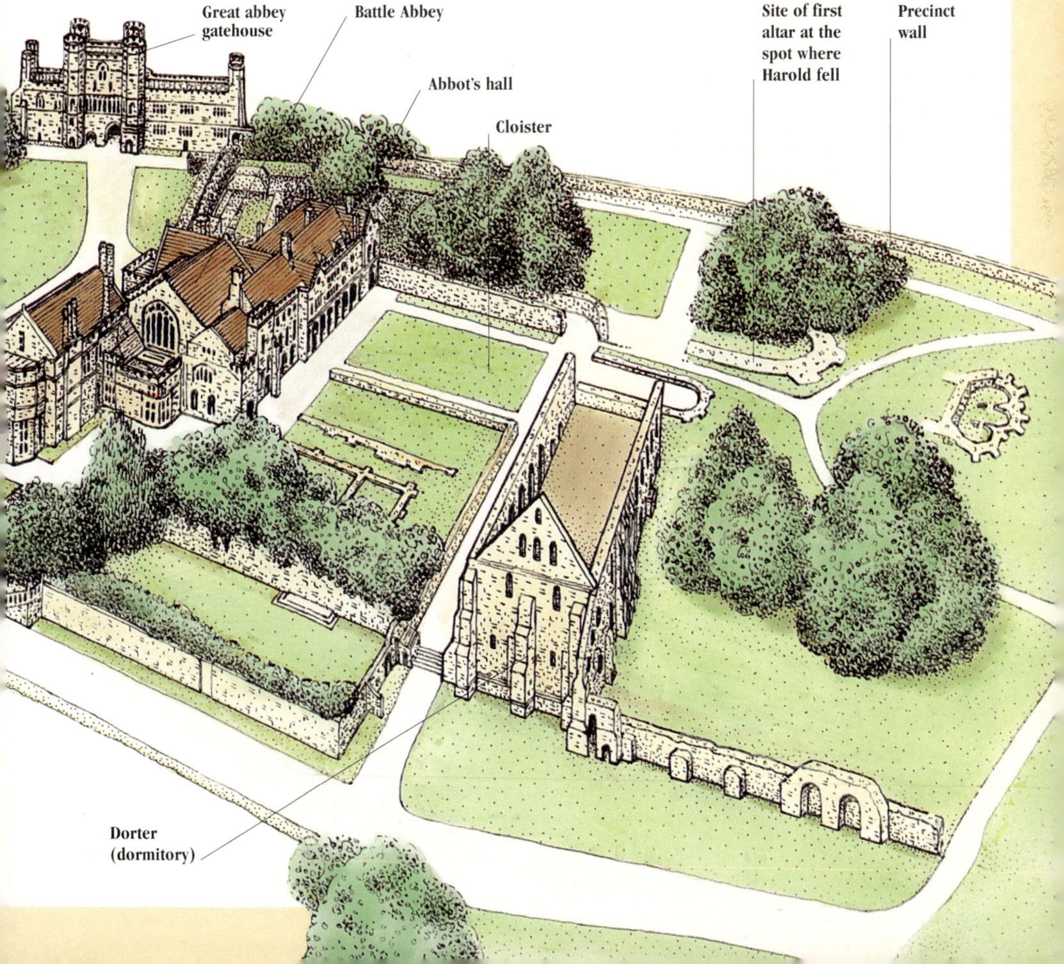

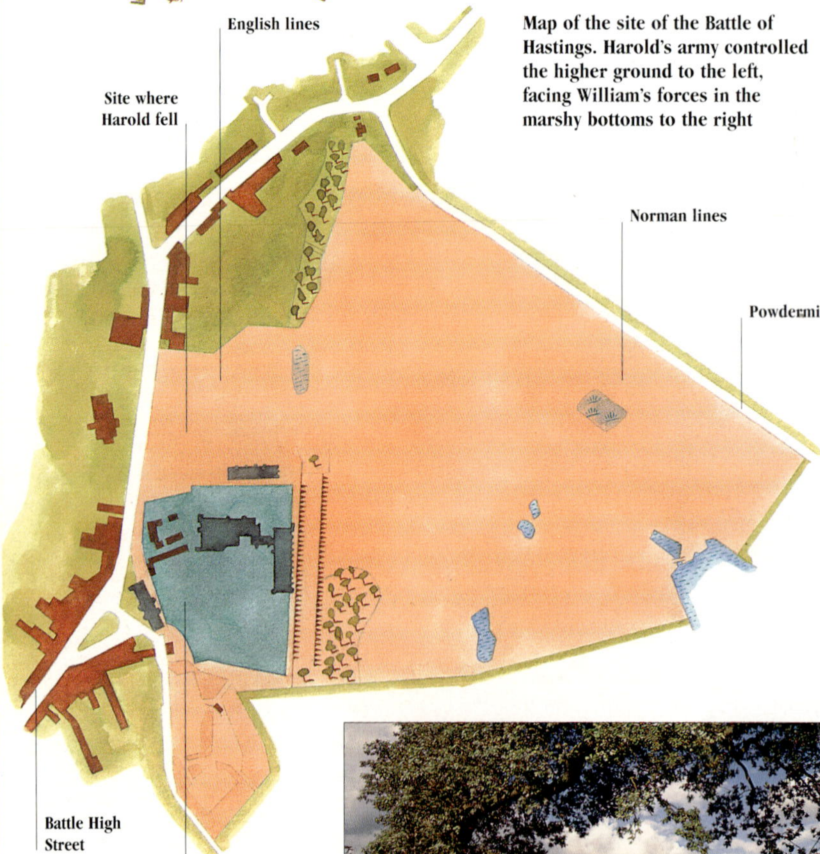

Map of the site of the Battle of Hastings. Harold's army controlled the higher ground to the left, facing William's forces in the marshy bottoms to the right

The site of the battle, with the abbey remains in the background

A re-enactment of the battle of Hastings (above)

The final assault by William was preceded by a devastating volley of arrows. Wave upon wave of archers shot up into the English ranks. The Bayeux Tapestry depicts an arrow hitting Harold in the eye. He did not – as popularly believed – die directly from that wound, but was cut down by a Norman sword, as shown in the tapestry's next scene.

Norman archer from the audio-visual re-enactment of the battle

With news of Harold's death, his army fled, the Normans in pursuit. Once William had quelled the nation in 1070, ruthlessly crushing any opposition to his rule, he decided to atone for the terrible loss of life at the Battle of Hastings. In the abbey that he founded, the high altar of the church was set on the exact spot where Harold fell.

Edward the Confessor

Portions of the abbey remain today, but little of the church or features dating back to the early Normans. The best-preserved and most impressive part is the Great Gatehouse, finest of all surviving medieval abbey entrances, built around 1338. The great hall, and other monastic buildings, were incorporated into the Tudor and Georgian house that occupied the site after Henry VIII's dissolution of the monasteries.

Abbot's Great Hall remodelled

Battle Abbey seal with the west front of the church

When Battle Abbey was dissolved, the site was given to Sir Anthony Browne, Henry VIII's master of the horse. The owners continued to remodel the abbey buildings for their home, although the principal area where the battle had been fought remained little touched. A generous gift from the USA enabled it to be purchased for the nation in 1976, 910 years after the date everyone remembers.

Exciting range of interactive displays and exhibitions, an audio-visual interpretation of the battle, and a new interactive audio tour of the history of the battlefield and abbey that guides you around the grounds.

Family Discovery Pack and free Children's Activity Sheet available.

Children's themed activity area with outdoor playground.

***Open** 1 April–31 Oct: daily, 10am–6pm (6pm/dusk in Oct). 1 Nov–31 March: daily, 10am–4pm (closed 24–26 Dec, 1 Jan). Film/audio-visual – '1066, The Battle of Hastings'; Abbot's Hall open to the public during school summer holidays only.*

***Entry** £3.50/£2.60/£1.80*

✆ 01424 773792

*P (charge payable) ∩ * (also available for the partially sighted, those in wheelchairs or with learning difficulties, and in French and German) ♿ (some steps) ⊙ 🚻 (nearby)*

Reconstructed Fireplace in the Gatehouse

Outside the Gatehouse in the early 19th century

Bayeux Tapestry

Interior of 'novices chamber' in the east range

William the Conqueror

➔ *At S end of Battle High St. (OS Map 199; ref TQ 749157.) Battle is reached by road by turning off A21 onto the A2100.*

Stage-coach South Coast/Maidstone & District 4/5 Maidstone–Hastings; Eastbourne Buses 28 BR Eastbourne–BR Rye; Hastings & District RE Group BR Rye–BR Battle summer Suns only (Tel: 01273 474747).

Battle ½m.

Tomb of Sir Anthony Browne, who was given Battle Abbey by Henry VIII in 1538

Calshot Castle

HAMPSHIRE (212, 3K)

This century, the fort has been part of both an RN and an RAF base. Spectacular views of the Solent can be seen from the roof. Henry VIII built this coastal fort to command the sea passage to Southampton. The barrack room has been restored to its pre-World War I artillery garrison appearance, complete with bunks and uniform.

Open *1 April–31 Oct: daily, 10am–6pm (6pm/dusk in Oct).*
Entry *£1.80/£1.40/90p.*
✆ *01703 892023*
On spit 2m SE of Fawley off B3053. (OS Map 196; ref SU 488025.)
Solent Blue Line X9, 39 Southampton-Calshot (passes BR Southampton) to within 1m (Tel: 01703 226235).

Calshot Castle (below) and the barrack room (right and far right).

Camber Castle

SUSSEX (213, 4O)

A rare example of an Henrician fort surviving in its original plan.

Open *7 June, 6 July, 17 Aug, 12 Oct: by guided tour only. Advance booking is required for tours (min. of 5 people, max. of 30), please telephone 01732 778000. Tours commence from Rye Heritage Centre.*
Entry *£2.00/£1.00.*
✆ *01732 778000*
Access across fields, off the A259, 1m S of Rye off harbour road. (OS Map 189; ref TQ 922185.)
From surrounding areas to Rye, thence 1¼m (Tel: 01273 474747).
Rye 1¼m.

Camber Castle

Carisbrooke Castle

ISLE OF WIGHT (212, 3K)

See pp 64–7 for full details.

Conduit House

Canterbury, KENT (213, 5P)

The Conduit House is the monastic waterworks which supplied nearby St Augustine's Abbey.

Open *Access very difficult. Please telephone 01732 778000 for further details.*

Entry *Free.*

Approximately 5–10 minutes' walk from St Augustine's Abbey. Situated within the new St Martin's Heights housing estate, St Martin's Avenue, Canterbury. (OS Map 179; ref TR 159585.)

East Kent C1/C2 from railway stations to bus station, thence C5 (Tel: 01227 472082).

Canterbury East or West, both 1½m.

Deal Castle

Deal Castle

KENT (213, 5P)

Crouching low and menacing, the huge, rounded bastions of this austere fort, built by Henry VIII, once carried 119 guns. It is a fascinating castle to explore, with long, dark passages, battlements, and a huge basement with an exhibition on England's coastal defences.

Free Children's Activity Sheet available.

Open *1 April–31 Oct: daily, 10am–6pm (6pm/dusk in Oct). 1 Nov–31 Mar: Wed–Sun, 10am–4pm (closed 24–26 Dec, 1 Jan).*

Entry *£2.80/£2.10/£1.40.*

01304 372762

(also available for the partially sighted, those with learning difficulties, and in French and German)

(courtyards & ground floor only, parking available)

SW of Deal town centre. (OS Map 179; ref TR 378521.)

From surrounding areas (Tel: 0800 696 996).

Deal ½m.

Donnington Castle

BERKSHIRE (212, 5K)

Built in the late 14th century, the twin towered gatehouse of this castle survives amidst some impressive earthworks.

Open *Any reasonable time.*

Entry *Free.*

(steep slopes within grounds)

1m N of Newbury off B4494. (OS Map 174; ref SU 461694.)

Newbury Buses 110, 118 from Newbury (passes close to BR Newbury) (Tel: 01635 40743).

Newbury 1¼m.

Dover Castle

KENT (213, 4P)

See pp 70–7 for full details.

Dymchurch Martello Tower

KENT (213, 4O)

One of many artillery towers which formed part of a chain of strongholds intended to resist invasion by Napoleon. It is fully restored, with an original 24-pounder gun on the roof.

Open *5–8 April: daily, 12–4pm. May–July: weekends, 12–4pm. 1–31 Aug: daily, 12–4pm. For further details please telephone 01732 778000. (Open with the assistance of Shepway District Council.)*

Entry *£1.00/80p/50p.*

Access from High Street, not from seafront. (OS Map 189; ref TR 102294.)

Stagecoach East Kent 11, 12/A, Stagecoach South Coast 711 Folkestone– Hastings (passes close to BR Folkestone Central) (Tel: 0800 696 996).

Sandling 7m; Dymchurch (R H & D Rly), adjacent.

Carisbrooke Castle

The Redvers Arms

From time immemorial, whosoever controlled Carisbrooke controlled the Isle of Wight. The castle sits at the very heart of the island, and has been a fixture since its foundation as a Saxon camp during the 8th century. Carisbrooke's royal connections date from the end of the 13th century when it was purchased from the Redvers family by Edward I. For a brief period the castle occupied the centre of the national and political stage when Charles I was imprisoned there in 1648, before being taken for trial and execution in London the following year. His story is commemorated in the Charles I rooms and in the many exhibits relating to his imprisonment.

The compact set of castle buildings demonstrates every phase of construction from the Saxon era to the present. Remnants of the Saxon wall run below the shell of the stone Norman keep, high on its artificial mound. The discomfort of the keep was diminished with the building of a great hall and private apartments for the Redvers family, who ruled the island and Carisbrooke from 1100 to 1293. The last of them, the young Countess Isabella, was a most ambitious builder. She was among the first in the country to put glass into domestic windows. Remains of her beautiful chapel show an individual taste. The castle fell into royal hands when Edward I bought it on Isabella's death.

Sir George Carey (left), governor of Carisbrooke from 1552 to 1603, and a replica of his seal (below)

The castle was refortified in the 16th century against the threat of invasion by Catholic Spain in 1588. When Spain threatened to invade England again in 1599, Sir George Carey, the Governor, persuaded Elizabeth I to improve the defences still further.

The 12th-century keep, on its artificial mound, towers above the later great hall and private apartments (right)

Charles I and Governor Hammond (above) and the windows put in 1856 to replace the one through which Charles tried to escape (left)

Although Carisbrooke saw no action in the English Civil War, it housed the defeated King Charles I in 1647–8. The castle was prepared for its new inhabitant while the government decided his future. Charles tried escaping twice, before he was taken to London to be tried.

Less distinguished prisoners had been used to tread the waterwheel, drawing water up the well's 49-metre (161-feet) depth. In the 18th century donkeys were introduced and they are still there today, providing a very popular attraction for visitors. One of the castle's museums is dedicated to Princess Beatrice, Victoria's daughter, governor 1896–1944, and symbol of a continuing royal presence felt throughout the Isle of Wight. A new interactive museum in the Old Coach House, displaying the history of the castle, rounds off a pleasant visit.

Charles I's daughter Elizabeth, who died at Carisbrooke of pneumonia in 1650

St Nicholas Chapel (left) and an Edwardian decoration from it (above)

Open *1 April–31 Oct: daily, 10am–6pm (6pm/dusk in Oct). 1 Nov–31 March: daily, 10am–4pm (closed 24–26 Dec, 1 Jan).*

Entry *£3.80/£2.90/£1.90.*

01983 522107

('Keepers Kitchen'; normally open summer season only) (also in French and German) (grounds & lower levels only)

1¼m SW of Newport.
(OS Map 196; ref SZ 486877.)

Southern Vectis 9C/S from Newport in summer or 7/A/B/C, 16B from Newport, Yarmouth & Ventnor to within ¼m (Tel: 01983 562264).

Ryde Esplanade 9m; Wootton (IoW Steam Rly) 3m.

Fishbourne (Wightlink) 6m; Ryde (Wightlink) 8m; Yarmouth (Wightlink) 9m (Tel: 01705 827744).

Free Children's Activity Sheet available.

An exciting CD Rom unit provides information on the castles of England, their functions and purpose.

Tactile (braille) orientation model in courtyard.

Donkey Centre.

A donkey was first used to draw water using the treadmill in the 18th century. There are now four at work at Carisbrooke.

The Norman Keep, built before 1136

Eynsford Castle

KENT (213, 5N)

One of the first stone castles built by the Normans. The moat and remains of the curtain wall and hall can still be seen.

***Open** Any reasonable time.*
***Entry** Free.*

In Eynsford off A225. (OS Map 177; ref TQ 542658.)

Kentish Bus 13, 415 BR Eynsford–Dartford (Tel: 0800 696 996).

Eynsford 1m.

Farnham Castle Keep

Farnham Castle Keep

SURREY (212, 5L)

A motte and bailey castle which has been in continuous occupation since the 12th century.

***Open** 1 April–30 Sept: daily, 10am–6pm.*
***Entry** £2.00/£1.50/£1.00.*
01252 713393

½m N of Farnham town centre on A287. (OS Map 186; ref SU 839474.)

From surrounding areas (Tel: 01737 223000).

Farnham ¾m.

Faversham Stone Chapel

KENT (213, 5O)

The remains of a small medieval church incorporating part of a 4th-century Romano-British pagan mausoleum.

***Open** Any reasonable time.*
***Entry** Free.*

1¼m W of Faversham on A2. (OS Map 178; ref TQ 992614.)

Maidstone & District/Kent Coach 333 Maidstone–Faversham (passes BR Faversham) (Tel: 0800 696 996).

Faversham 1½m.

Flowerdown Barrows

HAMPSHIRE (212, 4K)

Round barrows of a Bronze Age burial site which were once part of a larger group.

***Open** Any reasonable time.*
***Entry** Free.*

In Littleton, 2½m NW of Winchester off A272. (OS Map 185; ref SU 459320.)

Stagecoach Hampshire Bus 68/A/C from Winchester (passes BR Winchester) (Tel: 01256 464501).

Winchester 2m.

Fort Brockhurst

HAMPSHIRE (212, 3K)

This was a new type of fort, built in the 19th century to protect Portsmouth with formidable fire-power. Largely unaltered, the parade ground, gun ramps and moated keep can all be viewed. An exhibition illustrates the history of Portsmouth's defences.

See nesting swans, geese and ducks, and look out for ghostly activity in Prisoner Cell No 3!

Fort Brockhurst (aerial view)

View the RAF Gosport Aviation Heritage Exhibition.
Open *1 April–30 Sept: daily, 10am–6pm (closed 24–26 Dec, 1 Jan). Closed 1–2pm.*
Entry *£2.00/£1.50/£1.00.*
01705 581059
(grounds & ground floor only; for
Off A32, in Gunner's Way, Elson, on N side of Gosport. (OS Map 196; ref SU 596020.)
Provincial 1–7 Fareham–Gosport Ferry (passes BR Fareham, also Gosport Ferry links with BR Portsmouth & Southsea) (Tel: 01962 868944).
Fareham 3m.

Fort Cumberland

HAMPSHIRE (212, 3K)

Constructed in the shape of a wide pentagon by the Duke of Cumberland in 1746. The fort was occupied by the Royal Marines until 1973 and is perhaps the most impressive piece of 18th-century defensive architecture remaining in England.

Open *27 July, 27 Sept: by guided tour only. Advance booking is required for tours, please telephone 01732 778000.*
Entry *£2.00/£1.00.*
In the Eastney district of Portsmouth on the estuary approach via Henderson Road, a turning off Eastney Road, or from the Esplanade. (OS Map 196; ref SZ 682992.)
Blue Admiral 16, Stagecoach Coastline 21 BR Portsmouth Harbour–Hayling Ferry (Tel: 01705 650967).
Fratton 2m.

Horne's Place Chapel

Appledore, KENT (213, 4O)

This 14th century domestic chapel was once attached to the manor house. The house and chapel are privately owned and visitors are requested to respect the owners' privacy.

Open *Wed only, 10am–5pm.*
Entry *Free.*
(nearby)
1½m N of Appledore. (OS Map 189; ref TQ 957307.)
Appledore 2½m.

Horne's Place Chapel

Dover Castle

The white cliffs of Dover are among England's most celebrated sights. On top of the cliffs stands Dover Castle, once described as 'the key to the kingdom'. It is one of the country's largest castles, and has the longest recorded history of any major fortress in Britain. The story stretches almost without break from the Iron Age to the nuclear age. Every era has left its physical mark: the Roman lighthouse, fortified Anglo-Saxon town, stout Norman keep, Tudor defences, Georgian barracks, and the underground structures from which the Dunkirk evacuation was masterminded.

Interior of St Mary-in Castro

Underground tunnels

St Mary-in-Castro and *Pharos*

Dover Castle is a sturdy reminder of some of the toughest fighting days in England's past. Although William the Conqueror strengthened the defences that Harold built, the main masonry dates from the 12th century. The monumental keep was built for Henry II, as were the walls of the Inner Bailey, and the eastern part of the outer curtain wall.

Henry II

Their designs were innovative, with regularly spaced towers for the Inner Bailey, and the curtain wall's gatehouses and flanking towers. The works were completed under Henry III.

Unique to Dover Castle are underground tunnels, originally cut in the 13th century, which reached their culmination in the secret wartime tunnels.

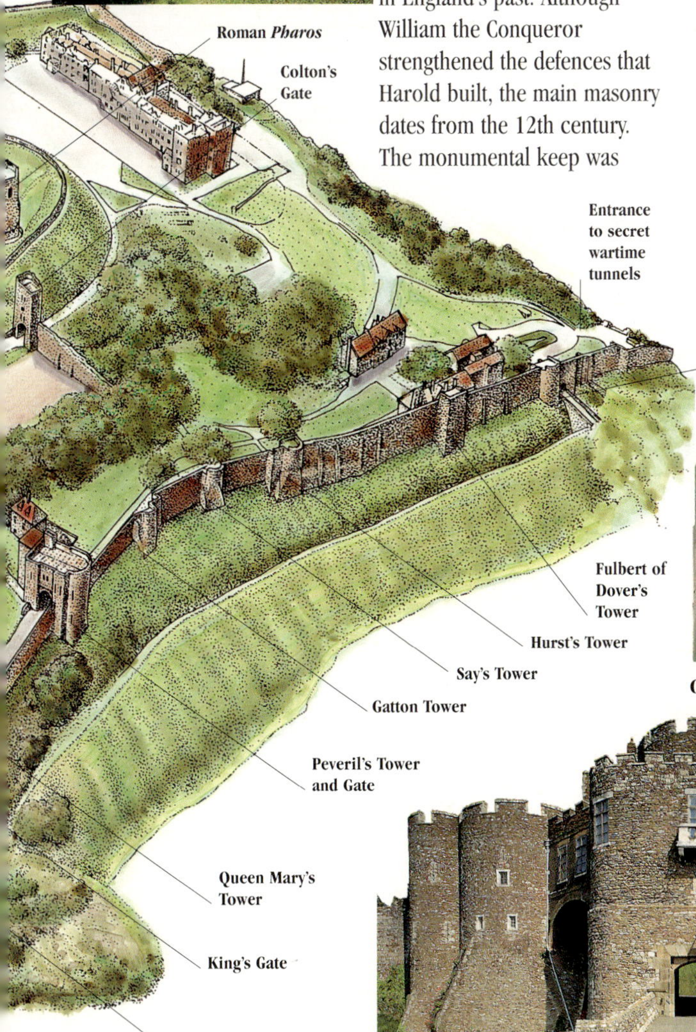

Canon's Gate (the Caponier)

Constable's Gate

The keep, the central strong tower built in the 1180s, is the obvious starting point for visitors. Its three-towered forebuilding, carrying the entry staircase and two chapels, is one of the most elaborate of all. The upper chapel, reserved for the royal family's use, is especially fine, with its rich decoration and its style of Norman, crossing over into Gothic. The former royal apartments, with their great central halls and more intimate chambers, are still most impressive in their monumental scale, despite having lost most of their original decoration.

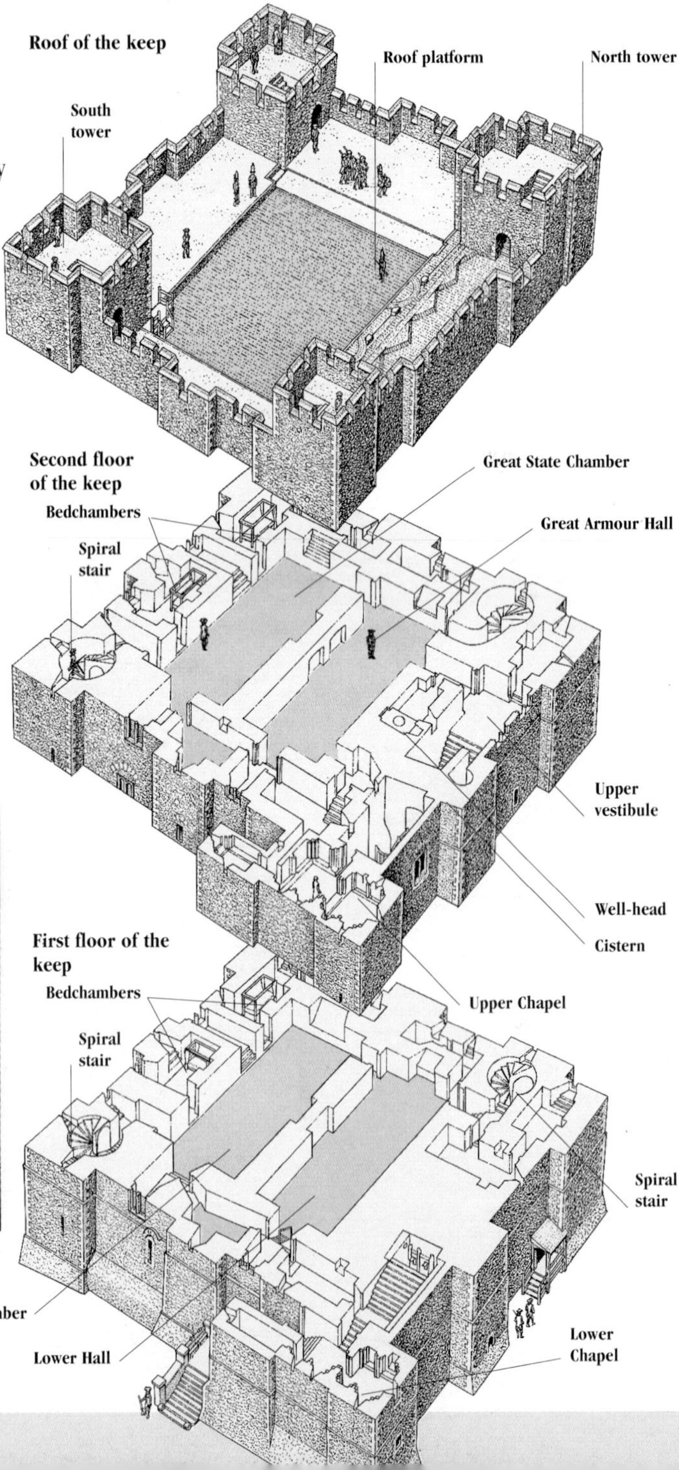

Spiral stairs leading to all floors of the keep

Although most of the medieval buildings, other than the gates and walls, have gone, Henry III's great hall survives. It is incorporated into the Georgian barracks which are one of the features of Dover's continued military importance long after many other castles had fallen into picturesque decay. Queen Elizabeth's 'Pocket Pistol' is a survival of the Tudor age of defence. A great gun, 7.3 metres (24 feet) long, it was actually made in 1544 for Henry VIII.

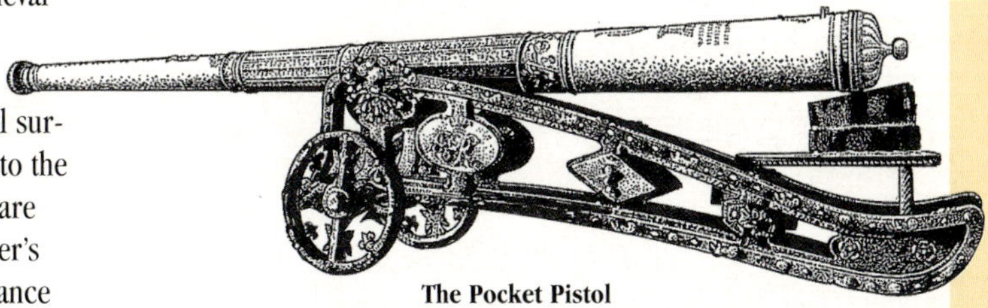

The Pocket Pistol

Prince of Wales, later George V, a notable Constable

The castle's outer defences, which were innovative in military design, provide a fascinating, and lengthy, walk through history.

The Avranches Tower, purpose-built in the 1180s for archers, is approached via the magazines and the artillery works of the Napoleonic Wars. The Bell Battery, originally for six guns, was built as part of the programme of refortification that began in the 1750s.

On the cliff edge, with panoramic views over the town and out to sea, there are the remains of the Admiralty Lookout and Signal Station used in both World Wars.

Soldiers and sailors have guarded the English approaches from this spot for well over 800 years. Dover Castle has something for everyone interested in the nation's past.

A view of the castle featuring the curtain wall, Peverell's Tower and the keep

Secret wartime tunnels

Whoever first had the idea of tunnelling under Dover Castle can hardly have anticipated the dramas that would unfold underground. The rabbit warren of tunnels has been the centre of military operations from the Napoleonic Wars almost to the present. The Dunkirk evacuation in 1940 was its finest hour.

Visitors may experience for themselves what military life was like underground.

Tunnelling operations began in earnest in 1797 when Dover was fortified in readiness for a French invasion. Seven tunnels (running with damp and prone to collapse) were dug for the soldiers and officers who were filling both castle and town to overflowing.

When French threats ended, the tunnels fell into disuse until they came back into their own in World War II.

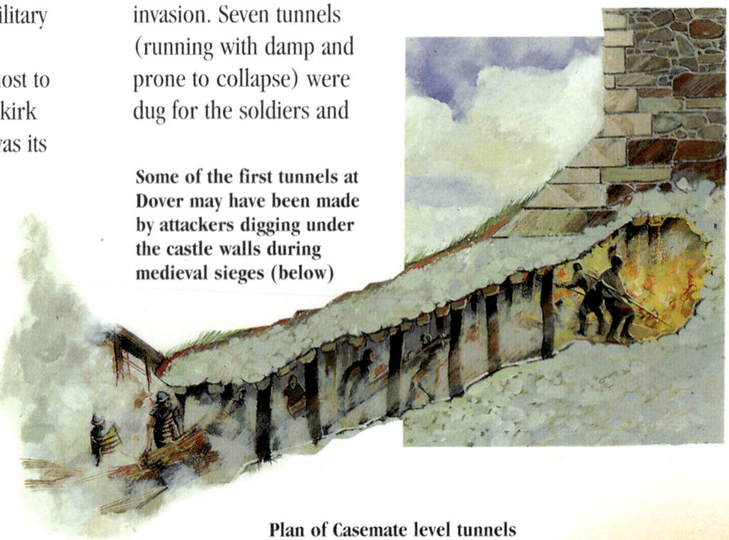

Some of the first tunnels at Dover may have been made by attackers digging under the castle walls during medieval sieges (below)

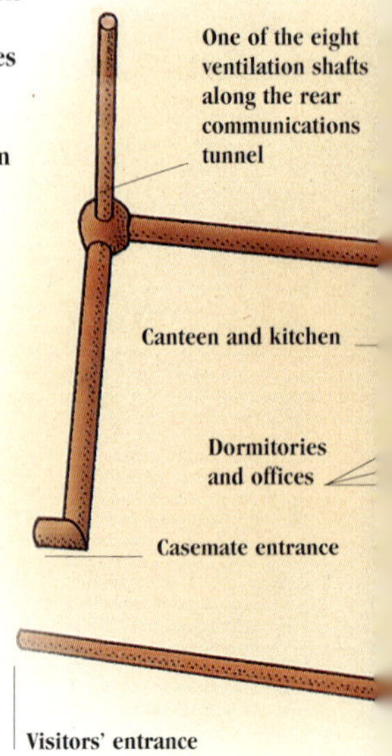

Plan of Casemate level tunnels showing the layout of the operation rooms and services as they were in mid-1943. These, together with the Annexe level above, are open to the public

Entrance to secret wartime tunnels (left)

Coastal artillery operations room during World War II (below)

Spy artefacts from World War II

Air ducts in a Napoleonic tunnel

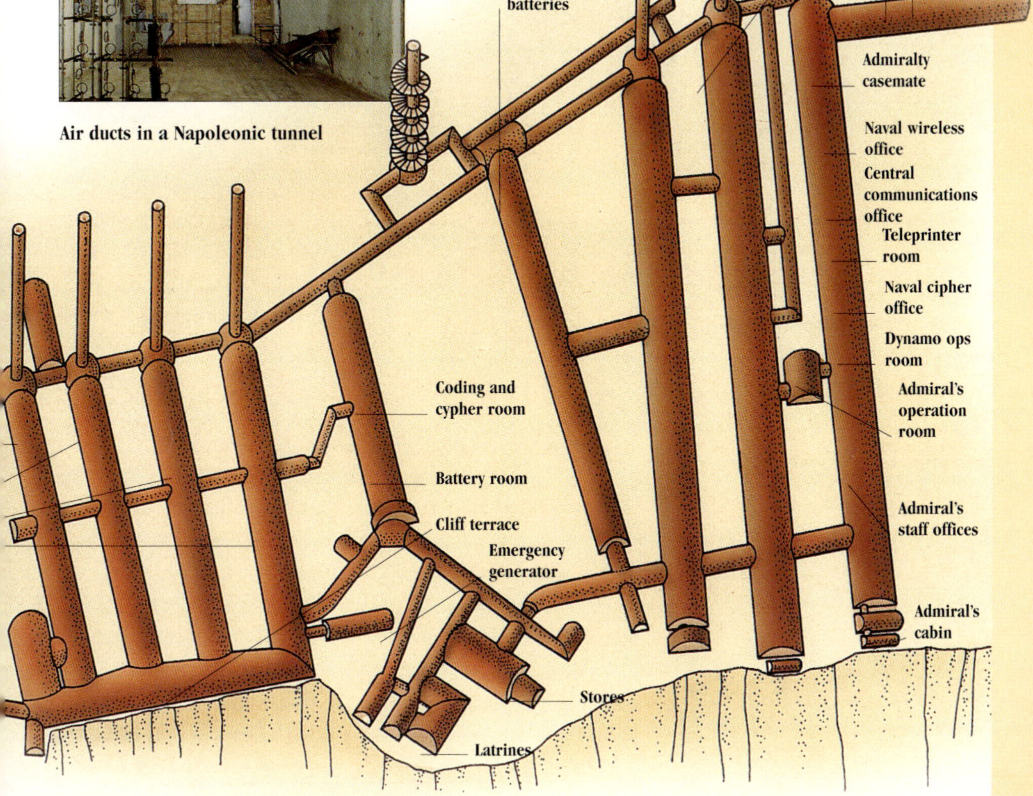

Vice-Admiral Ramsay, who was commanding the Straits of Dover, occupied the underground tunnels from the outbreak of war. In May 1940, as France fell before the German advance, these tunnels became the nerve centre for Operation Dynamo – the evacuation of the British Expeditionary Force (BEF) and French troops from Dunkirk's beaches.

World War II gun embrasures on the eastern ramparts

Winston Churchill and Admiral Ramsay plotting in the tunnels

Casemate level, with graffiti from different periods on the walls (left)

Ramsay and his staff worked round the clock for nine days. On 26 May some 400,000 troops were awaiting rescue. The best estimate was that 45,000 could be brought back. Dunkirk was ablaze. Pleasure craft, fishing boats, sailing barges streamed across the Channel as tenders from the beaches. The Allied forces and rescue ships were sitting targets. Yet, by 4 June, all were evacuated. In total, 338,000 men came back: the BEF and 139,000 French soldiers.

Under sustained German air attack, Dover's tunnels acquired a new importance as shelter for the Combined Headquarters. Additional tunnels were dug, telecommunications systems were installed, and even a hospital was established. Hundreds of men and women worked and lived underground in unpleasant conditions, damp and piercingly cold.

With the end of the War, the tunnels were adapted as a Regional Seat of Government in the event of nuclear catastrophe, finally abandoned by the Home Office in 1984. In the 1990s, the tunnels' wartime secrets are open for all to see.

Anti-aircraft operations room

Reconstructed repeater station

The Princess of Wales' Royal Regiment, a lively exhibition of regimental history from the 1600s to the present day. Children's play area in the basement of the keep. Making History: Re-creating the Past – an exhibition which explores the way experts re-created the past. Live and Let Spy exhibition in the Keep.

Exciting CD Rom unit with information on English castles' functions and purpose.

Open *1 April–31 Oct: daily, 10am–6pm (6pm/dusk in Oct). 1 Nov–31 March: daily, 10am–4pm (closed 24–26 Dec, 1 Jan).*

Entry *£6.00/£4.50/£3.00. (includes admission to secret wartime tunnels, by guided tour only – last tour begins at 5pm (summer) and 3pm (winter).*

01304 201628

*(The Keep Restaurant; for private functions tel: 01304 205830) (Two separate tours – for grounds only and for medieval underground works only – available in French, German and Japanese. * (underground hospital.) (courtyard & grounds – some very steep slopes)*

On E side of Dover. (OS Map 179; ref TR 326416.)

Stagecoach East Kent 90 from BR Dover Priory (Tel: 0800 696 996).

Dover Priory 1½m.

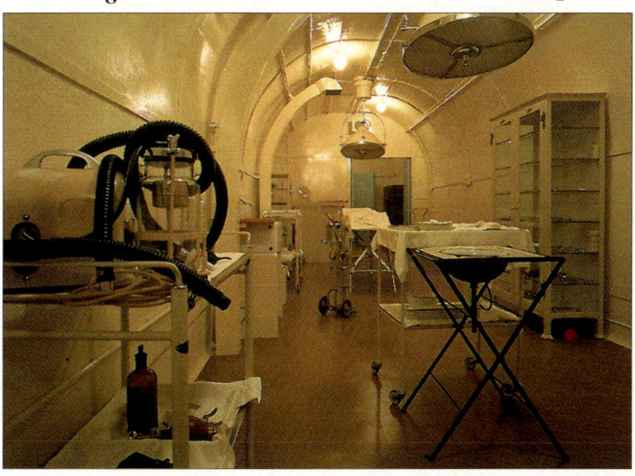

The underground hospital on the Annexe level (left)

Hurst Castle

HAMPSHIRE (211/212, 3J)

This was one of the most sophisticated fortresses built by Henry VIII, and later strengthened in the 19th and 20th centuries, to command the narrow entrance to the Solent. There is an exhibition in the castle, and two huge 38-ton guns from the fort's armaments.

Open *April–June: daily, 10am–5.30pm. July–Aug: daily, 10am–6pm. Sept–Oct: daily, 10am–5.30pm.*
Entry *£2.00/£1.50/£1.00.*
01590 642344
('Castle Cafe'; weekends only April and May, daily June–Sept)
On Pebble Spit S of Keyhaven. Best approached by ferry from Keyhaven, telephone 01590 642500 (June–Sept, 9am–2pm) or answerphone 01425 610784, for ferry details. (OS Map 196; ref SZ 319898.)
Wilts & Dorset 123/4 Bournemouth–Lymington (passes BR New Milton) to within 2½m, or 1m to ferry (Tel: 01202 673555).
Lymington Town 4½m to Keyhaven, 6½m to Fort.

Hurst Castle (above right)and a 38-ton gun (above) from the armaments

King James's and Landport Gates

Portsmouth, HAMPSHIRE (212, 3K)

These gates were once part of the 17th-century defences of Portsmouth.

Open *Exterior any reasonable time.*
Entry *Free.*
King James's Gate: forms entrance to United Services Recreation Ground (officers) on Park Rd; Landport Gate: as above, men's entrance on St George's Rd. (OS Map 196; King James's Gate ref SU 638000, Landport Gate ref SU 634998.)
From surrounding areas (Tel: 01962 868944).
Portsmouth Harbour ¼m.

Kit's Coty House and Little Kit's Coty House

KENT (213, 5N)

Ruins of two prehistoric burial chambers, taking their name from the Celtic phrase for 'tomb in the woods'.

Open *Any reasonable time.*
Entry *Free.*
W of A229 2m N of Maidstone. (OS Map 188; ref TQ 745608 & 745604.)

Kit's Coty House (left)

Maidstone & District 101, 126, BR Maidstone East–Gillingham (Tel: 0800 696 996).
Aylesford 2½m.

Knights Templar Church

Dover, KENT (213, 4P)

Standing across the valley from Dover Castle are the foundations of a small circular 12th-century church.

Open *Any reasonable time.*
Entry *Free.*

On the Western Heights above Dover.
(OS Map 179; ref TR 313408.)
Dover Priory ¾m.

Maison Dieu

Lullingstone Roman Villa

KENT (213, 5N)

See pp 80–3 for full details.

Maison Dieu

Ospringe, KENT (213, 5O)

This forerunner of today's hospitals remains largely as it was in the 16th century with exposed beams and an overhanging upper storey. It contains an exhibition about Ospringe in Roman times.

Open *1 April–31 Oct: weekends and Bank Holidays, 2–5pm. For further details contact The Faversham Society on 01795 534542. Keykeeper in winter. (Open with the assistance of The Faversham Society.)*
Entry *Free.*

In Ospringe on A2 ½m W of Faversham.
(OS Map 178; ref TR 002608.)
Maidstone & District/Kent Coach 333, Maidstone–Faversham (passes BR Faversham) (Tel: 0800 696 996).
Faversham ¾m.

Lullingstone Roman Villa

When Lullingstone villa was discovered in 1939, in the fertile valley of the River Darent in Kent, it was one of the most exciting archaeological finds of the century. The original villa, with timber walls built on flint bases, dates from the end of the 1st century AD in the years of prosperity fifty to a hundred years after the Emporer Claudius had invaded Britain (AD 43). Kent was one of the areas favoured by the Romans, and it was there that they built some of their earliest villas – or country estates. It was embellished, extended and even rebuilt during more than 300 years of occupation. The remains that are visible today include a wonderful mosaic floor, a sequence of bath-houses, and layers of changing religious observance – from a shrine and Romano-Celtic mausoleum to a Christian church – making the villa a priceless window into the world of the Roman settlers.

A bronze flagon found in the mausoleum

The rest of the bath complex: hot-water bath, hot room, tepid room and cold room

Large cold plunge bath

Recreation room

The villa's original plan was a block of rooms, fronted by a verandah, with projecting wings, one of which had a cellar. Although the main house was extended and remodelled twice, the same basic shape was retained.

At each remodelling, the baths were extended and made more comfortable. The famed fastidiousness of the Romans is reflected in the sequence of *caldarium* (hot room), *tepidarium* (tepid room), and *frigidarium* (cold room), as well as what was probably a hot dry room or *laconicum*.

Panel of geometric patterns that lies between the Europa and Bellerophon mosaics

Bronze hub cap found at the villa

One panel depicts the Rape of Europa, a scene from the *Aeneid*, with Jupiter, in the shape of a bull, abducting Europa to ravish her. The other depicts Bellerophon on his winged horse Pegasus killing the Chimaera, the fire-breathing monster of legend.

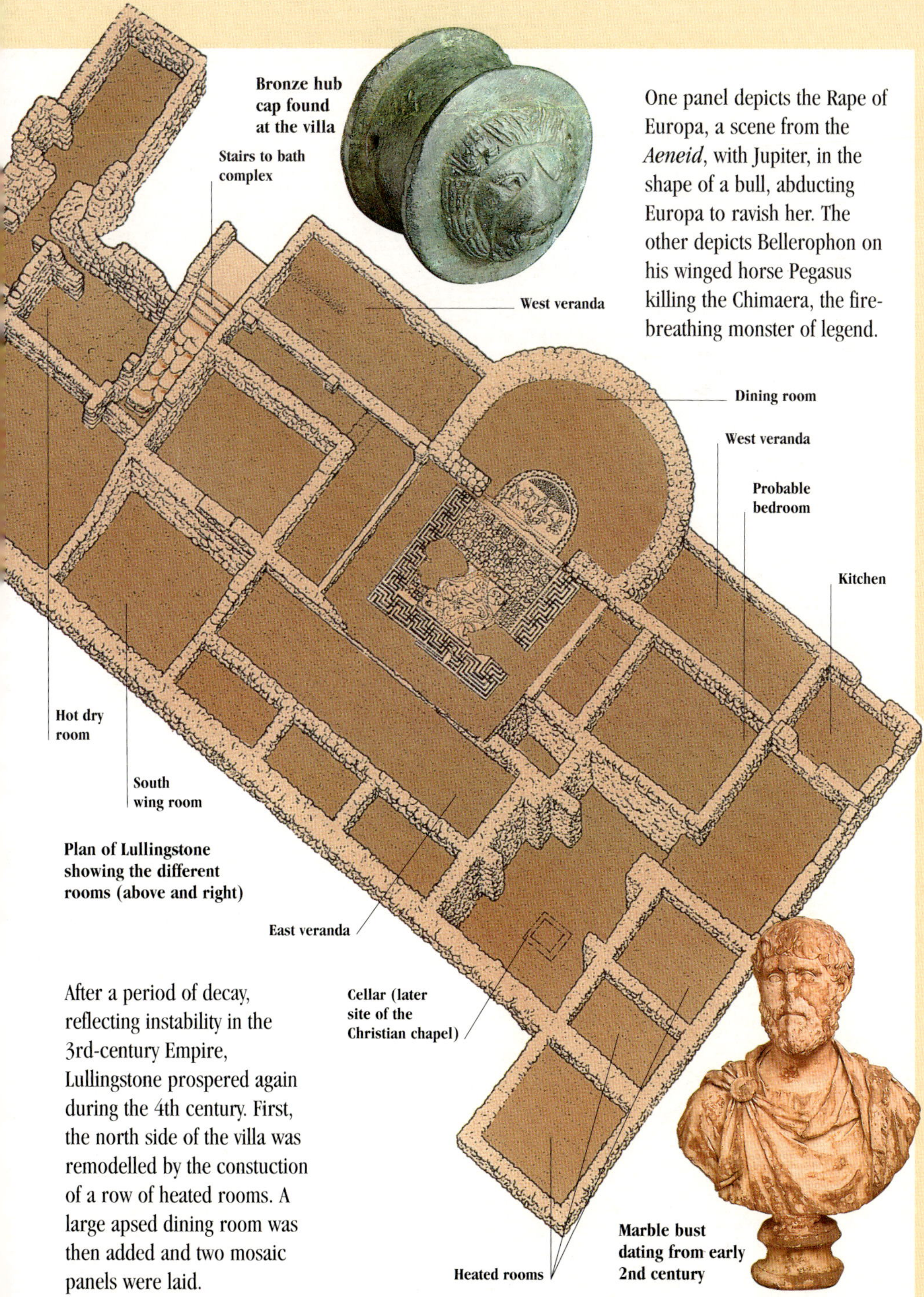

Plan of Lullingstone showing the different rooms (above and right)

After a period of decay, reflecting instability in the 3rd-century Empire, Lullingstone prospered again during the 4th century. First, the north side of the villa was remodelled by the constuction of a row of heated rooms. A large apsed dining room was then added and two mosaic panels were laid.

Marble bust dating from early 2nd century

The vestiges of the painting of three water nymphs in the cellar.

Spring, one of the seasonal figures in the mosaic floor

Bone inlay head of Medusa

Whenever they improved the bathing facilities, the occupants of Lullingstone also demonstrated that godliness was next to cleanliness. The mausoleum built in the grounds, in the form of a Romano-Celtic temple, contained a young man and woman buried in state.

There is evidence of a shrine from the earliest period of occupation. Frescoes of water nymphs have been uncovered in the cellar, and two finely carved Greek marble busts found there may be from an earlier generation. Grave offerings and other relics found during excavations (including human and animal skeletal remains) are also evidence of the different religions practised there.

The owners later adopted Christianity. They turned some of the rooms into a chapel, with wall paintings depicting the sacred monogram of Christ and his worshippers at prayer.

From the end of the 4th century, disaster gradually overtook Lullingstone. A serious fire destroyed a substantial portion of the house, the Roman imperial system decayed, and by 420 the villa had been abandoned.

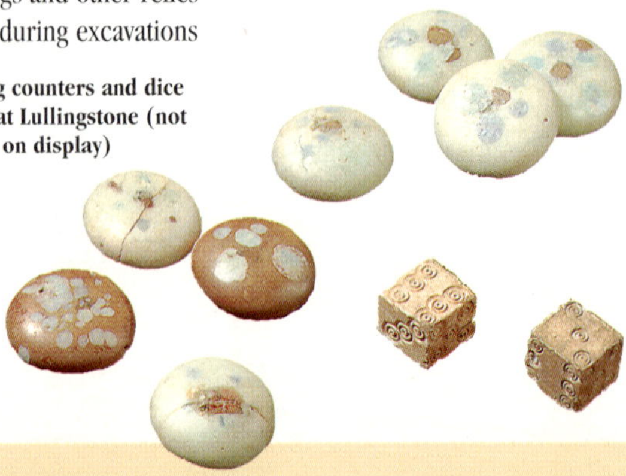

Gaming counters and dice found at Lullingstone (not always on display)

Jupiter abducting Europa, as depicted in the mosaic floor

Only the mausoleum's remains survived, which were incorporated into an early Christian church. Some materials from the villa were used to build the rest of the church, while soil, washed down the hillside, covered what remained. Suspicions of the existence of a substantial Roman building were borne out by the villa's proper discovery some 1500 years after its original inhabitants had fled. They left behind them one of the finest of all survivals from the centuries of Roman rule.

Marble bust dating from the later 2nd century

Free Children's Activity Sheet available.

Open *1 April–31 Oct: daily, 10am–6pm (6pm/dusk in Oct). 1 Nov–31 March: daily, 10am–4pm (closed 24–26 Dec, 1 Jan).*

Entry *£2.00/£1.50/£1.00*

✆ 01322 863467

(also available in French and German)

½m SW of Eynsford off A225 off junction 3 of M25. Follow A20 towards Brands Hatch. (OS Map 177; ref TQ 529651.)

Eynsford ¾m.

The villa viewed from the south (left) with the hot dry room of the bath complex in the foreground

A seasonal figure, with ears of corn, depicted in the mosaic floor

Medieval Merchant's House

(OS Map 196; ref SU 419112.)
Southampton Citybus 17A/B, 27 from BR Southampton (Tel: 01703 553011).
Southampton ¾m.

Milton Chantry

Gravesend, KENT (213, 5N)

A small 14th-century building which housed the chapel of the leper hospital and the chantry of the de Valence and Montechais families. It later became a tavern and in 1780 part of a fort.

Open *1 March–31 Dec: Tues–Fri and bank holidays,*

Medieval Merchant's House

Southampton, HAMPSHIRE (212, 4K)

The life of a prosperous merchant in the Middle Ages is vividly evoked by the brightly painted cabinets, chests and colourful wall hangings authentically re-created for this faithfully restored 13th-century town house, originally built as a shop and home for wine merchant John Fortin.

Free Children's Activity Sheet available.

Open *1 April–31 Oct: daily, 10am–6pm (6pm/dusk in Oct).*
Entry *£2.00/£1.50/£1.00.*

01703 221503
(one step)
58 French Street, ¼m S of city centre just off Castle Way (between High St and Bugle St)

Netley Abbey

Netley Abbey East window

1–5pm; Sat–Sun, 10am–5pm. Keykeeper (Tel: 01474 564422). (Open with assistance of Gravesham Borough Council.)

Entry *Free.*

In New Tavern Fort Gardens E of central Gravesend off A226. (OS Map 177; ref TQ 652743).

From surrounding areas (Tel: 0800 696 996.)

Gravesend ¾m.

Netley Abbey

HAMPSHIRE (212, 4K)

A 13th century Cistercian abbey converted in Tudor times for use as a house. Watch out for ghostly figures drifting amongst the ruins.

Old Soar Manor

Plaxtol, KENT (213, 5N)

The remains of a late 13th century knight's manor house, comprising the two-storey solar and chapel. There is an exhibition to visit.

Old Soar Manor

Open *Any reasonable time.*

Entry *Free.*

01705 527667

(nearby, across road near estuary)

In Netley, 4m SE of Southampton, facing Southampton Water. (OS Map 196; ref SU 453089.)

Southampton Citybus 16/A. BR Southampton-Hamble (Tel: 01703 553011).

Netley 1m.

Northington Grange

Northington, HAMPSHIRE

See The Grange.

Open *1 April–30 Sept: daily, 10am–6pm (Site maintained, managed and owned by the National Trust.)*

Entry *Free.*

0892 890651

(Limited) (National Trust Kent & East Sussex office)

1m E of Plaxtol. (OS Map 188; ref TQ 619541.)

Wealden Beeline 222 BR Borough Green–BR Tunbridge Wells; East Surrey 404 Sevenoaks–Plaxtol; on both alight E end of Plaxtol, thence ¾m by footpath (Tel: 0800 696 996).

Borough Green & Wrotham 2½m.

Pevensey Castle (above and right)

Osborne House

ISLE OF WIGHT (212, 3K)

See pp 88–93 for full details.

Pevensey Castle

SUSSEX (213, 3N)

Medieval castle including remains of an unusual keep enclosed within its walls, originally dating back to the 4th-century Roman fort Anderida.

***Open** 1 April–31 Oct: daily, 10am–6pm (6pm/dusk in Oct). 1 Nov–31 March: Wed–Sun, 10am–4pm (closed 24–26 Dec, 1 Jan). Closed 1–2pm in winter.*

***Entry** £2.00/£1.50/£1.00.*

01323 762604

(charge payable) (nearby) ('Castle Cottage Tearoom and Restaurant')

In Pevensey off A259.

(OS Map 199; ref TQ 645048.)

Eastbourne Buses 28, Stagecoach South Coast 18, 711/4 from Eastbourne (Tel: 01273 474747).

Pevensey & Westham or Pevensey Bay, both ½m.

Portchester Castle West Front

Portchester Castle

HAMPSHIRE (212, 3K)

A residence for kings and a rallying point for troops, this grand castle has a history stretching back nearly 2,000 years. There are Roman walls, the most complete in Europe, substantial remains of the castle and an exhibition telling the story of Portchester.

Free Children's Activity Sheet and CD Rom unit with information on the castles of England.

***Open** 1 April–31 Oct: daily, 10am–6pm (6pm/dusk in Oct). 1 Nov–31 March: daily, 10am–4pm (closed 24–26 Dec, 1 Jan).*

***Entry** £2.50/£1.90/£1.30.*

01705 378291

(grounds & lower levels only) in car park

(Local pubs provide refreshment)

On S side of Portchester off A27, Junction 11 on M27.

(OS Map 196; ref SU 625046.)

Red Admiral 65/A, 67 Fareham-Southsea to within

¼m (Tel: 01705 650967).
Portchester 1m.

Reculver Towers and Roman Fort

KENT (213, 5P)
Standing in a country park, a 12th-century landmark of twin towers and the walls of a Roman fort.

Open *Any reasonable time (external viewing only).*
Entry *Free.*
01227 3 66444
(ground floor only – long slope up from car park)
01227 3 66444.
At Reculver 3m E of Herne Bay. (OS Map 179; ref TR 228694.)
East Kent/Regent 635 from Herne Bay (Tel: 0800 696 996).
Herne Bay 4m.

Richborough Castle

KENT (213, 5P)
This fort and township date back to the Roman landing in AD43. The fortified walls and the massive foundations of a triumphal arch which stood 25 m (80 ft) high still survive.

Open *1 April–31 Oct: daily, 10am–6pm (6pm/dusk in Oct). 1–31 Nov: daily, 10am–4pm.*
Entry *£2.00/£1.50/£1.00.*
01304 612013
1½m N of Sandwich off A257. (OS Map 179; ref TR 324602.)
Sandwich 2m.

Richborough Roman Amphitheatre

KENT (213, 5P)
Remains associated with the nearby 3rd-century castle.

Open *Difficult access through farmed field. Please telephone Richborough Castle (01304 612013) for details.*
Entry *Free.*
1¼m N of Sandwich off A257, Junction 7 of M2, onto A2. (OS Map 179; ref TR 321598.)
Sandwich 1¾ m.

Richborough Castle and bust

Rochester Castle with the tide out

Rochester Castle

KENT (213, 5N)
Founded on the Roman city wall, this Norman bishop's castle was an important royal stronghold.

Open *1 April–30 Sept: daily, 10am–6pm. 1 Oct–31 March: daily, 10am–4pm (closed 24–26 Dec, 1 Jan). (Site managed by Rochester upon Medway City Council.)*
Entry *£2.50/£2.00/£1.30.*
E (public, in castle grounds)
01634 402276
By Rochester Bridge (A2), Junction 1 of M2 and Junction 2 of M25. (OS Map 178; ref TQ 742686.)
From surrounding areas (Tel: 0800 696 996).
Rochester ½m.

Osborne House

Osborne House was 'a place of one's own, quiet and retired', for Queen Victoria and Prince Albert. They found tranquillity on the Isle of Wight, far from the formality of court life at Buckingham Palace and Windsor Castle. The house they built for themselves and their large family was set among terraced gardens which they filled with treasured mementoes. Victoria died at Osborne in 1901, still mourning her beloved Albert, who had died in early middle age. Edward VII gave the house to the nation shortly afterwards. With recent restoration, it has become one of the most evocative memorials to Britain's longest-reigning monarch.

Osborne House from the east with the Italian garden and terraces prior to their restoration to how they were at the end of Queen Victoria's reign

With royalty, most things are relative. When visitors see Osborne for the first time, knowing that the young Victoria and Albert had wanted a modest country home, they are surprised by its scale and magnificence. The house is set on rising ground overlooking the Solent, where the ships that helped Britannia rule the waves sailed to and fro. Two tall towers in an Italian style dominate, above fountains set on terraces and rolling wooded parkland. Inside, magnificence abounds — the Indian room, marbled pillars, gilding, statuary, grand paintings. The full, even stuffed-full, interiors seem typically Victorian, but the contents remind us that this family had links with all the crowned heads of Europe.

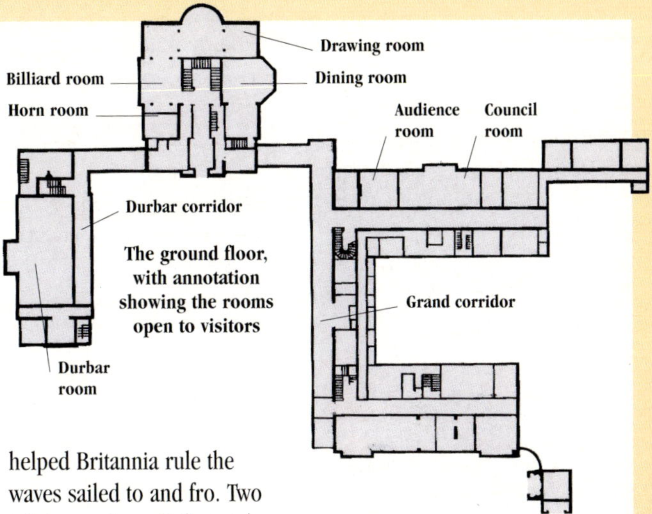

The ground floor, with annotation showing the rooms open to visitors

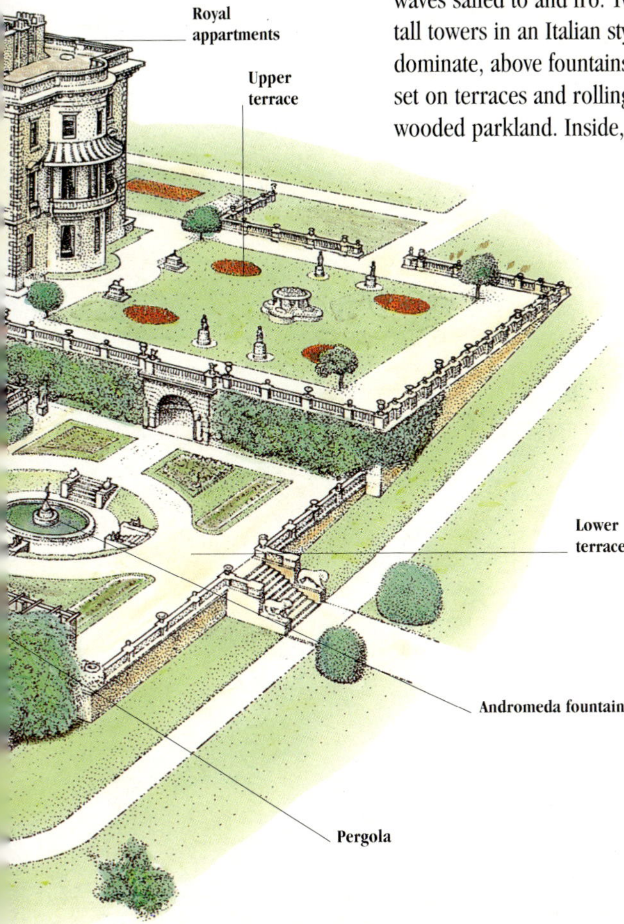

Marble Winged Victory and bronze statue, both in the Grand corridor

Despite the idea of cosy domesticity at Osborne, the formality of monarchy and its role as head of the British empire, are never far away.

Victoria and Albert married in 1840, three years after the young queen had come to the throne. They were dismayed by the places they were expected to live in. Windsor was a rambling old castle, with smelly drains – their typhoid germs killed Prince Albert in 1861.

Victoria and Albert bought Osborne in 1845, and began to dismantle the existing relatively small house. Its ambitious replacement was the work of Thomas Cubitt, best known for his buildings in London.

Prince Albert (right) and Queen Victoria (far right), Britain's longest-reigning monarch

The Grand Corridor

Cubitt's striking Italianate towers dominate the architectural composition of Osborne

Queen Victoria's bedroom (right)

This Michelangelo inspired French clock (above) graces the dining room (left)

The new house was Italianate, rather than in the Gothic idiom one often associates with the Victorians. The first part was ready for occupation by 1846 and the main structure was completed by 1851. This speed was the result of both Cubitt's skill and Albert's unflagging Teutonic zeal. Osborne's completion was also the year of the Great Exhibition – Albert's greatest achievement – held in the Crystal Palace in Hyde Park. Victoria and Albert with their many children embodied the family ideal and helped restore respect for the monarchy following its low esteem under George IV and William IV. Queen Victoria enthused to her uncle Leopold, King of the Belgians, that Albert had 'raised monarchy to the highest pinnacle of respect, and rendered it popular beyond what it ever was in this country'. Although of necessity state affairs and Privy Council meetings took place at Osborne, it was essentially a family holiday home. The queen had her first experience of sea bathing there – she liked it until she put her head under the water.

One of Queen Victoria's many medicines

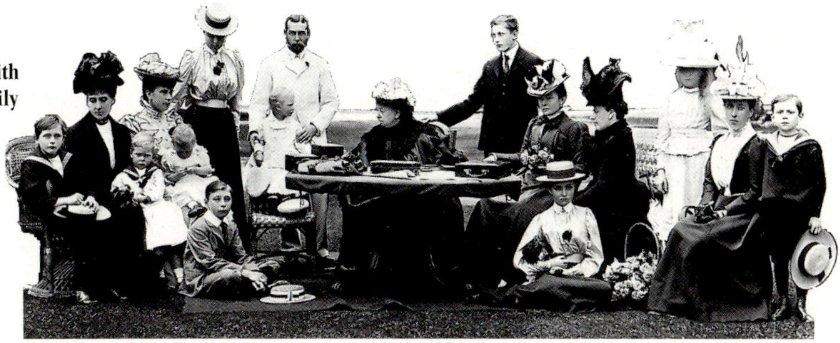

Queen Victoria photographed with many of her family in 1898

Victoria and Albert's nine children were given more freedom at Osborne. They could play in their own little home, Swiss Cottage, which was given to them on Victoria's birthday in 1854. As a memento of their youth Victoria commissioned marble sculptures of their infant arms, which still lie in ghostly display.

A new routine helped ease painful memories after Albert died and Victoria went into the mourning from which she never fully emerged. Growing numbers of grand- and great-grand-children filled the house at Christmas, while Princess Beatrice, Victoria's youngest daughter, became her mother's companion. The princess lived in the Durbar wing, Osborne's last addition, built by craftsmen from India in 1890–91 to provide more formal state rooms.

The Durbar room, the last addition to Osborne

Queen Victoria died on 22 January 1901 on a couch bed in the Queen's Bedroom. The private royal suite was closed to all except members of the royal family until the Queen gave permission in 1954 for full public access.

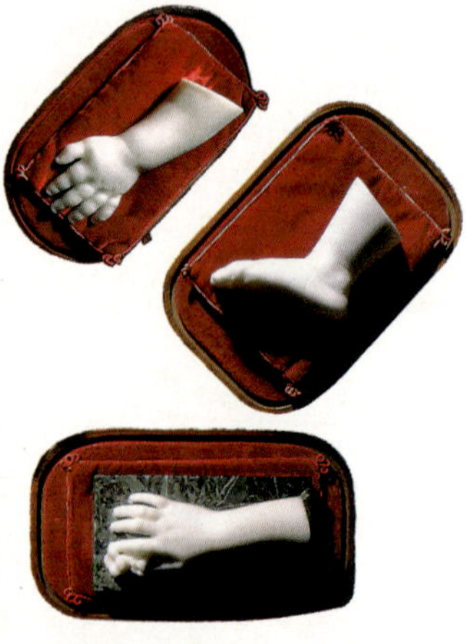

Marble replicas of Queen Victoria's children's arms and legs (above) and the drawing room (left)

A hand-coloured marble bust given to Albert by Victoria as a birthday gift in 1856

Enjoy a Victorian carriage ride to the Swiss Cottage area.
Free Children's Activity Sheet available.

Open *1 April–30 Sept: daily, House, 10am–5pm (last admission 4.30pm), Grounds, 10am–6pm (last admission 5pm). 1 Oct–31 Oct: daily, House and Grounds, 10am– 5pm/ dusk (last admission 4pm).*
Entry *House and Grounds £6.00/ £4.50/£3.00. Grounds only £3.50/ £2.60/£1.80 (separate ticket available April–May, Sept–Oct only).*
01983 200022
('Keepers Kitchen')
(exterior and ground floor only; vehicles with disabled passengers may set them down at the house entrance before returning to car park)

1m SE of East Cowes. (OS Map 196; ref SZ 516948.)
Southern Vectis 4 Ryde–E Cowes, 5 Newport–E Cowes (Tel: 01983 523831).
Ryde Esplanade 7m; Wootton (IoW Steam Rly) 3m.
East Cowes (Red Funnel) 1½m (Tel: 01703 330333); Fishbourne (Wightlink) 4m; Ryde (Wightlink) 7m (Tel: 01705 827744).

A German musical box (left), recalling Albert's origins

A model shopfront (above) on display in Swiss Cottage (below)

St Augustine's Abbey crypt

Royal Garrison Church

Portsmouth, HAMPSHIRE (213, 3K)

Originally a hospice for pilgrims, this 16th-century chapel became the Garrison Church after the Dissolution. Expertly restored in the 1860s but fire-bombed in 1941, the chancel survived and there is still plenty to see.

Open *1 April–30 Sept: Mon–Fri, 11am–4pm.*
Entry *Free.*

On Grand Parade S of Portsmouth High St.
(OS Map 196; ref SU 633992.)
From surrounding areas (Tel: 01962 868944).
Portsmouth Harbour ¼m.

St Augustine's Abbey

Canterbury, KENT (213, 5O)

Founded in 598, this was one of the earliest monastic sites in southern England. There are remarkable remains of the foundations of the original 6th-century churches, the Norman church and medieval monastery.

Open *1 April–31 Oct: daily, 10am–6pm (6pm/dusk in Oct). 1 Nov–31 March: daily, 10am–4pm (closed 24–26 Dec, 1 Jan).*
Entry *£1.50/£1.10/80p.*
01227 767345
(some steps) (nearby)
In Longport ¼m E of Cathedral Close.
(OS Map 179; ref TR 154578.)
From surrounding areas (Tel: 0800 696 996).
Canterbury East & West, both ¾m.

St Augustine's Cross

Ebbsfleet, KENT (213, 5P)

19th-century cross, in Celtic design, marking the traditional site of St Augustine's landing in 597.

Open *Any reasonable time.*
Entry *Free.*

2m E of Minster off B29048. (OS Map 179; ref TR 340641.)
Thanet Bus 01 Ramsgate–Canterbury (Tel: 0800 696 996).
Minster 2m.

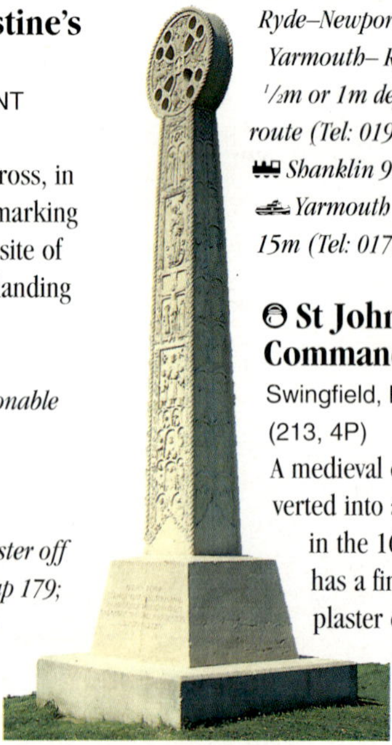

St Augustine's Cross

St Catherine's Oratory

ISLE OF WIGHT (212, 3K)

Affectionately known as the Pepperpot, this 14th-century lighthouse, erected following the wreck of the wine ship *St Marie* of Bayonne, stands on the highest point of the island.

Open *Any reasonable time (external viewing only).*
(Site maintained and managed by the National Trust.)
Entry *Free.*

¾m NW of Niton.
(OS Map 196; ref SZ 494773.)
Southern Vectis 16/B Ryde–Newport, 7/A Yarmouth–Ryde, to within ½m or 1m depending on route (Tel: 01983 562264).
Shanklin 9m.
Yarmouth (Wightlink) 15m (Tel: 01705 827744).

St John's Commandery

Swingfield, KENT (213, 4P)

A medieval chapel, converted into a farmhouse in the 16th century. It has a fine moulded plaster ceiling and a remarkable timber roof.

Open *By appointment only; tel. 01732 778000 for details.*
Entry *Free.*
⊗
➲ *2m NE of Densole off A260. (OS Map 179; ref TR 232440.)*
🚌 *East Kent 16 BR Folkestone Central–Canterbury to within 1m (Tel: 0800 696 996).*
🚆 *Kearsney 4m.*

St Leonard's Tower

St Leonard's Tower

West Malling, KENT (213, 5n)

An early and particularly fine example of a Norman tower keep, built *c.*1080 by Gundulf, Bishop of Rochester.

Open *Any reasonable time (external viewing only).*
Entry *Free.*
♿ *(grounds only)* ⊗
➲ *On unclassified road W of A228. (OS Map 188; ref TQ 675570.)*
🚌 *Maidstone & District 70 from Maidstone, Mercury 151 from Chatham (Tel: 0800 696 996).*
🚆 *West Malling 1m.*

Silchester Roman City Walls and Amphitheatre

HAMPSHIRE (212, 5K)

The best preserved Roman town walls in Britain, almost one-and-a-half miles around, with an impressive, recently restored amphitheatre.

Open *Any reasonable time.*
Entry *Free.*
⊗
➲ *On minor road 1m E of Silchester. (OS Map 175; ref SU 643624.)*
🚌 *Stagecoach Hampshire Bus 44, 53 from Basingstoke (passes BR Bramley) to within 1m (Tel: 01256 464501).*
🚆 *Bramley or Mortimer, both 2¾m.*

Sutton Valence Castle

KENT (213, 5O)

The ruins of a 12th-century stone keep built to monitor the important medieval route across the Weald from Rye to Maidstone.

Open *Any reasonable time.*
Entry *Free.*
⊗
➲ *5m SE of Maidstone in Sutton Valence village on A274. (OS Map 188; ref TR 815491.)*
🚌 *Maidstone & District/ Nu-Venture/Chalkwell 12 Maidstone–Tenterden (pass BR Headcorn) (Tel: 0800 696 996).*
🚆 *Headcorn 4m, Hollingbourne 5m.*

Temple Manor

Rochester, KENT (213, 5N)

The 13th-century manor house of the Knights Templar.

Open *2 days notice is required, please telephone 01634 827980 for details. (Site managed by Rochester upon Medway City Council.)*
Entry *Free.*
P ♿ *(grounds only)* ⊗
➲ *In Strood (Rochester) off A228. (OS Map 178; ref TQ 733686.)*
🚌 *From surrounding areas (Tel: 0800 696 996).*
🚆 *Strood ¾m.*

The Grange

Northington, HAMPSHIRE
(212, 4K)
Magnificent neoclassical country house, built at the beginning of the 18th century.

Open *Any reasonable time (exterior viewing only).*
Entry *Free.*
P ♿ *(with assistance)*
4m N of New Alresford off B3046.
(OS Map 185; ref SU 562362.)
Oakley Buses 309 Basingstoke–Alresford to within ½m (passes close to BR Basingstoke) (Tel: 01256 780731).
Winchester 8m.

The Grange

Titchfield Abbey

HAMPSHIRE (212, 4K)
Remains of a 13th-century abbey overshadowed by a grand Tudor gatehouse.

Open *1 April–31 Oct: daily, 10am–6pm (6pm/dusk in Oct). 1 Nov–31 March: daily, 10am–4pm. (Site managed by The Titchfield Abbey Society.)*
Entry *Free.*
P ♿

½m N of Titchfield off A27.
(OS Map 196; ref SU 541067.)
Solent Blue Line 26 Fareham–Southampton (Tel: 01703 226235).
Fareham 2m.

Titchfield Abbey

Upnor Castle

KENT (213, 5N)
Well preserved 16th-century gun fort, built to protect Queen Elizabeth I's warships. However in 1667 it failed to resist the Dutch navy, which stormed up the Medway destroying half the English fleet.

Open *1 April–30 Sept: daily, 10am–6pm. Closed 12–1pm. Please telephone 01634 827980 for further details. (Site managed by Rochester upon Medway City Council.)*
Entry *£2.50/ £1.90/£1.30.*
01634 718742
P *(at a slight distance from castle – park before village)*
♿ *(grounds only)*
At Upnor, on unclassified road off A228.
(OS Map 178; ref TQ 758706.)
Mercury 197 from BR Chatham; otherwise 120, 191/4/6 Chatham-Hoo, alight Wainscott, thence 1m (Tel: 0800 696 996).
Strood 2m.

Walmer Castle and Gardens

KENT (213, 5P)
One of the many forts built along the south coast by Henry VIII, it has since been transformed into an elegant stately home. As the residence of the Lords Warden of the Cinque Ports, Walmer was used by the Duke of Wellington and is still used today by HM the Queen Mother. The delightful gardens are at their best in summer when the herbaceous borders are in full bloom.

Open *1 April–31 Oct: daily, 10am–6pm (6pm/dusk in Oct). 1 Nov–31 Mar: Wed–Sun, 10am–4pm (closed Jan–Feb and*

when Lord Warden in residence).
Entry *£3.80/£2.90 /£1.90.*
☎ 01304 364288
🚻 🅿 *(nearby approach to castle)*
🎧 *(also available for the partially sighted, those with learning difficulties, and in French and German)* ♿ *(courtyard & garden only, parking available)* ⊗ 🛍
➜ *On coast S of Walmer on A258. Junction 13 off M20 or from M2 to Deal.*
(OS Map 179; ref TR 378501.)
🚌 *From surrounding areas (Tel: 0800 696 996).*
🚆 *Walmer 1m.*

Waverley Abbey

SURREY (212, 4L)

First Cistercian house in England, founded in 1128. The remaining ruins date from the 13th century.

Open *Any reasonable time.*
Entry *Free.*
🅿 *(limited)* ⊛
➜ *2m SE of Farnham off B3001 and off junction 10 of M25.*
(OS Map 186; ref SU 868453.)
🚆 *Farnham 2m.*

Western Heights

Dover, KENT (213, 4P)

Parts of moat of 19th-century fort built to fend off a French invasion. Now incorporated into White Cliffs Countryside Project.

Open *Any reasonable time.*
Entry *Free.*
⊛ 🅿
➜ *Above Dover town on W side of Harbour.*

Walmer Castle (right) and profile of the Duke of Wellington (below)

(OS Map 179; ref TR 312408.)
🚆 *Dover Priory ¾m.*

Wolvesey Castle

Wolvesy, HAMPSHIRE (212, 4K)

One of the greatest medieval buildings in England, Wolvesey was

the Bishops's of Winchester chief residence. Its extensive ruins still reflect their importance and immense wealth.

Open *1 April–31 Oct: daily, 10am–6pm (6pm/dusk in Oct).*
Entry *£1.50/£1.10/80p.*
☎ 01962 854766
♿ ⊛
➜ *¾m SE of Winchester Cathedral, next to the Bishop's Palace; access from College St.*
(OS Map 185; ref SU 484291.)
🚌 *From surrounding areas (Tel: 01962 868944).*
🚆 *Winchester ¾m.*

Yarmouth Castle

ISLE OF WIGHT (212, 3J)

This last addition to Henry VIII's coastal defences was completed in 1547. It houses exhibitions of paintings of the Isle of Wight and photographs of old Yarmouth.

⊛ Picnic spot with views over the Solent.
Open *1 April–31 Oct: daily, 10am–6pm (6pm/dusk in Oct). Closed 1–2pm.*
Entry *£2.00/£1.50/£1.00.*
☎ 01983 760678
♿ *(ground floor only)*
⊛ 🅿 *(coach & car park 200yds, limited roadside of 1hr)*
➜ *In Yarmouth adjacent to car ferry terminal.*
(OS Map 196; ref SZ 354898.)
⛴ *Yarmouth (Wightlink) adjacent (Tel: 01705 827744).*

Albert Memorial: a model (below) and a gilded angel (below right)

Albert Memorial

Kensington,
GREATER LONDON
(212, 6M)

An elaborate national memorial by George Gilbert Scott to commemorate the Prince Consort. Its site at the southern end of Kensington Gardens links it with the greatest achievement of Albert's lifetime, the Great Exhibition of 1851. It was inaugurated in 1872 but not finally completed until 1876. The figure of the Consort sits on a pyramid of 868 brick arches and has above it a lofty Gothic canopy supported by Granite columns. Its ornate statuary includes the Parnassus frieze, representations of the Continents, the Industrial Arts, the Greater Sciences, and the four greater Christian and four moral Virtues, surmounted by the realm of the spirit and the Christian afterlife. The memorial is currently undergoing extensive conservation and repair by English Heritage, but the Visitor Centre is open.

Open *1 April–30 Sept: daily, 10am–6pm. 1 Oct–31 March: daily, 9am–3.30pm.*
Entry *Free.*
Frequent from surrounding areas (Tel: 0171 222 1234).
Victoria 1½m.
Tube *South Kensington ½m.*

Chiswick House (right) and a portrait of Inigo Jones (below), the pioneer of the Palladian style.

Chapter House

Westminster Abbey,
GREATER LONDON

See Pyx Chamber, Chapter House and Abbey Museum.

Chiswick House

Chiswick, GREATER LONDON (212, 5M)

Palladian villa built *c.*1728 for Lord Burlington, a great promoter of the Palladian style first pioneered in England by Inigo Jones. The interior decoration is by William Kent, as are the beautiful Italianate gardens, with classical statues and neoclassical temples. Both house and gardens are undergoing extensive restoration.

An exhibition, with a film, tells the story of the house and gardens, and Lord Burlington.

Open *1 April–31 Oct: daily, 10am–6pm (6pm/dusk in Oct). 1 Nov–31 March: Wed–Sun, 10am–4pm (closed 24–26 Dec, 1 Jan). Closed 1–2pm.*
Entry *£2.50/£1.90/£1.30.*
0181 995 0508
(in grds) (off west-bound A4) (also available for the partially sighted, those with learning difficulties, and in French and German)
(exterior & ground floor only)
Burlington Lane, W4.
190, 290 Hammersmith–Richmond; E3 Greenford–Chiswick (Tel: 0171 222 1234).
Chiswick ½m.

Coombe Conduits

Kingston-Upon-Thames, GREATER LONDON (212, 5M)

Built by Henry VIII to supply water to Hampton Court Palace, three miles away, Coombe Conduits consists of two small buildings (one now a ruin) connected by an underground passage.

Open *By appointment only. Please contact Head Custodian at Marble Hill House on 0181 892 5115.*
Entry *Free.*

Frequent from surrounding areas (Tel: 0171 222 1234).
Kingston-upon-Thames ¼m.

Eltham Palace

Eltham, GREATER LONDON (213, 5M)
See pp 100–1 for full details.

Jewel Tower

Westminster, GREATER LONDON (213, 5M)

Built *c.*1365 to house the personal treasure of Edward III and formerly part of the Palace of Westminster. It was subsequently used as a storehouse and government office. There is an exhibition, 'Parliament Past and Present'.

Open *1 April–31 Oct: daily, 10am–6pm (6pm/dusk in Oct). 1 Nov–31 March: daily, 10am–4pm (closed 24–26 Dec, 1 Jan). Closed 1–2pm.*
Entry *£1.50/£1.10/80p.*
0171 222 2219
Opposite S end of Houses of Parliament (Victoria Tower).
Frequent from surrounding areas (Tel: 0171 222 1234).
Westminster ¼m.
Tube *Charing Cross ¾m, Victoria and Waterloo, both 1m.*

Jewel Tower

ELTHAM PALACE

The vast hunting park where English monarchs once pursued stags has now been submerged in the suburbs of south-east London. Today Eltham Palace is a fascinating blend of old and new, a 1930s country house incorporating the remains of a great medieval royal palace. From the 15th-century Great Hall, where Erasmus met the future Henry VIII, the visitor steps straight into the lost pre–War world with a suite of striking Art Deco interiors designed for the Courtauld family by fashionable decorators of the 1930s.

Edward II

Now, for the first time, both parts of the Palace are open to the public, together with the delightful garden created around the medieval bridges and moat by the Courtaulds. This extraordinary juxtaposition of royal palace and 30s-style interiors makes Eltham unique.

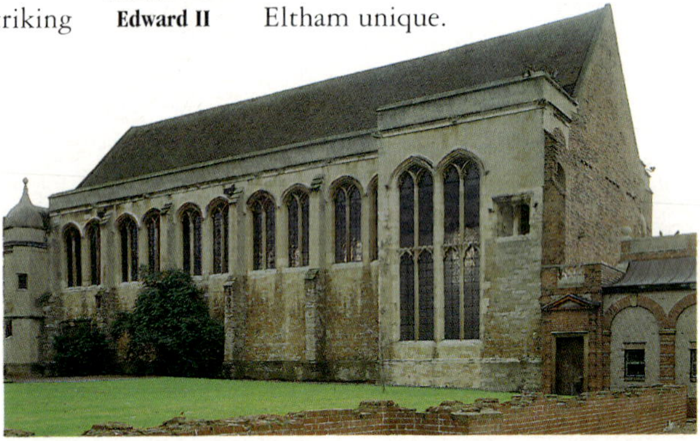

Eltham Palace as it is today

Eltham's royal connection began in 1305, when it was given to the future Edward II. It may even have been here that the Order of the Garter was founded in 1347.

Eltham's heyday was in the 15th century. Around 1480 Edward IV built the Great Hall, the principal surviving building, and the bridge across the moat. The former is one of the finest examples of a late medieval hall. Elaborate pendants decorate its magnificent hammer-beam roof. Henry VIII's court stayed at Eltham many times, but it waned in royal favour, partly because nearby Greenwich Palace was more accessible.

Sold off after Charles I's execution, the palace fell into decay. The task of preservation, begun in 1828, was completed in the 1930s when Stephen Courtauld, of the textile family, was granted a lease. The resulting house, built from 1933–37, is one of the most unusual of that era. Outside there are echoes of Wren's work at Hampton Court.

The remains of the Palace in 1735

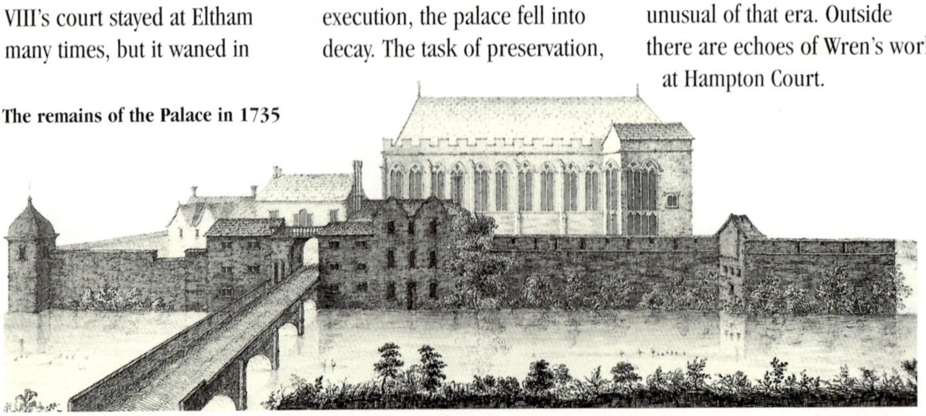

Edward IV, who built the Great Hall

The interior has magnificent rooms, its walls inlaid with exotic woods, the surfaces having the sweeping lines of great ocean liners. The Courtaulds left Eltham during the war, and it was then used by the Royal Army Education Corps from 1945. With their departure, English Heritage is now able to open all Eltham's doors to everyone.

The Great Hall

A 1930s bedroom in the Courtauld House

The medieval bridge over the moat (below)

Open *1 April–30 Sept: Thurs, Fri & Sun only, 10am–6pm. 3 Oct–30 March: Thurs, Fri & Sun only, 10am–4pm (6pm/dusk in Oct).*
Entry *House and gardens £4.00/£3.00/£2.00. Gardens only £2.00/£1.50/£1.00. House and Great Hall only £2.50/£1.90/£1.25.*
✆ 0181 294 2621 or 0181 294 2548 (in opening hours).
➲ 3/4m N of A20 off Court Yard, SE9.
Frequent from surrounding areas (Tel: 0171 222 1234).
Eltham or Mottingham, both 1/2m.

Kenwood

Hampstead, GREATER LONDON (212, 6M)

See pp 104–5 for full details.

London Wall

Tower Hill, GREATER LONDON (213, 6M)

The best preserved piece of the Roman Wall, heightened in the Middle Ages, which formed part of the eastern defences of the City of London.

Open *Any reasonable time.*
Entry *Free.*

Near Tower Hill underground station, EC3.
Frequent from surrounding areas (Tel: 0171 222 1234).
Fenchurch Street ¼m.
Tube *Tower Hill, adjacent.*

Marble Hill House

Twickenham, GREATER LONDON (212, 5M)

A magnificent Thames-side Palladian villa built 1724–29 for Henrietta Howard, Countess of Suffolk, and set in 66 acres of parkland. The Great Room, recently restored, has lavish gilded decoration and architectural paintings by Panini. The house also contains an important collection of early Georgian furniture, the Lazenby Bequest Chinoiserie collection and an 18th-century lacquer screen. There is an exhibition with a film about the house, grounds, and the life and times of Henrietta Howard.

Marble Hill House: the Great Room

Marble Hill House

Free Children's Activity Sheet available.

Open *1 April–31 Oct: daily, 10am–6pm (6pm/dusk in Oct). 1 Nov–31 March: Wed–Sun, 10am–4pm (closed 24–26 Dec, 1 Jan). Closed 1–2pm.*

Entry *£2.50/£1.90/£1.30.*

0181 892 5115

('Coach House Cafe', normally open summer season only) *(at Richmond end of Marble Hill Park)*
(exterior & ground floor only; toilets)

Richmond Road, Twickenham.
Frequent from surrounding areas (Tel: 0171 222 1234).
St Margarets ½m.

Pyx Chamber, Chapter House and Abbey Museum

Westminster Abbey, GREATER LONDON (213, 6M)

The Chapter House, built by the royal masons in 1250 and faithfully restored in the 19th century, contains some of the finest examples of medieval English sculpture to be seen. The building is octagonal, with a central column, and still has its original floor of glazed tiles. Its uses have varied, but in the 14th century it served as a meeting place for the Benedictine monks of the

Chapter House: the Virgin

Abbey, and also for members of Parliament. The 11th-century Pyx Chamber now houses the Abbey treasures, reflecting its use as the strong-room of the Exchequer from the 14th to 19th centuries. The Abbey museum contains medieval royal effigies.

Open *1 April–30 Sept: daily, 10am–5.30pm. 1 Oct–31 March: daily, 10am–4pm (closed 24–26 Dec, 1 Jan). Liable to be closed at short notice on State occasions. Pyx Chamber opens at 10.30am all year.*
Entry *£2.50/£1.90/£1.30.*
0171 222 5897

Approach either through the Abbey or through Dean's Yard and the cloister.
Frequent from surrounding areas (Tel: 0171 222 1234).
Victoria and Charing Cross both ¾m, Waterloo 1m.
Tube *Westminster ¼m.*

Ranger's House

Blackheath,
GREATER LONDON
(213, 5M)

A handsome red brick villa built *c*.1700, on the edge of Greenwich Park, with a splendid bow-windowed gallery. A new Architectural Study Centre is open in the Coach House, displaying an interesting collection of domestic architectural features from London dwellings of the 17th–19th centuries.

Open *1 April–31 Oct: daily, 10am–6pm (6pm/dusk in Oct). 1 Nov–31 March: Wed–Sun, 10am–4pm (closed 24–26 Dec, 1 Jan). Closed 1–2pm.*
Entry *£2.50/£1.90/£1.30.*
0181 853 0035
(in Chesterfield Walk; limited) (lift available)

Chesterfield Walk, Blackheath, SE10.
LT 53 Oxford Circus–Plumstead (Tel: 0171 222 1234).
Maze Hill ½m.

Rangers House (above) and a medallion of Lord Chesterfield (left)

Winchester Palace

Southwark,
GREATER LONDON
(213, 6M)

The west gable end, with its unusual round window, is the prominent feature of the remains of the Great Hall of this 13th-century town house of the Bishops of Winchester, damaged by fire in 1814.

Open *Any reasonable time.*
Entry *Free.*

Near Southwark Cathedral, at corner of Clink St & Storey St, SE1.
Frequent from surrounding areas (Tel: 0171 222 1234).
and ***Tube*** *London Bridge ¼m.*

KENWOOD

Lord Mansfield's lion

Standing in splendid, landscaped grounds on the edge of Hampstead Heath, Kenwood contains the most important private collection of paintings ever given to the nation. There is a selection of Old Masters, among the finest a self-portrait by Rembrandt, and paintings by such eminent British artists as Turner, Reynolds and Gainsborough. The outstanding neoclassical house was itself remodelled by Robert Adam, 1764–73, who created the magnificent library. Many rooms contain displays of neo-classical furniture. Outside, the historic landscaped park, with sloping lawns and a lake form a perfect setting to the lakeside concerts held here in the summer.

In the 18th century Kenwood was occupied by a succession of Scottish lords. For the great judge, Lord Mansfield, Robert Adam transformed the brick house into a majestic villa. Later Earls of Mansfield remodelled the parkland and Kenwood remained in the family until 1922. When developers attempted to buy the estate, the grounds were saved by public purchase; the brewing magnate Edward Cecil Guinness, first Earl of Iveagh, bought the house and bequeathed it and his picture collection to the nation in 1927.

Free Children's Activity Sheet available.
Open *1 April–31 Oct: daily, 10am–6pm (6pm/dusk in Oct). 1 Oct–31 March: daily, 10am–4pm (closed 24–25 Dec).*
Entry *Free.*
0181 348 1286
('Brewhouse and Garden Café') (also available for the partially sighted and those with learning difficulties)
(ground floor only; toilets)

The concert bowl by the lake, venue for perfect summer concerts

Stucco decoration on Adam's south front (right) and the south front itself (far right)

The landscape of Kenwood (below)

Rembrandt's self-portrait

Pre-booked group tours avaialble.

Hampstead Lane, NW3.

LT 210 BR Finsbury Park–Golders Green (Tel: 0171 222 1234).

Hampstead Heath 1½m.

***Tube** Archway and Golders Green.*

Audley End House and Park

ESSEX (213/214, 7N)

See pp 108–11 for full details.

Baconsthorpe Castle

NORFOLK (215, 10O)

The remains of the gatehouses of a large 15th-century fortified manor house, partly surrounded by a moat.

Open *All year: daily, 10am–4pm.*
Entry *Free.*

¾m N of village of Baconsthorpe off unclassified road 3m E of Holt. (OS Map 133; ref TG 122382.)

Sheringham 4½m.

Berney Arms Windmill

Berney Arms Windmill

NORFOLK (215, 9P)

A wonderfully situated marsh mill, one of the best and largest remaining in Norfolk, with seven floors, making it a landmark for miles around. Built to grind a constituent of cement, it was in use until 1951, ending its days pumping water to drain surrounding marshes.

Open *1 April–30 Sept: daily, 9am–5pm. Closed 1–2pm.*
Entry *£1.00/ 80p/50p.*
01493 700605

3½m NE of Reedham on N bank of River Yare. Accessible by boat from Haven Bridge, Great Yarmouth (Tel: Mermaid Cruises 01493 728876) or by footpath from Halvergate (3½m). (OS Map 134; ref TG 465051.)

Berney Arms ¼m.

Binham Priory

NORFOLK (215, 10O)

Extensive remains of a Benedictine priory, of which the original nave of the church still continues in use as the parish church.

Open *Any reasonable time.*
Entry *Free.*

¼m NW of village of Binham-on-Wells road off B1388. (OS Map 132; ref TF 982399.)

Sanders, Wells Community Bus, Eastern Counties 778, 780 from Wells-next-the-Sea (Tel: 01603 613613).

Binham Wayside Cross

NORFOLK (215, 10O)

Medieval cross marking the site of an annual fair held until the 1950s.

Open *Any reasonable time.*
Entry *Free.*

On village green adjacent to Priory. (OS Map 132; ref TF 982399.)

Baconsthorpe Castle

Sanders, Wells Community Bus, Eastern Counties 778, 780 from Wells-next-the-Sea (Tel: 01603 613613).

Binham Priory

Blakeney Guildhall

NORFOLK (215, 10O)

The surviving basement, most likely used for storage, of a large 14th-century building, probably a merchant's house.

Open *Any reasonable time.*
Entry *Free.*

In Blakeney off A149. (OS Map 133; ref TG 030441.)

Sanders Coaches, Eastern Counties Coastliner from BR Sheringham (Tel: 01603 613613).

Sheringham 9m.

Burgh Castle

NORFOLK (215, 9P)

Impressive walls, with projecting bastions, of a Roman fort built in the late 3rd century as one of a chain to defend the coast against Saxon raiders.

Open *Any reasonable time.*
Entry *Free.*

At far W end of Breydon Water, on unclassified road 3m W of Great Yarmouth. (OS Map 134; ref TG 475046.)

Eastern Counties 219, Great Yarmouth Transport 23 from Great Yarmouth (Tel: 01603 613613).

Great Yarmouth 5m.

Bury St Edmunds Abbey

SUFFOLK (215, 8O)

A Norman tower and 14th-century gatehouse of a ruined Benedictine abbey. The Visitor Centre has interactive displays.

Open *Abbey all year: weekdays, 7.30am–dusk, weekends and Bank Holidays, 9am–dusk. For opening hours of Visitor Centre please telephone 01284 763110. (Site managed by St Edmundsbury Borough Council.)*
Entry *Free.*

E end of town centre. (OS Map 155; ref TL 858642.)

From surrounding areas (Tel: 01473 265676).

Bury St Edmunds 1m.

Bury St Edmunds Abbey

AUDLEY END

Audley End was one of the great wonders of the nation when it was built by the first Earl of Suffolk, Lord Treasurer to James I. It was on the scale of a great royal palace, and soon became one when Charles II bought it in 1668 after Suffolk's fall from power. That fickle monarch did not appreciate what he had acquired, and within a generation substantial parts of the house had been demolished. Even so, what remains is in itself one of the most significant Jacobean houses in England. Successive owners have since placed their stylistic imprint both within the graceful exterior and in the surrounding parkland.

As we see it now, Audley End's interior with its historic picture collecton and furniture is largely the product of its owner in the mid-19th century, the third Lord Braybrooke. The challenge for the visitor today is to piece together the many changes over time that have created such a harmonious whole.

The first Lord Braybrooke (left) remodelled Audley End in the late 18th century

The rooms at Audley End are a blend of many generations of taste – the differences sometimes subtly combined, sometimes dramatically exploited. The main structure has remained remarkably little-altered since the main front court was demolished in 1708, and the east wing came down in 1735.

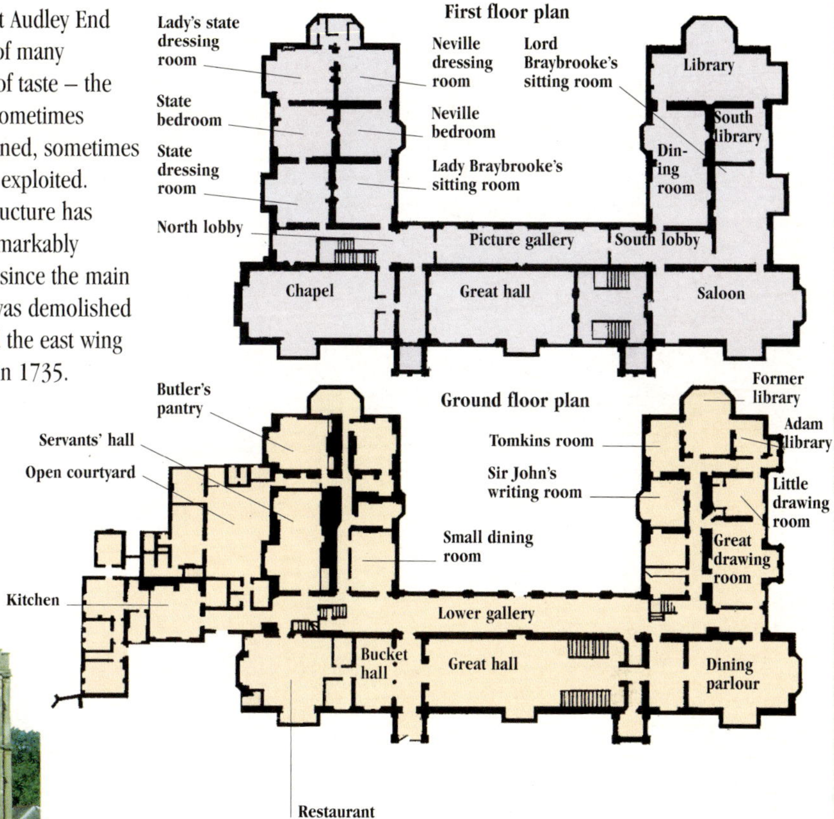

Audley End as it is today (left) and how it was in 1676 (below)

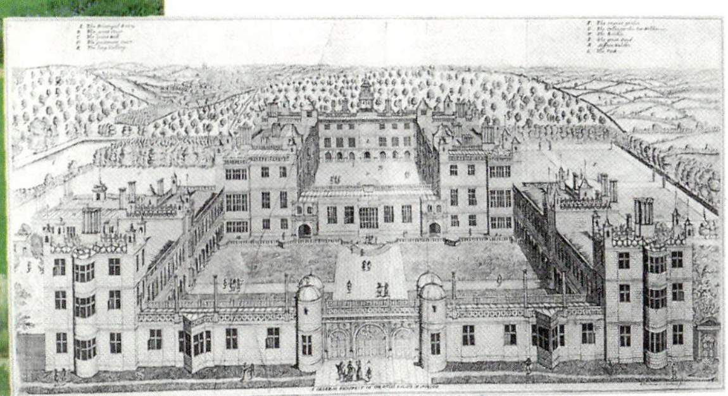

Some rooms have been changed only in small ways, especially the huge Hall and the Saloon with their Jacobean plasterwork and wooden carvings. Other parts of the house, notably the state apartments and bedchambers, have been redecorated time and again. In the 1760s Adam brought his individual brand of graceful neoclassical architecture to the house, while Lancelot 'Capability' Brown transformed the parkland.

Audley End and the Ring Hill Temple **painted by William Tomkins** ***c.*** **1785**

The fourth Lord Braybrooke was more interested in archaeology and ornithology than redecorating, but the fifth Lord made some minor alterations in the 1860s. The ninth Lord Braybrooke resumed possession after its requisition in World War II, but found the burden too great and in 1948 it was sold to English Heritage's predecessor, the Ministry of Works.

Adam's library (right) was dismantled in 1825

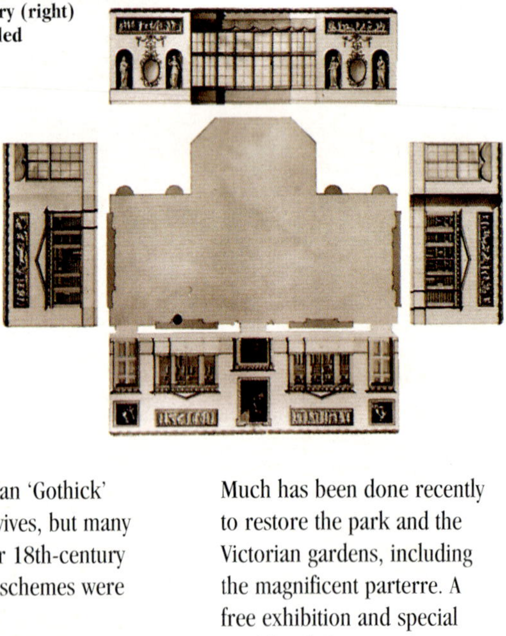

Sir John Griffin Griffin, later fourth Baron Howard de Walden and first Baron Braybrooke, introduced sweeping changes before he died in 1797. The third Baron Braybrooke, who inherited house and title in 1825, stamped his taste equally firmly and with longer-lasting results. He installed his huge picture collection, filled the rooms with furnishings, and reinstated some of the original Jacobean feel to the state rooms.

The Georgian 'Gothick' chapel survives, but many of the other 18th-century decorative schemes were replaced.

Much has been done recently to restore the park and the Victorian gardens, including the magnificent parterre. A free exhibition and special guidebook focus on the extensive grounds, with their lake, river and ornamental gardens. On a summer weekend, Audley End's beauty and historical continuity are readily apparent.

Coats of arms adorn the plaster ceiling in the great hall

Stuffed birds were the main legacy of the fourth Lord Braybrooke

⊕ A quiz for all the family to complete as they explore the house and grounds.
⊕ Facilities for babies.
⊕ Family Discovery Pack available.

Open *1 April–30 Sept: Wed–Sun and Bank Holidays, 12 noon–6pm; park and gardens open at 10am. Last admissions 5pm.*

Entry *to house and grounds £5.50/£4.10/£2.80. Grounds only £3.30/£2.50/ £1.30.*

☎ 01799 522399

(Audley End Restaurant)

(substantial ground-floor area and gardens only)

(also available for the partially sighted and those with learning difficulties and in French and Japanese). French and German guide books available. No photography allowed within house.

1m W of Saffron Walden on B1383 (M11 exits 8, 9 Northbound only, & 10). (OS Map 154; ref TL 525382.)

Hedingham/Viceroy 59 from BR Audley End, Eastern National 301, Townlink 504 Bishops Stortford–Saffron Walden (Tel: 01345 000333).

Audley End 1¼m.

Fireworks frequently light up the summer sky at Audley End

The Doll's House (right) is a miniature version of the Victorian high life at Audley End

Caister Roman Site

NORFOLK (215, 9P)

The remains of a Roman site, possibly a fort, including part of a defensive wall, a gateway and buildings along a main street.

Open *Any reasonable time. (Site managed by Great Yarmouth Borough Council.)*
Entry *Free.*

Near Caister-on-Sea, 3m N of Great Yarmouth. (OS Map 134; ref TG 518125.)
Great Yarmouth Transport 8, 16/7, Eastern Counties 223, 622–6, 701/5/7, 723/6 (Tel: 01603 613613).
Great Yarmouth 3m.

Castle Acre: Bailey Gate

NORFOLK (215, 9N)

The north gateway to the medieval planned town of Acre with rounded flint towers.

Open *Any reasonable time.*
Entry *Free.*

In Castle Acre, at E end of Stocks Green, 5m N of Swaffham. (OS Map 132; ref TF 817152.)

Castle Acre Castle

NORFOLK (215, 9O)

The remains of a Norman manor house, which became a castle with earthworks, set by the side of the village.

Open *Any reasonable time.*
Entry *Free.*

At E end of Castle Acre 5m N of Swaffham. (OS Map 132; ref TF 819152.)

Castle Acre Priory

NORFOLK (215, 9N)

The great west front of the 12th-century church of this Cluniac priory still rises to its full height and is elaborately decorated. The delightful walled herb garden, recreated to show herbs used in medieval times for both culinary and medicinal purposes, should not be missed.

Castle Acre Priory

Open *1 April–31 Oct: daily, 10am–6pm (6pm/dusk in Oct). 1 Nov–31 March: Wed–Sun, 10am–4pm (closed 24–26 Dec, 1 Jan). Closed 1–2pm in winter.*
Entry *£2.50/£1.90/£1.30.*
01760 755394
(also available in French)
(ground floor & grounds only)
¼m W of village of Castle Acre, 5m N of Swaffham. (OS Map 132; ref TF 814148.)

Castle Acre Priory

Castle Rising Castle

NORFOLK (215, 10N)

A fine mid 12th-century domestic keep, set in the centre of massive defensive earthworks. The keep walls stand to their original height and many of the fortifications are still intact.

Castle Rising Castle

__Open__ 1 April–31 Oct: daily, 10am–6pm (6pm/dusk in Oct). 1 Nov–31 March: Wed–Sun, 10am–4pm (closed 24–26 Dec, 1 Jan). Closed 1–2pm in winter.

__Entry__ £2.00/£1.50/£1.00.

01553 631330

(exterior only; toilets)

4m NE of King's Lynn off A149.

(OS Map 132; ref TF 666246.)

Eastern Counties 410/1 King's Lynn–Hunstanton (Tel: 01553 772343).

King's Lynn 4½m.

Church of the Holy Sepulchre

Church of the Holy Sepulchre

Thetford, NORFOLK (215, 8O)

The ruined nave of a priory church of the Canons of the Holy Sepulchre, the only surviving remains in England of a house of this order.

__Open__ Any reasonable time.

__Entry__ Free.

On W side of Thetford off B1107.

(OS Map 144; ref TL 865831.)

From surrounding areas (Tel: 01603 613613).

Thetford ¾m.

Cow Tower

Norwich, NORFOLK (215, 9P)

A circular brick tower, which once formed part of the 14th-century city defences.

__Open__ Any reasonable time.

__Entry__ Free.

In Norwich, near cathedral.

(OS Map 134; ref TG 240091.)

From surrounding areas (Tel: 01603 613613).

Norwich ½m.

Creake Abbey

NORFOLK (215, 10O)

The ruins of the church of an Augustinian abbey.

__Open__ Any reasonable time.

__Entry__ Free.

1m N of North Creake off B1355.

(OS Map 132; ref TF 856395.)

Bus: Wells Community Bus, Sanders, Dunthorne Wells-next-the-Sea–Fakenham, Mon, Thu, Sat (Tel: 01603 613613).

Denny Abbey

CAMBRIDGESHIRE

(214, 10N)

What at first appears to be an attractive stone-built farm-house is actually the remains of a 12th-century Benedictine abbey which, at different times, also housed the Knights Templar and Franciscan nuns.

Open *1 April–30 Sept: daily, 12pm–5pm.*
Entry *£1.50/£1.10/80p.*
01223 860489
(grounds & ground floor only)
6m N of Cambridge on A10. (OS Map 154; ref TL 495684.)
Cambus 109 Cambridge–Ely (passes close to BR Water-beach) (Tel: 01223 423554).
Waterbeach 3m.

Duxford Chapel

CAMBRIDGESHIRE

(214, 8N)

A medieval chapel once part of the Hospital of St John.

Open *Telephone 01799 522 842 for details of opening arrangements.*

Denny Abbey

Framlingham Castle (above) and a re-creation of life there in Tudor times (right)

Entry *Free.*
Adjacent to Whittlesford station off A505. (OS Map 154; ref TL 486472.)
Whittlesford, adjacent.

Framlingham Castle

SUFFOLK (215, 8P)

A superb 12th-century castle which, from the outside, looks almost the same as when it was built. From the continuous curtain wall, linking 13 towers, there are excellent views over Framlingham and the charming reed-fringed mere. At different times, the castle has been a fortress, an Elizabethan prison, a poor house and a school. The many alterations over the years have led to a pleasing mixture of historical styles. The Lanman Museum, containing a local history collection, can be seen for a small extra charge.

Walk along the full length of the towering castle walls. Activity book for children available.

Open *1 April–31 Oct: daily, 10am–6pm (6pm/dusk in Oct). 1 Nov–31 March: daily, 10am–4pm (closed 24–26 Dec, 1 Jan).*
Entry *£2.50/ £1.90/£1.30.*
01728 724189
(grounds & ground floor only) *
In Framlingham on B1116. (OS Map 156; ref TM 287637.)
Eastern Counties/Ipswich Buses 71, 80/1, 82/A/B from

Ipswich (passes close to BR Woodbridge, except Sundays) (Tel: 01473 265676).
Wickham Market 6½m; Saxmundham 7m.

Grime's Graves

NORFOLK (215, 9O)

These remarkable Neolithic flint mines, unique in England, comprise over 300 pits and shafts. The visitor can descend some 10m (30ft) by ladder into one excavated shaft, and look along the radiating galleries, where the flint for making axes and knives was extracted.

Climb down into a prehistoric flint mine.

Open *1 April–31 Oct: daily, 10am–6pm (6pm/dusk in Oct). 1 Nov–31 March: Wed–Sun, 10am–4pm (closed 24–26 Dec, 1 Jan). Last visit to pit 20 minutes before closing. Closed 1–2pm.*

Entry *£1.50/£1.10/80p.*

01842 810656

(exhibition area only; access track rough)

7m NW of Thetford off A134. (OS Map 144; ref TL 818898.)

Eastern Counties/Whippet/Wayland 200/1 Thetford Mildenhall, alight Santon Downham thence 2m (Tel: 01473 265676).

Brandon 3½m.

Grime's Graves

Hadleigh Castle

ESSEX (213, 6N)

The curtain wall and two towers, which survive almost to their full height, overlook the Essex marshes and Thames estuary.

Open *Any reasonable time.*

Entry *Free.*

01760 755161

(hilly)

¾m S of A13 at Hadleigh. (OS Map 178; ref TQ 810860.)

Thamesway and Southend Transport services from surrounding areas to within ½m (Tel: 0345 000 333).

Leigh-on-Sea 1½m by footpath.

Hill Hall

ESSEX (213, 6N)

Now partly roofed, this fine Elizabethan mansion has some of the earliest Renaissance decoration in the country. Rare wall paintings of mythological and biblical subjects date from the same period. The house is surrounded by parklands landscaped by Repton.

Open *The Hall is undergoing major building works and is not normally open to the public. Any open day will be announced in the members' magazine,* Heritage Today, *and the local press.*

Entry *Free.*

01992 561657

(ground floor and grounds).

3m E of Epping on unclassified road to Theydon Mount. From M11 – Junc. 7, S on B1393 to Epping, then as above. (OS Map 167; ref TQ 489994.)

Tube *Epping 2½m.*

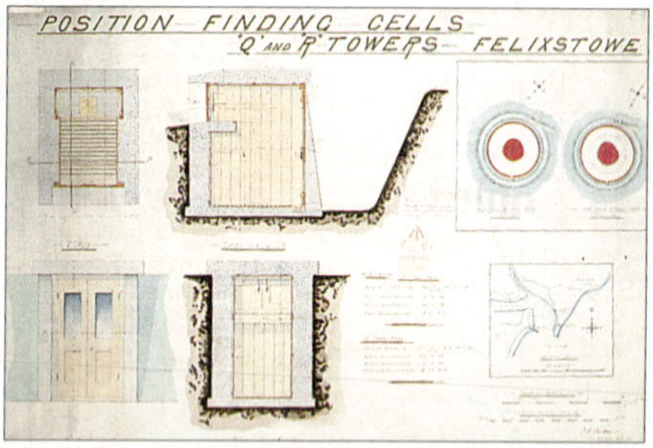

Landguard Fort (above) and a historic plan of the site (right)

Isleham Priory Church

CAMBRIDGESHIRE
(215, 8N)

Rare example of an early Norman church. It has survived little altered despite being later converted to a barn.

Open *Any reasonable time. Keykeeper (please follow instructions shown at site or telephone regional office 01604 730320 for details).*
Entry *Free.*

In Isleham, 16m NE of Cambridge on B1104.
(OS Map 143; ref TL 642744.)
Cambus 122 Cambridge–Soham (Tel: 01223 423554).
Newmarket 8½m; Ely 9m.

Landguard Fort

Felixstowe, SUFFOLK
(213/215, 7P)

An 18th-century fort, with later additions. There is a museum of World War memorabilia.

Open *Museum, 28 May–1 Oct: Wed & Sun only, 2–5pm (in addition, 1 Aug–5 Sept: Thurs). Guided tours of fort Wed, Sun & Thurs (as stated above) 2.15pm & 4pm.*
Entry *Museum adults 75p/children 30p. Fort adults £1.50/children 60p (no unaccompanied children). English Heritage members 80p.*
01394 286403 (evenings)

1m S of Felixstowe near docks.
(OS Map 169; ref TM 284318.)
Eastern Counties 75–9 Ipswich–Felixstowe Dock to within ¾m (but with F4 from Felixstowe to Fort Summer Suns only) (Tel: 01473 253734).
Felixstowe 2½m.

Leiston Abbey

SUFFOLK (215, 8P)

The remains of this abbey for Premonstratensian canons include a restored chapel.

Open *Any reasonable time.*

Isleham Priory

Entry *Free.*

1m N of Leiston off B1069. (OS Map 156; ref TM 445642.)

Eastern Counties/ Eastern National 80/1, 168-9, Country Travel 80 Ipswich–Aldeburgh (passes close to BR Saxmundham) (Tel: 01473 265676).

Saxmundham 5m.

Lexden Earthworks and Bluebottle Grove

Colchester, ESSEX

(213/215, 7O)

Parts of a series of earthworks, once encompassing 12 square miles, which protected Iron Age Colchester and were subsequently added to by the conquering Romans.

Open *Any reasonable time. (Sites managed by Colchester Borough Council.)*

Longthorpe Tower (above) and one of the wall paintings (left)

Entry *Free.*

2m W of Colchester off A604. (OS Map 168; ref TL 965246 [Lexden Earthworks] and TL 975245 [Bluebottle Grove].)

Colchester Transport 5/A from BR Colchester (Tel: 01206 44449).

Colchester or Colchester Town, both 2½m.

Longthorpe Tower

CAMBRIDGESHIRE

(214, 9M)

The finest example of 14th-century domestic wall paintings in northern Europe. The tower, with the Great Chamber that contains the paintings, is part of a fortified manor house.

Open *July–Aug: weekends only, 10am–6pm. Closed 1–2pm.*

Entry *£1.00/80p/50p.*

01733 268482

2m W of Peterborough on A47. (OS Map 142; ref TL 163983.)

Viscount 14, Searles/ Newborough 303, Viscount 367 Peterborough–Oundle (Tel: 01733 54571); Midland Fox/Woods 747 Peterborough–Leicester, Blands 304 from Peterborough (Tel: 01533 511411).

Peterborough 1½m.

Mistley Towers

ESSEX (213/215, 7O)

The remains of a church designed by Robert Adam and built in 1776. It was unusual in having towers at both the east and west ends.

Open *Key available from Mistley Quay Workshops (Tel: 01206 393884).*

Entry *Free.*

(exterior only)

On B1352, 1½m E of A137 at Lawford, 9m E of Colchester. (OS Map 169; ref TM 116320.)

Eastern National 102-4 Colchester–Harwich (Tel: 0345 000 333).

Mistley ¼m.

Mistley Towers

Moulton Packhorse Bridge

SUFFOLK (215, 8N)

Medieval four-arched bridge spanning the River Kennett.

Open *Any reasonable time.*

Entry *Free.*

P

In Moulton off B1085, 4m E of Newmarket. (OS Map 154; ref TL 698645.)

Kennett 2m.

North Elmham Chapel

NORFOLK (215, 10O)

Remains of a Norman chapel converted into a fortified dwelling and enclosed by earthworks in the late 14th century by the notorious Bishop of Norwich, Hugh le Despencer.

Open *Any reasonable time.*

Entry *Free.*

6m N of East Dereham on B1110. (OS Map 132; ref TF 988217.)

Old Merchant's House, Row 111 House and Greyfriars' Cloisters

Interior of Old Merchant's House

Great Yarmouth, NORFOLK (215, 9P)

Two 17th century-Row Houses, a type of building unique to Great Yarmouth, containing original fixtures and displays of local architectural fittings salvaged from bombing in 1942–43. Nearby are the remains of a Franciscan friary, with a rare vaulted cloister, accidentally discovered during bomb damage repairs.

Open *1 April–14 April: Sun–Fri 10am–5pm. 27 May–29 Sept: Sun–Fri, 10am–5pm. Closed 1–2pm. Tours start from Row 111 house.*

Entry *£1.50/£1.10/80p.*

Great Yarmouth, make for

South Quay along riverside and dock, ½m inland from beach. Follow signs to dock and south quay. (OS Map 134; ref TG 525072 [Houses] and TG 525073 [Cloisters].)

From surrounding areas (Tel: 01603 613613).

Great Yarmouth ½m.

Orford Castle

SUFFOLK (215, 8P)

A royal castle built for coastal defence in the 12th century. A magnificent keep survives almost intact with three immense towers reaching to 30m (90 feet). Inside there are many rooms to explore.

Free Children's Activity Sheet available

Orford Castle

CD Rom unit with information on English castles.

Open *1 April–31 Oct: daily, 10am–6pm (6pm/dusk in Oct). 1 Nov–31 March: daily, 10am–4pm (closed 24–26 Dec, 1 Jan). Closed 1–2pm in winter.*

Entry *£2.00/£1.50/£1.00.*

013944 50472

In Orford on B1084 20m NE of Ipswich. (OS Map 169; ref TM 419499.)

Belle 160, Eastern Counties 122, Suffolk County Villager Woodbridge–Orford (passes close to BR Woodbridge); Suffolk County Bus 651 Ipswich–Orford (Tel: 01473 265676).

Wickham Market 8m.

Prior's Hall Barn

Widdington, ESSEX (213/214, 7N)

One of the finest surviving medieval barns in south-east England and representative of the aisled barns of north-west Essex.

Open *1 April–30 Sept: Sat & Sun, 10am–6pm. Telephone 01799 522842 for further details.*

Entry *Free.*

In Widdington, on unclassified road 2m SE of Newport, off B1383. (OS Map 167; ref TL 538319.)

Eastern National 301 Bishops Stortford–Saffron Walden (Tel: 0345 000 333).

Newport 2m.

Prior's Hall Barn, Widdington

St Botolph's Priory

Colchester, ESSEX (215, 7O)

The nave, with an impressive arcaded west end, of the first Augustinian priory in England.

Open *Any reasonable time. (Site managed by Colchester Borough Council.)*

Entry *Free.*

Colchester, near Colchester Town station. (OS Map 168; ref TL 999249.)

From surrounding areas (Tel: 0345 000 333).

Colchester Town, adjacent.

St John's Abbeygate

St James's Chapel

Lindsey, SUFFOLK
(213/215, 7O)

A little 13th-century chapel with thatched roof and lancet windows.

Open *All year: daily, 10am–4pm.*
Entry *Free.*
(single step).
On unclassified road ½m E of Rose Green, 8m E of Sudbury. (OS Map 155; ref TL 978443.)
Suffolk Bus 156 from Ipswich–Ely, Sun only (Tel: 01473 265676).
Sudbury 8m.

St John's Abbey Gate

Colchester, ESSEX
(213/215, 7O)

This fine abbey gatehouse, in East Anglian flintwork, survives from the Benedictine abbey of St John.

Open *Any reasonable time. (Site managed by Colchester Borough Council.)*
Entry *Free.*
On S side of central Colchester. (OS Map 168; ref TL 998248.)
From surrounding areas (Tel: 0345 000 333).
Colchester Town ¼m.

St Olaves Priory

NORFOLK (215, 9P)

Remains of an Augustinian priory founded nearly 200 years after the death in 1030 of the patron saint of Norway, after whom it is named.

Open *Any reasonable time.*
Entry *Free.*
5½m SW of Great Yarmouth on A143. (OS Map 134; ref TM 459996.)
Haddiscoe 1¼m.

Saxtead Green Post Mill

SUFFOLK (215, 8P)

A fine example of a post mill, where the superstructure turns on a great post to face the wind. The mill is still in working order and you can climb the wooden stairs to the various floors, which are full of fascinating mill machinery.

Open *1 April–30 Sept: Mon–Sat, 10am–6pm. Closed 1–2pm.*
Entry *£1.50/£1.10/80p.*
01728 685789
2½m NW of Framlingham on A1120. (OS Map 156; ref TM 253645.)

Saxtead Green Post Mill

Eastern Counties 82, 99, 120 from Ipswich (passes close to BR Woodbridge) (Tel: 01473 265676).
Wickham Market 9m.

Thetford Priory

NORFOLK (215, 8N)

The 14th-century gatehouse is the best preserved part of this Cluniac priory built in 1103. The extensive remains include the plan of the cloisters.

Open *Any reasonable time.*
Entry *Free.*
On W side of Thetford near station.

Boscobel House: portrait of Charles II

Buildwas Abbey

SHROPSHIRE (217, 9G)

Set beside the River Severn, against a backdrop of wooded grounds, are extensive remains of this Cistercian abbey begun in 1135. The remains include the church which is almost complete except for the roof.

Open *1 April–31 Oct: daily, 10am–6pm (6pm/dusk in Oct). 1 Nov–31 March: Wed–Sun, 10am–4pm (closed 24–25 Dec, 1 Jan). Please telephone 01743 701101 for further details.*
Entry *Free.*

On S bank of River Severn on B4378, 2m W of Iron Bridge. (OS Map 127; ref SJ 642044.)

Williamsons X96 Birmingham–Shrewsbury (passes close to BR Telford Central) (Tel: 0345 056 785).

Telford Central 6m.

Bushmead Priory

BEDFORDSHIRE (214, 8M)

A rare survival of the medieval refectory of an Augustinian priory. Its original timber-framed roof is almost intact and contains interesting wall paintings and stained glass.

Open *July–Aug: weekends only, 10am–6pm. Closed 1–2pm.*
Entry *£1.50/£1.10/80p.*
01525 866152 (weekends only)

On classified road near Colmworth, 2m E of B660. (OS Map 153; ref TL 115607.)

St Neots 6m.

Cantlop Bridge

SHROPSHIRE (217, 9G)

Single-span cast-iron road bridge over the Cound Brook, designed by the great engineer Thomas Telford.

Buildwas Abbey from the west

Open *Any reasonable time.*
Entry *Free.*

¾m SW of Berrington on unclassified road off A458. (OS Map 126; ref SJ 517062.)

Shrewsbury 5m.

Chichele College

NORTHAMPTONSHIRE (214, 8L)

Parts of a quadrangle remain of this college for secular canons, founded in 1422.

Open *Quadrangle any reasonable time.*

Bushmead Priory

For chapel please contact keykeeper, Mrs C. Jones, 22 Lancaster St., Higham Ferrers; tel. 01933 317182. (Site managed by East Northamptonshire District Council.)
Entry *Free.*

In Higham Ferrers, on A6. (OS Map 153; ref SP 960687.)

Stagecoach United Counties 46/A, X94 from Wellingborough (Tel: 01604 36681).

Wellingborough 5m.

Clun Castle

SHROPSHIRE (217, 8F)

The remains of a four-storey keep and other buildings of this border castle.

Open *Any reasonable time.*
Entry *Free.*

In Clun, off A488, 18m W of Ludlow. (OS Map 137; ref SO 299809.)
Midland Red West 741–5, 773 from Ludlow (passes close to BR Ludlow) (Tel: 0345 056 785).
Hopton Heath 6½m; Knighton 6½m.

Croxden Abbey

STAFFORDSHIRE (214/217, 10J)

Remains of a Cistercian abbey founded in 1176.

Open *Any reasonable time.*
Entry *Free.*

5m NW of Uttoxeter off A522. (OS Map 128; ref SK 065397.)
Uttoxeter 6m.

Clun Castle

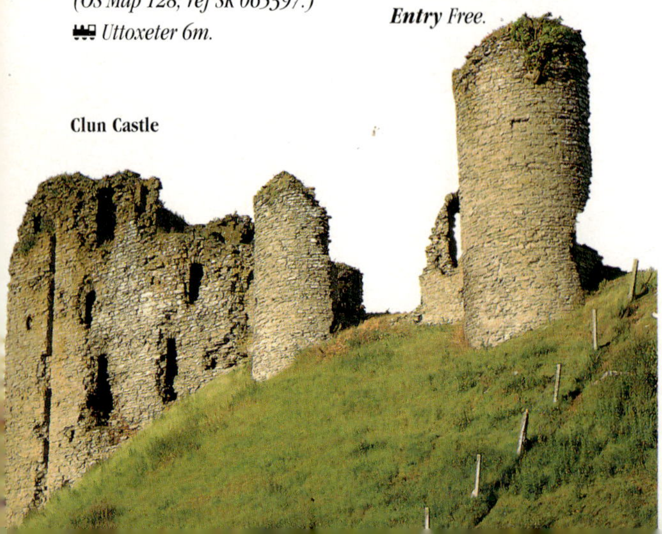

De Grey Mausoleum

Flitton, BEDFORDSHIRE (214, 7L)

The tombs in De Grey Mausoleum

A remarkable treasure-house of sculpted tombs and monuments from the 16th to 19th centuries, dedicated to the de Grey family of Wrest Park.

Open *Weekends only. Please contact keykeeper, Mr Stimpson, 3 Highfield Road, Flitton (Tel: 01525 860094). Access through Flitton Church.*
Entry *Free.*
01799 522842

Flitton, attached to church, on unclassified road 1½m W of A6 at Silsoe. (OS Map 153; ref TL 059359.)
Flitwick 2m.

Deddington Castle

OXFORDSHIRE (214/217, 7K)

Extensive earthworks conceal remains of 12th-century castle.

Open *Any reasonable time.*
Entry *Free.*

S of B4031 on E side of Deddington, 17m N of Oxford on A423. (OS Map 151; ref SP 471316.)
Midland Red X59 Oxford–Banbury to within ½m (Tel: 01788 535555).
King's Sutton 5m.

Edvin Loach Old Church

HEREFORD & WORCESTER (217, 8G)

Peaceful and isolated 11th-century church remains.

Open *Any reasonable time.*
Entry *Free.*

4m N of Bromyard on unclassified road off B4203. (OS Map 149; ref SO 663585.)

Eleanor Cross

Geddington, NORTHAMPTONSHIRE (214, 9L)

One of a series of famous

Eleanor Cross

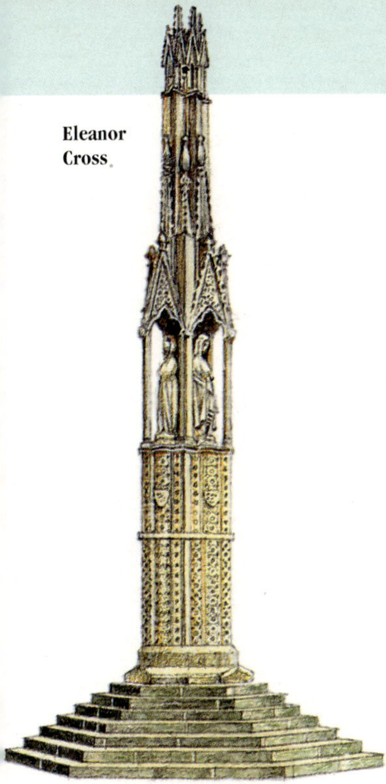

crosses erected by Edward I to mark the resting places of the body of his wife, Eleanor, when brought for burial from Harby in Nottinghamshire to Westminster Abbey.

Open *Any reasonable time.*
Entry *Free.*

In Geddington, off A43 between Kettering and Corby. (OS Map 141; ref SP 896830.)
Stagecoach United Counties 8 Kettering–Corby. (Tel: 01604 36681).
Kettering 4m.

Gainsborough Old Hall

LINCOLNSHIRE (214, 12L)

A large medieval house with a magnificent Great Hall and suites of rooms. A collection of historic furniture and a re-created medieval kitchen are on display.

Open *Easter Sunday–31 Oct: Mon–Sat, 10am–5pm, Sun 2pm–5.30pm. 1 Nov–Easter Saturday, Mon–Sat, 10am–5pm (closed Good Friday, 24–26 Dec, 1 Jan). (Site managed by Lincolnshire County Council.)*
Entry *£1.75/95p/95p (no reduction for students/unemployed).*
01427 612669
(most of ground floor)

In Gainsborough, opposite the Library. (OS Map 121; ref SK 815895.)
From surrounding areas (Tel: 01522 553135).
Gainsborough Central ½m, Gainsborough Lea Road 1m.

Geddington, Eleanor Cross

See Eleanor Cross.

Goodrich Castle

HEREFORD & WORCESTER (217, 7G)

Remarkably complete, magnificent red sandstone castle with 12th-century keep and extensive remains from the 13th and 14th centuries.

Free Children's Activity Sheet available.
Open *1 April–31 Oct: daily, 10am–6pm (6pm/dusk in Oct). 1 Nov–31 March: daily, 10am–4pm (closed 24–26 Dec, 1 Jan). Closed 1–2pm.*
Entry *£2.20/£1.70/£1.10.*
01600 890538

5m S of Ross-on-Wye off A40. (OS Map 162; ref SO 579199.)
Stagecoach Red & White 61 Monmouth-Gloucester to within ½m (passes close to BR Gloucester) (Tel: 0345 125 436).

Goodrich Castle

Halesowen Abbey

WEST MIDLANDS (217, 8H)
Remains of an abbey founded by King John in the 13th century, now incorporated into a 19th-century farm.

Open *July–August: weekends only, 10am–6pm.*
Entry *£1.00/80p/50p.*
P *(rough grass between church and infirmary)*
Off A456 Kidderminster road, 6m W of Birmingham city centre. (OS Map 139; ref SO 975828.)
West Midlands Travel 9, 19 Birmingham–Stourbridge (Tel: 0121 200 2700).
Old Hill 2½m.

Hardwick Old Hall

DERBYSHIRE (214/217, 11K)
This large ruined house, finished in 1591, still displays Bess of Hardwick's innovative planning and interesting decorative plasterwork. The views from the top floor over the country park and 'New' Hall are spectacular.

Hardwick Old Hall

Ideal for children and schools.
Open *1 April–31 Oct: Wed–Sun, 10am–6pm (6pm/dusk in Oct).*
Entry *£1.50/£1.10/80p. National Trust members admitted free. (Site maintained and managed by English Heritage, and owned by the National Trust. Joint ticket available for the New Hall and Gardens and the Old Hall.)*
P *(£2.00 vehicle entry charge for access to National Trust Estate, refundable on a visit to Hardwick New Hall)*
9½m SE of Chesterfield, off A6175. (OS Map 120; ref SK 463638.)
E Midland/Trent X2, 63 Chesterfield–Nottingham to within 1½m (Tel: 01332 292200).
Chesterfield 9½m.

Halesowen Abbey (right) and infirmary (below)

Haughmond Abbey

SHROPSHIRE (217, 9G)
The extensive remains of this 12th-century Augustinian abbey include the Chapter

Haughmond Abbey: the Abbot's Chamber (below) and a detail of the Chapter House (right)

House, which retains its late-medieval timber ceiling, and some fine medieval sculpture.

Open *1 April–30 Sept: daily, 12–5pm.*
Entry *£1.50/£1.10/80p.*
01743 709661

3m NE of Shrewsbury off B5062.
(OS Map 126; ref SJ 542152.)
Midland 519 Shrewsbury–Newport (Tel: 0345 056 785).
Shrewsbury 3½m.

Hob Hurst's House

DERBYSHIRE (214/217, 11J)

A square prehistoric burial mound with an earthwork ditch and outer bank.

Open *Any reasonable time.*
(Site managed by the Peak Park Joint Planning Board.)
Entry *Free.*

From unclassified road off B5057, 9m W of Chesterfield.
(OS Map 119; ref SK287692.)
Whites X66, Hulleys X67, 170 from Chesterfield, to within 2m (Tel: 0132 292200).
Chesterfield 9m.

Houghton House

BEDFORDSHIRE (214, 7L)

Reputedly the inspiration for 'House Beautiful' in Bunyan's *Pilgrim's Progress*, the remains of this early 17th-century mansion still convey elements that justify the description, including work attributed to Inigo Jones.

Open *Any reasonable time.*
Entry *Free.*

1m NE of Ampthill off A421, 8m S of Bedford.
(OS Map 153; ref TL 039394.)
Stagecoach United Counties 142/3 BR Flitwick–Bedford to within ½m (Tel: 01604 20077).
Flitwick or Stewartby, both 3m.

Iron Bridge

SHROPSHIRE (217, 9G)

The world's first iron bridge and Britain's best-known industrial monument. Cast in Coalbrookdale by local ironmaster Abraham Darby, it was erected across the River Severn in 1779.

Open *Any reasonable time.*
Entry *Free.*

In Ironbridge, adjacent to A4169.
(OS Map 127; ref SJ 672034.)
Frequent from Telford passes close to BR Telford Central or Wellington Telford West) (Tel: 0345 056 785).
Telford Central 5m.

Iron Bridge

Jewry Wall

Leicester,
LEICESTERSHIRE
(214, 9K)

One of the largest surviving lengths of Roman wall in the country. Over 9 metres (30 feet) high, it formed one side of the exercise hall of the civic baths.

Open *Any reasonable time.*
Entry *Free.*

In St Nicholas St W of Church of St Nicholas.
(OS Map 140; ref SK 583044.)
From surrounding areas (Tel: 0116 251 1411).
Leicester 3/4m.

Kenilworth Castle (217, 8J)

See pp 132–5 for full details.

Kirby Hall

NORTHAMPTONSHIRE
(214, 9L)

Outstanding example of a large, stone-built Elizabethan mansion, begun in 1570 with 17th-century alterations. The fine gardens, currently being restored, are home to beautiful peacocks.

Open *1 April–31 Oct: daily, 10am–6pm (6pm/dusk in Oct). 1 Nov–31 March: Wed–Sun, 10am–4pm (closed 24–26 Dec, 1 Jan). Closed 1–2pm.*
Entry *£2.00/£1.50/£1.00.*
01536 203230
(grounds, gardens & ground floor only.)

On unclassified road off A43 4m NE of Corby.
(OS Map 141; ref SP 926927.)

Kirby Hall: through the forecourt entrance towards the inner court

Kirby Hall from the Great Garden

Kirby Muxloe Castle

LEICESTERSHIRE
(214, 9K)

Picturesque, moated, brick-built castle begun in 1480 by William, Lord Hastings.

Open *Any reasonable time (closed 24–26 Dec, 1 Jan). Please telephone 01604 730320 for details.*
Entry *Free.*

4m W of Leicester off B5380.
(OS Map 140; ref SK 524046.)
Midland Fox 63, Citybus 152/3 from Leicester (Tel: 0116 251 1411).
Leicester 5m.

Langley Chapel

SHROPSHIRE (217, 9G)

A delightful medieval chapel, standing alone in a field, with a complete set of early 17th-century wooden fittings and furniture.

Open *Any reasonable time (closed 24–26 Dec, 1 Jan).*
Entry *Free.*

1 1/2m S of Acton Burnell, on unclassified road off A49 9 1/2m S of Shrewsbury.
(OS Map 126; ref SJ 538001.)
Boultons/Timeline from Shrewsbury, Tues, Sat only, to within 1 1/2m (Tel: 0345 056 785).
Shrewsbury 7 1/2m.

Leicester Jewry Wall

See Jewry Wall.

Leigh Court Barn

HEREFORD & WORCESTER (217, 8H)

Magnificent 14th-century timber-framed barn, built for the monks of Pershore Abbey. It is the largest of its kind in Britain.

Leigh Court Barn

Open *1 April–30 Sept: Thurs–Sun, 10am–6pm.*
Entry *Free.*

5m W of Worcester on unclassified road off A4103. (OS Map 150; ref 784534.)

Midland Red West 417, 421/2/3/5 from Worcester to within 1m (Tel: 0345 125 436).

Worcester Foregate Street 5m.

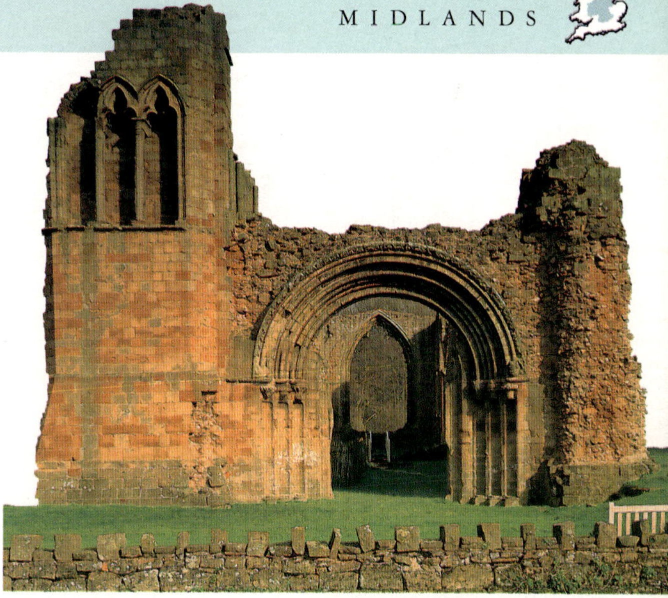

Lilleshall Abbey: the West Front

Lilleshall Abbey

SHROPSHIRE (217, 9H)

Extensive and evocative ruins of an abbey of Augustinian canons, including remains of the 12th- and 13th-century church and the cloister buildings, surrounded by green lawns and ancient yew trees.

Open *Any reasonable time.*
Entry *Free.*

On unclassified road off A518, 4m N of Oakengates. (OS Map 127; ref SJ 738142.)

Midland/Timeline 80–4, 481–3 Telford–Stafford (passes close to BR Telford Central & Stafford) to within 1m (Tel: 0345 056 785).

Oakengates 4½m.

Langley Chapel

KENILWORTH CASTLE

Queen Elizabeth I *did* sleep here! The massive, red sandstone castle, which seems positively to glow in the early morning and evening light, was the Warwickshire power base of the best beloved of all her courtiers, Robert Dudley, Earl of Leicester. Among the buildings that remain are those that he built or rebuilt to entertain his queen and sustain his noble dignity. Other parts of Kenilworth, dating back to the 12th century, are powerful statements of its former strength and the way that it once dominated this part of the Midlands. Kenilworth Castle has always been intimately linked with some of the most important names in English history. Today, with some of its Tudor gardens, its impressive Norman 'keep' and John of Gaunt's Great Hall, it is the largest castle ruin in England.

An arrow slit on Lunn's Tower

The first castle at Kenilworth was built about 50 years after the Norman conquest by Geoffrey de Clinton, chamberlain to Henry I. Henry II took over the castle – as well as nearby Warwick – 50 years later, to make both ready against attack from his son's rebel army, and it remained in royal hands when the rebellion ended. The castle was radically extended by King John in the 13th century, and he also transformed the surrounding mere (great lake) into one of its most glorious features.

Artist's impression of Kenilworth Castle today

George Gascoigne, Robert Dudley's pageant-master

Entrance to the keep (above)

Kenilworth was one of the four royal castles which were to be handed over to the barons under the terms of the Magna Carta. John, however, somehow managed to avoid surrendering the castle, which stayed in royal hands until 1253, when it was given to Simon de Montfort by Henry III. The de Montforts turned against the Crown in the Barons' War in 1266, and the castle was besieged. The defenders were well stocked with food and arms and had the added protection of the Great Mere, although a water-borne assault was attempted. They managed to hold out for almost nine months before disease took its toll and they were forced to surrender.

Entrance to Leicester's Gatehouse (right)

Kenilworth remained in royal hands. In a coup, Edward II was briefly imprisoned there, before being taken to Berkeley Castle and hideously murdered in 1326. John of Gaunt, a giant of English history, rebuilt the castle palatially in the 1390s. Henry V retired there after winning the Battle of Agincourt 20 years later. He built himself a banqueting house, The Pleasuance, on the other side of the lake. Henry VIII had it dismantled and moved the Pleasuance buildings back into the main castle.

Leicester's building

A civil war pikeman (right)

The castle took centre stage again in the 16th century, when it was acquired by the Dudley family. John Dudley, Duke of Northumberland and effectively ruler of England in the reign of the boy-king Edward VI, was executed for trying to place his daughter-in-law Lady Jane Grey on the throne in 1553. Dudley's son Robert was a great favourite of Elizabeth I. Kenilworth was given back to him and he transformed it into a place fit for her to visit. Tales woven by Sir Walter Scott, in his novel *Kenilworth* (1821), around Dudley, his wife (who died in mysterious circumstances) and the Virgin Queen still give extra glamour to the castle.

Kenilworth never saw quite such glories again. Following the Battle of Edgehill in the Civil War it was partially demolished by Parliamentary troops to make it useless as a stronghold.

The castle from the south at sunset (below)

Over the years Kenilworth was allowed to fall into ruin, and the lake to drain away. The castle was saved for the nation in 1938. It remains a powerful reminder of great men, their glories, pleasures and rebellions, and offers glorious views over a countryside now at peace.

Re-enactment of life in the Civil War at Kenilworth

A quiz for all the family to complete as they explore the castle.

Family Discovery Pack and Free Children's Activity Sheet available.

An exciting CD Rom unit provides information on the castles of England, their functions and purpose.

Open *1 April–31 Oct: daily, 10am–6pm (6pm/dusk in Oct). 1 Nov–31 March: daily, 10am–4pm (closed 24–26 Dec, 1 Jan).*
Entry *£2.50/£1.90/£1.30*
01926 852078
(also available for the partially sighted and those with learning difficulties and in French, German and Japanese)

Ornamental arrow slit on the water tower

In Kenilworth.
(OS Map 140; ref SP 278723.)
Midland Red/Stratford Blue X16-9; Stagecoach G & G X12, West Midlands Travel 12A/C Coventry–Leamington Spa (passes close to BR Coventry & Leamington Spa) (Tel: 01788 535555).
Warwick 5m.

Re-enactment of a Civil War battle at Kenilworth

Lincoln Bishop's Old Palace

Lincoln, LINCOLNSHIRE
(214/219, 11L)

The remains of this medieval palace of the Bishops of Lincoln are in the shadow of Lincoln Cathedral. You can climb the stairs to the Alnwick Tower, explore the undercroft and see the vineyard, which is one of the most northerly in Europe.

Ideal for children and schools.
Open *1 April–30 Sept: daily, 12–5pm.*
Entry *£1.00/80p/50p.*
01522 527468

S side of Lincoln Cathedral.
(OS Map 121; ref SK 981717.)
From surrounding areas (Tel: 01522 553135).
Lincoln 1m.

Longtown Castle

HEREFORD & WORCESTER
(217, 7F)

An unusual cylindrical keep built *c*.1200, with walls 4.5 metres (15 feet) thick.

Open *Any reasonable time.*
Entry *Free.*

4m WSW of Abbey Dore.
(OS Map 161; ref SO 321291.)

Longtown Castle

Lyddington Bede House

LEICESTERSHIRE
(214, 9L)

Set among picturesque golden stone cottages, beside the handsome parish church of St Andrew, the Bede House was originally a medieval palace of the Bishops of Lincoln. It was later converted into an almshouse.

Lyddington Bede House

Open *1 April–30 Sept: daily, 10am–6pm. Closed 1–2pm.*
Entry *£1.50/£1.10/80p.*
☎ 0157282 2438
(ground-floor rooms only).
In Lyddington, 6m N of Corby, 1m E of A6003.
(OS Map 141; ref SP 875970.)
Midland Fox 'Rutland Flyer' Corby–Melton Mowbray (passes close to BR Oakham) (Tel: 0116 251 1411).

Mattersey Priory

NOTTINGHAMSHIRE (214/217/219, 11K)

Remains of a small Gilbertine monastery founded in 1185.

Open *Any reasonable time.*
Entry *Free.*
Rough access down drive ¾m long, 1m E of Mattersey off B6045, 7m N of East Retford.
(OS Map 112; ref SK 704896.)
Retford 7m.

Minster Lovell Hall and Dovecote

OXFORDSHIRE (217, 6J)

The handsome ruins of Lord Lovell's 15th-century manor house stand in a lovely setting on the banks of the River Windrush. A delightful medieval dovecote with nesting boxes is nearby.

Open *Any reasonable time.*
Entry *Free.*

Interior of Dovecote at Minster Lovell Hall

Adjacent to Minster Lovell church, 3m W of Witney off A40 (OS Map 164; ref SP 324114.)
Thames Transit 102 Witney–Carterton with connections from BR Oxford (Tel: 01865 772250).
Charlbury 7m.

Mitchell's Fold Stone Circle

SHROPSHIRE (217, 9F)

An air of mystery surrounds this Bronze Age stone circle, set on dramatic moorland and consisting of some 30 stones of which 15 are visible.

Open *Any reasonable time.*
Entry *Free.*
16m SW of Shrewsbury W of A488.
(OS Map 137; ref SO 306984.)
Minsterley 553 Shrewsbury–Bishop's Castle (passes close to BR Shrewsbury) to within 1m (Tel: 0345 056 785)
Welshpool 10m.

Moreton Corbet Castle

SHROPSHIRE (217, 10G)

A ruined medieval castle with the substantial remains of a splendid Elizabethan mansion.

Open *Any reasonable time.*
Entry *Free.*
In Moreton Corbet off B5063, 7m NE of Shrewsbury.
(OS Map 126; ref SJ 562232.)
Midland/PMT X64 Shrewsbury–Hanley (passes close to BR Shrewsbury & Stoke-on-Trent) (Tel: 0345 056 785).
Yorton 4m.

Minster Lovell Hall

Mortimer's Cross Water Mill

Mortimer's Cross Water Mill

HEREFORD & WORCESTER (217, 8G)

Intriguing 18th-century mill , still in working order, shows the process of corn milling. Set in a beautiful garden.

Open *1 April–30 Sept: Thurs, Sun & Bank Holidays only, 2–5.30pm. Parties by appointment at other times.*
Entry *£1.50/£1.00/50p.*
01568 708820
(exterior & ground floor only)
7m NW of Leominster on B4362.
(OS Map 148; ref SO 426637.)
Leominster 7½m.

Nine Ladies Stone Circle

Stanton Moor, DERBYSHIRE (214/217, 11J)

Once part of the burial site for 300–400 people, this Early Bronze Age circle is 15 metres (50 feet) across.

Open *Any reasonable time. (Site managed by the Peak Park Joint Planning Board.)*
Entry *Free.*
From unclassified road off A6, 5m SE of Bakewell. (OS Map 119; ref SK 253635.)
Hulleys 170 Matlock–Bakewell (passes close to BR Matlock), to within 1m (Tel: 01332 292200).
Matlock 4½m.

North Hinksey Conduit House

OXFORDSHIRE (217, 6K)

Roofed reservoir for Oxford's first water mains, built in the early 17th century.

Open *Any reasonable time (exterior only).*
Entry *Free.*
In North Hinksey off A34, 2½m W of Oxford. (OS Map 164; ref SP 494049.) Located off track leading from Harcourt Hill; use footpath from Ferry Hinksey Lane (near station).
Oxford 1½m.

North Leigh Roman Villa

OXFORDSHIRE (214/217, 7J)

The remains of a large and well-built Roman courtyard villa. The most important

North Hinksey Conduit House

feature is an almost complete mosaic tile floor, intricately patterned in reds and browns.

Tiled floor at North Leigh Roman Villa

Open *Grounds any reasonable time, no access to mosaic. Pedestrian access only from main road (550 metres).*
Entry *Free.*

2m N of North Leigh, 10m W of Oxford off A4095. (OS Map 164; ref SP 397154.)
Thames Transit 11 Oxford–Witney to within 1½m (Tel: 01865 772250).
Handborough 3½m.

Old Gorhambury House

HERTFORDSHIRE (212, 6M)

The remains of this Elizabethan mansion illustrate the impact of the Renaissance on English architecture.

Open *May–Sept: Thurs only, 2–5pm, or at other times by appointment.*
Entry *Free.*
01727 54051 (mornings only)

¼m W of Gorhambury House & accessible only through private drive from A4147 at St Albans (2m). (OS Map 166; ref TL 110077.)
Gade Valley 300 St Albans–Hemel Hempstead to start of drive. (Tel: 01992 556765).
St Albans Abbey 3m, St Albans 3½m.

Old Oswestry Hill Fort

SHROPSHIRE (217, 10F)

An impressive Iron Age fort of 68 acres defended by a series of five ramparts, with an elaborate western entrance and unusual earthwork cisterns.

Open *Any reasonable time.*
Entry *Free.*

1m N of Oswestry, accessible from unclassified road off A483. (OS Map 126; ref SJ 295310.)
Midland/Crosville Wales 2, D53, D63 from BR Gobowen (Tel: 0345 056 785).
Gobowen 2m.

Peveril Castle

DERBYSHIRE (214/217, 11J)

There are breathtaking views of the Peak District from this castle, perched high above the pretty village of Castleton. The great square tower stands almost to its original height.

Picnic spot of exceptional beauty. Free Children's Activity sheet available.
Open *1 April–31 Oct: daily, 10am–6pm (6pm/dusk in Oct). 1 Nov–31 March: Wed–Sun, 10am–4pm (closed 24–26 Dec, 1 Jan).*
Entry *£1.50/£1.10/80p.*
01433 620613

On S side of Castleton, 15m W of Sheffield on A625. (OS Map 110; ref SK 150827.)
Mainline/Hulleys/Chesterfield Transport 272/4 BR Sheffield-Castleton (Tel: 01332 292200).
Hope 2½m.

Peveril Castle

Rollright Stones

OXFORDSHIRE (214/217, 7J)

Three groups of stones, known as 'The King's Men', 'The Whispering Knights' and 'The King Stone', spanning nearly 2,000 years of the Neolithic and Bronze Ages.

Open *The King's Men any reasonable time by courtesy of the owner, who may levy a charge. The Whispering Knights & The King Stone any reasonable time, by footpath.*
Entry *Free.*
(in layby)
Off unclassified road between A44 and A3400, 2m NW of Chipping Norton near villages of Little Rollright and Long Compton. (OS Map 185; ref SP 297308.)

Roman Wall

St Albans, HERTFORDSHIRE (212, 6M)

Several hundred yards of the wall, built *c.*AD 200, which enclosed the Roman city of Verulamium. The remains of towers and foundations of a gateway can still be seen.

Open *Any reasonable time.*
Entry *Free.*
On S side of St Albans, ½m from centre off A4147. (OS Map 166; ref TL 135067.)
From surrounding areas (Tel: 01992 556765).
St Albans Abbey ½m, St Albans 1¼m.

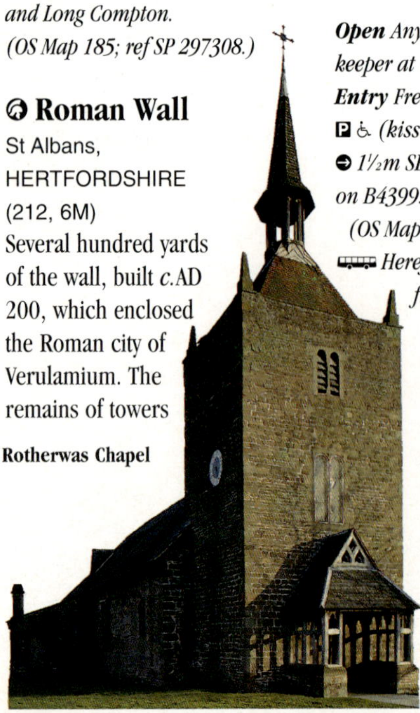

Rotherwas Chapel

Rotherwas Chapel

HEREFORD & WORCESTER (217, 7G)

This chapel dates from the 14th and 16th centuries and features an interesting mid-Victorian side chapel.

Open *Any reasonable time. Key-keeper at nearby filling station.*
Entry *Free.*
(kissing gate)
1½m SE of Hereford on B4399. (OS Map 149; ref SO 537383.)
Hereford Hopper 110/1/8 from City Centre (Tel: 0345 125 436).
Hereford 3½m.

Rufford Abbey

NOTTINGHAMSHIRE (214/217, 11K)

A 12th-century Cistercian abbey once largely concealed by a 17th-century country house. The demolition of the house in the 1950s revealed the remains of the abbey. It is set within Rufford Country Park, which has attractive grounds.

Open *1 April–31 Oct: daily, 10am–5pm. 1 Nov–31 March: daily, 10am–4pm (closed 24–26 Dec, 1 Jan).*
Entry *Free.*
01623 823148
craft centre
2m S of Ollerton off A614. (OS Map 120; ref SK 645646.)
Stagecoach East Midland 33 Nottingham–Worksop, Retford & District 136 Nottingham-Retford (Tel: 0115 924 0000).

Rushton Triangular Lodge

NORTHAMPTONSHIRE (214, 9L)

Extraordinary building built by the Catholic Sir Thomas Tresham on his return in 1593 from imprisonment for his religious beliefs. It symbolizes the Holy Trinity – it has three sides, three floors, trefoil windows and three triangular gables on each side.

Open *1 April–30 Sept: daily, 12–5pm.*
Entry *£1.00/80p/50p.*
01536 710761
1m W of Rushton, on unclassified road 3m from Desborough on A6.

(OS Map 141; ref SP 830831.) *Stagecoach United Counties 19 Kettering–Market Harborough, alight Desborough, thence 2m (Tel: 01604 20077).* *Kettering 5m.*

Rycote Chapel

OXFORDSHIRE (212/217, 6K)

This lovely 15th-century chapel, with exquisitely carved and painted woodwork, has many intriguing features, including two roofed pews and a musicians' gallery.

Open *1 April–30 Sept: weekends & Bank Holidays, 2–6pm.*
Entry *£1.50/£1.10/80p.*
(assistance required)
3m SW of Thame off A329. (OS Map 165; ref SP 667046.)
Oxford/Aylesbury Bus/ Motts 260, 280, X80 Oxford–Aylesbury (passes BR Haddenham & Thame Parkway) to within ¼m (Tel: 01296 38200).
Haddenham & Thame Parkway 5m.

Sibsey Trader Windmill

LINCOLNSHIRE (214/219, 11M)

An impressive old mill built in 1877, with its machinery and six sails intact. Flour milled on the spot can be bought there.

Open *Mill can be seen in action on 7 April, 21 April, 5 May, 26 May, 9 June, 23 June, 14 July, 28 July, 11 Aug, 25 Aug: 11am–5pm.*
Entry *£1.50/£1.00/70p.*
½m W of village of Sibsey, off A16 5m N of Boston. (OS Map 122; ref TF 345511.)
Various services and operators from Boston to Sibsey, thence ½m (Tel: 01522 553135).
Boston 5m.

Rycote Chapel

St Albans Roman Wall

See Roman Wall.

Stokesay Castle

SHROPSHIRE (217, 8G)

Wonderfully preserved example of a 13th-century fortified manor house situation in peaceful countryside. The castle now stands in a picturesque group with its own splendid timber-framed Jacobean gatehouse and the parish church.

Open *1 April–31 Oct: daily, 10am–6pm (6pm/dusk in Oct). 1 Nov–31 March: Wed–Sun, 10am–4pm (closed 24–26 Dec, 1 Jan). Closed 1–2pm in winter.*
Entry *£2.50/£1.90/£1.30.*
01588 672544
(gardens & great hall only) *(Refreshments)*
7m NW of Ludlow off A49. (OS Map 137; ref SO 436817.)
Midland Red West 435 Shrewsbury–Ludlow (Tel: 0345 056 785).
Craven Arms 1m.

Stokesay Castle

Sutton Scarsdale Hall

DERBYSHIRE (214/217, 11K)

Sutton Scarsdale Hall

The dramatic hilltop shell of a great early 18th-century baroque mansion.

Open *Any reasonable time.*
Entry *Free.*

Between Chesterfield and Bolsover, 1½m S of Arkwright Town.
(OS Map 120; ref SK 441690.)
Stagecoach E Midland 48 Chesterfield–Bolsover (Tel: 01332 292200).
Chesterfield 5m.

Tattershall College

LINCOLNSHIRE (214, 11M)

The remains of a grammar school for church choristers, built in the mid-15th century by Ralph, Lord Cromwell, the builder of nearby Tattershall Castle.

Open *Any reasonable time. (Site managed by Heritage Lincolnshire.)*
Entry *Free.*

In Tattershall (off Market Place) 14m NE of Sleaford on A153.
(OS Map 122; ref TF 213577.)
Brylaine Boston–Woodhall Spa (passes close to BR Boston) (Tel: 01522 553135).
Ruskington 10m.

Uffington Castle, White Horse and Dragon Hill

OXFORDSHIRE (217, 6J)

A group of sites lying along the Ridgeway, an old prehistoric route. There is a large Iron Age camp enclosed within ramparts, a natural mound known as Dragon Hill and the spectacular White Horse, cut from turf to reveal chalk.

Open *Any reasonable time. (Site managed by the National Trust.)*
Entry *Free.*

S of B4507, 7m W of Wantage.
(OS Map 174; ref SU 301866.)

Wall Roman Site (Letocetum)

STAFFORDSHIRE (214/217, 9J)

The remains of a staging post, alongside Watling Street. Foundations of an inn and bath-house can be seen, and there is a display of finds in the site museum.

Open *1 April–31 Oct: daily, 10am–6pm (6pm/dusk in Oct). Closed 1–2pm.*
Entry *£1.50/£1.10/80p. National Trust members admitted free. (Site maintained and managed by English Heritage, and owned by the National Trust.)*
01543 480768

Off A5 at Wall near Lichfield.
(OS Map 139; ref SK 099067.)
Shenstone 1½m.

Wayland's Smithy

OXFORDSHIRE (217, 6J)

Wall Roman Site: the bath-house

Near to the Uffington White Horse lies this evocative Neolithic burial site, surrounded by a small circle of trees. It is an unusual site in that two grave types lie one upon the other.

Open *Any reasonable time. (Site managed by the National Trust.)*
Entry *Free.*

On the Ridgeway ¾m NE of B4000 Ashbury–Lambourn road. (OS Map 174; ref SU 281854.)

Wenlock Priory

SHROPSHIRE (217, 9G)

The ruins of a large Cluniac priory in an attractive garden setting featuring delightful topiary. There are substantial remains of the early 13th-century church and Norman chapter house.

Open *1 April–31 Oct: daily, 10am–6pm (6pm/dusk in Oct). 1 Nov–31 March: Wed–Sun, 10am–4pm (closed 24–26 Dec, 1 Jan). Closed 1–2pm in winter.*
Entry *£2.00/£1.50/£1.00.*
01952 727466
(also available for the partially sighted, those with learning difficulties, and in French and German)

Wenlock Priory, a carved panel

In Much Wenlock. (OS Map 127; ref SJ 625001.)
Midland Red West 436/7, King Offa 836 Shrewsbury–Bridgnorth (passes close to BR Shrewsbury) (Tel: 0345 056 785).
Telford Central 9m.

White Ladies Priory

SHROPSHIRE (217, 9H)

The ruins of the late 12th-century church of a small priory of Augustinian canonesses.

Open *Any reasonable time.*
Entry *Free.*

1m SW of Boscobel House off unclassified road between A41 and A5, 8m NW of Wolverhampton. (OS Map 127; ref SJ 826076.)
Cosford 2½m.

White Ladies Priory

Wigmore Castle

HEREFORD & WORCESTER
(217, 8G)

There has been a castle at Wigmore since the 1060s, and the present ruins date from the late 13th and early 14th centuries, when the Mortimers were at the height of their power. The castle was dismantled in 1643 by parliamentary troops during the Civil War, and remains very much as it was left then.

Open *Telephone 01604 730320 for further details.*
Entry *Free.*

11m NW of Leominster, 14m SW of Ludlow off W side of A4110. (OS Map 137; ref SO 408693.)

Leominster 11m.

Wingfield Manor

DERBYSHIRE (214/217, 11J)

Huge, ruined, medieval country mansion built in mid-15th century. Mary Queen of Scots was imprisoned at Wingfield in 1569. Most of the manor has been unoccupied since the 1770s, but the late-Gothic Great Hall (with its superb vaulted undercroft) and the 'High Tower' are fine testaments to Wingfield in its heyday.

Open *The manor incorporates a private working farm. Visitors are requested to respect the privacy of the owners and refrain from visiting outside official opening hours. For details on opening times please telephone 01604 730326 (for 24 hour information) or 01773 832060 (property itself), before visiting.*
Entry *£2.50/£1.90/£1.30.*

(Great Hall and grounds, steep approach 600 metres). Orientation leaflet available.

17m N of Derby, 11m S of Chesterfield on B5035 ½m S of South Wingfield. From M1 – Junc 28, W on A38, A615 (Matlock Road) at Alfreton and turn onto B5035 after 1½m. (OS Map 119; ref SK 374548.)

Whites/Stagecoach E Midland 140, 254 Matlock–Alfreton (Tel: 01332 292200).

Alfreton and Mansfield Parkway 4m.

Witley Court

HEREFORD & WORCESTER
(217, 8H)

Spectacular ruins of a once great house. An earlier Jacobean manor house was converted in the 19th century into a vast Italianate mansion with porticoes by John Nash. The adjoining church, by James Gibbs, has a remarkable 18th-century baroque interior. The gardens were equally elaborate and contained immense stone fountains, which survive today. The largest, the Poseidon Fountain, will be restored to working order.

Witley Court: the Poseidon fountain

Open *1 April–31 Oct: daily, 10am–6pm (6pm/dusk in Oct). 1 Nov–31 March: Wed–Sun, 10am–4pm (closed 24–26 Dec, 1 Jan). Closed 1–2pm. Special evening guided tours available during 1996; please telephone property for details.*
Entry *£2.50/£1.90/£1.30.*
01299 896636
(not managed by English Heritage) (exterior & grounds only, poor access up long, rough drive)
10m NW of Worcester on A443.
(OS Map 150; ref 769649.)
Droitwich Spa 8½m.

Wrest Park House and Gardens

BEDFORDSHIRE (214, 7M)

Acres of wonderful gardens originally laid out in the early 18th century, including the Great Garden, with charming buildings and ornaments, and the delightfully intricate French Garden, with statues and fountain. The house, once the home of the de Grey family whose Mausoleum at Flitton is nearby, was inspired by 18th-century French chateaux.

Open *1 April–30 Sept: weekends & Bank Holidays only, 10am–6pm.*
Entry *£2.50/£1.90/£1.30.*
01525 860152
('Refreshments')
¾m E of Silsoe off A6, 10m S of Bedford.
(OS Map 153; ref TL 093356.)
Stagecoach United Counties X1, X2, X52 BR Luton–Bedford to within ½m (Tel: 01604 20077).
Flitwick 4m.

Wroxeter Roman City

SHROPSHIRE (217, 9G)

The excavated centre of the fourth largest city in Roman Britain, with impressive remains of the 2nd-century municipal baths.

Education Centre (holiday time only). Free Children's Activity Sheet available.
Open *1 April–31 Oct: daily, 10am–6pm (6pm/dusk in Oct). 1 Nov–31 March: Wed–Sun, 10am–4pm (closed 24–26 Dec, 1 Jan). Closed 1–2pm in winter.*
Entry *£2.50/£1.90/£1.30.*
01743 761330
At Wroxeter, 5m E of Shrewsbury on B4380.
(OS Map 126; ref SJ 568088.)
Williamsons X96 Birmingham–Shrewsbury (passes close to BR Telford Central) (Tel: 0345 056 785).
Shrewsbury 5½m; Wellington Telford West 6m.

Wroxeter Roman City (above) and a carved stone head (right)

Wrest Park House and Gardens

Aldborough Roman Town

NORTH YORKSHIRE (219, 14K)

The principal town of the Brigantes, the largest tribe in Roman Britain. The delightfully located remains include parts of the Roman defences and two mosaic pavements. A museum displays finds from the site.

Brick tile from Aldborough Roman Town

Open *1 April–31 Oct: daily, 12–5pm.*
Entry *£1.40/£1.10/70p. Winter, grounds only, admission free.*
01423 322768
(summer only)
¾m SE of Boroughbridge, on minor road off B6265 within 1 m of junction of A1 and A6055.
(OS Map 99; ref SE 405661.)
United 142 BR York–Ripon (Tel: 01325 468771).

Ambleside Roman Fort

CUMBRIA (218/220, 15G)

The remains of this 1st- and 2nd-century fort were built to guard the Roman road between Brougham and Ravenglass.

Open *Any reasonable time. (Site managed by the National Trust.)*
Entry *Free.*
200 yds W of Waterhead car park, Ambleside.
(OS Map 90; ref NY 376033.)
Stagecoach Cumberland 518, 555, W1 from BR Windermere (Tel: 01946 63222).
Windermere 5m.

Arthur's Round Table

CUMBRIA (218/220, 15G)

A prehistoric circular earthwork bounded by a ditch and an outer bank.

Open *Any reasonable time.*
Entry *Free.*
At Eamont Bridge, 1m S of Penrith.
(OS Map 90; ref NY 523284.)
Penrith 1½m.

Auckland Castle Deer House

Bishop Auckland, COUNTY DURHAM (218/220, 16J)

A charming building erected in 1760 in the park of the Bishops of Durham so that deer could shelter and find food.

Open *Park opening times*
1 April–30 Sept: daily, 10am–6pm.
1 Oct–31 March: daily, 10am–4pm (closed 24–26 Dec, 1 Jan).

Assorted pottery vessels from Aldborough Roman Town

Aydon Castle

Entry *Free.*

◈

➲ *In Auckland Park, Bishop Auckland, N of town centre on A68. (OS Map 93; ref NZ 216305.)*

🚌 *From surrounding areas (Tel: 0191 383 3337).*

🚆 *Bishop Auckland 1m.*

Aydon Castle

NORTHUMBERLAND

(220, 17H)

One of the finest fortified manor houses in England, built in the late 13th century. Situated in a position of great natural beauty, its remarkably intact state is due to its conversion to a farmhouse in the 17th century. The castle celebrates its 700th Anniversary in 1996.

Open *1 April–31 Oct: daily, 10am–6pm (6pm/dusk in Oct). Closed 1–2pm.*

Entry *£1.80/£1.40/90p.*

☎ 01434 632450

(ground floor)

➲ *1m NE of Corbridge, on minor road off B6321 or A68. (OS Map 87; ref NZ 002663.)*

🚆 *Corbridge 4m – approach by bridleparth from W side of Aydon Road, immediately N of Corbridge bypass.*

Baguley Hall

GREATER MANCHESTER

(217/218, 11H)

A medieval timber-framed hall house dating from the 14th century, with 18th- and 19th-century additions. An extensive programme of repair is being carried out, with access on advertised open days only.

Open *Please ring 0191 261 1585 for details.*

Entry *Free.*

➲ *6m S of Manchester, in Hall Lane, Baguley, near Wythenshawe (E of junction 3 of M56, off A560). (OS Map 109; ref SJ 815893.)*

🚌 *Frequent from surrounding areas (Tel: 0161 228 7811).*

🚆 *Gatley 2½m.*

Barnard Castle

COUNTY DURHAM

(218/220, 15H)

The substantial remains of this large castle stand on a rugged escarpment overlooking the River Tees. You can still see parts of the 14th-century Great Hall and the cylindrical 12th-century tower, built by the Baliol family.

Open *1 April–31 Oct: daily, 10am–6pm (6pm/dusk in Oct). 1 Nov–31 March: Wed–Sun, 10am–4pm (closed 24–26 Dec, 1 Jan). Closed 1–2pm in winter.*

Entry *£2.00/£1.50/£1.00.*

☎ 01833 638212

(in town)

➲ *In Barnard Castle. (OS Map 92; ref NZ 049165.)*

🚌 *United 75/A, X75 Darlington–Barnard Castle (passes close to BR Darlington) (Tel: 01325 468771).*

Barnard Castle

Beeston Castle

Beeston Castle

CHESHIRE (217/218, 11G)

The castle commands exceptional views of the surrounding countryside. There is an introductory exhibition at the bottom of the hill.

Free Children's Activity Sheet available.

Open *1 April–31 Oct: daily, 10am–6pm (6pm/dusk in Oct). 1 Nov–31 March: daily, 10am–4pm (closed 24–26 Dec, 1 Jan).*

Entry *£2.30/£1.70/£1.20.*

01829 260464

11m SE of Chester on minor road off A49 or A41. (OS Map 117; ref SJ 537593.)

Cheshire Bus C83, L2 from Chester (Tel: 01244 60266).

Chester 10m.

Belsay Hall Castle and Gardens

NORTHUMBERLAND (220, 17J)

See pp 150–3 for full details.

Berwick-upon-Tweed Barracks

NORTHUMBERLAND (220, 19H)

Among the earliest purpose-built barracks, these have changed very little since 1717. The barracks house 'By Beat of Drum', an exhibition which re-creates scenes such as a British infantryman's life in a barrack room, the Museum of the King's Own Scottish Borderers, the Borough Museum with its imaginative exhibitions and part of the Burrell Collection.

Berwick Barracks: Ravensdown

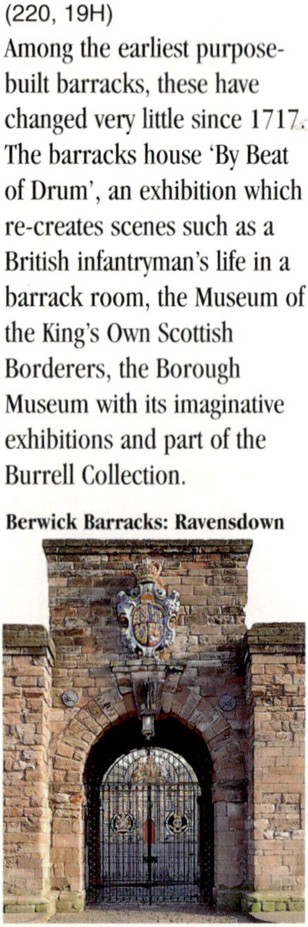

A lively exhibition, 'By Beat of Drum'. Imaginative and colourful display at Borough Museum.

Open *1 April–31 Oct: daily, 10am–6pm (6pm/dusk in Oct). 1 Nov–31 March: Wed–Sun, 10am–4pm (closed 24–26 Dec, 1 Jan). Closed 1–2pm in winter. (Museum of Kings Own Scottish Borderers open Mon–Sat, 10am–4pm.)*

Entry *£2.30/£1.70/£1.20.*

01289 304493

On the Parade, off Church St, Berwick town centre. (OS Map 75; ref NT 994535.)

From surrounding areas (Tel: 01670 533128).

Berwick-upon-Tweed ¼m.

Berwick-upon-Tweed Castle

NORTHUMBERLAND (220, 19H)

Remains of 12th-century castle.

Open *Any reasonable time.*

Entry *Free.*

Adjacent to Berwick railway station, W of town centre, accessible also from river bank. (OS Map 75; ref NT 994535.)

see **Berwick-upon-Tweed Barracks**.

Berwick-upon-Tweed Main Guard

NORTHUMBERLAND (220, 19H)

Georgian Guard House near the

quay. An exhibition celebrates the 150th anniversary of the railway coming to Berwick-upon Tweed. *The Story of a Border Garrison Town* is a permanent display of the history of the town and its fortifications.

Berwick Castle: the White Wall and Breakneck Stair.

Open *1 April–14 April (including Good Friday) and 6 May–30 Sept: Sat–Thurs, 11am–4pm. (Site managed by Berwick Civic Society.)*

Entry *Free.*

♿

➲ *Surrounding Berwick town centre on N bank of River Tweed. (OS Map 75; ref NT 994535.)*

🚌 🚆 *see* **Berwick-upon-Tweed Barracks**.

Berwick-upon-Tweed Ramparts

NORTHUMBERLAND (220, 19H)

Remarkably complete, 16th-century town fortifications, with gateways and projecting bastions.

Open *Any reasonable time.*

Entry *Free.*

♿ *(🚻 & P in town centre)*

➲ *Surrounding Berwick town centre on N bank of River Tweed. (OS Map 75; ref NT 994535.)*

🚌 🚆 *see* **Berwick-upon-Tweed Barracks**.

Berwick Ramparts

Bessie Surtees House

TYNE & WEAR (219/220, 16J)

Two 16th- and 17th-century merchants' houses. One is a remarkable and rare example of Jacobean domestic architecture. An exhibition about these buildings is on the first floor.

Bessie Surtees House

Open *Weekdays only 10am–4pm (closed Bank Holidays).*

Entry *Free.*

☎ *0191 261 1585*

🚻

➲ *41–44 Sandhill, Newcastle. (OS Map 88; ref NZ 252639.)*

🚌 *From surrounding areas (Tel: 0191 232 5325).*

🚆 *Newcastle ½m. Metro: Central Station ½m.*

Belsay Hall

The beautiful honey-coloured stone from which Belsay Hall is built came from its own quarries in the grounds. Those quarries have since become the unusual setting for one of a series of spectacular gardens, the property's finest feature, deservedly listed Grade I in the Register of Gardens. The house itself was innovative, built between 1810 and 1817 in a style derived directly from Ancient Greece. The spirit of innovation continues in 1996, when a major craft exhibition, 'Living at Belsay', will furnish the hall's main rooms with work commissioned from contemporary regional and national craftsworkers. It is one of the highlights of the Year of Visual Arts.

The thirty acres of magnificent landscaped grounds and gardens are Belsay's particular glory. The quarry gardens and the Cragwood Walk are the most special features. Sir Charles Monck, who built the present hall, saw the potential of the stone quarries, and introduced many rare and fine specimens into them to make a garden.

Succeeding generations extended the quarry and added to its planting. They made a green gorge, its sheer walls hung with exotic plants and

The great arch in the quarry garden

A quiet corner of the garden

the floor dotted with ferns. It is an adventure in itself to explore its paths and shady corners. Rhododendrons are among Belsay's special features; many beautiful examples grow in the quarry, as well as in the woodland and rhododendron gardens created later in the 19th century. These wilder areas are separated by a ha-ha ditch from the more formal terraces at the front of the Hall, with their beds of roses, lilies, lavender and other fragrant and brightly-coloured plants.

English Heritage has made great efforts to return Belsay's gardens, which suffered from neglect after World War II, to their former state, to complement the great house.

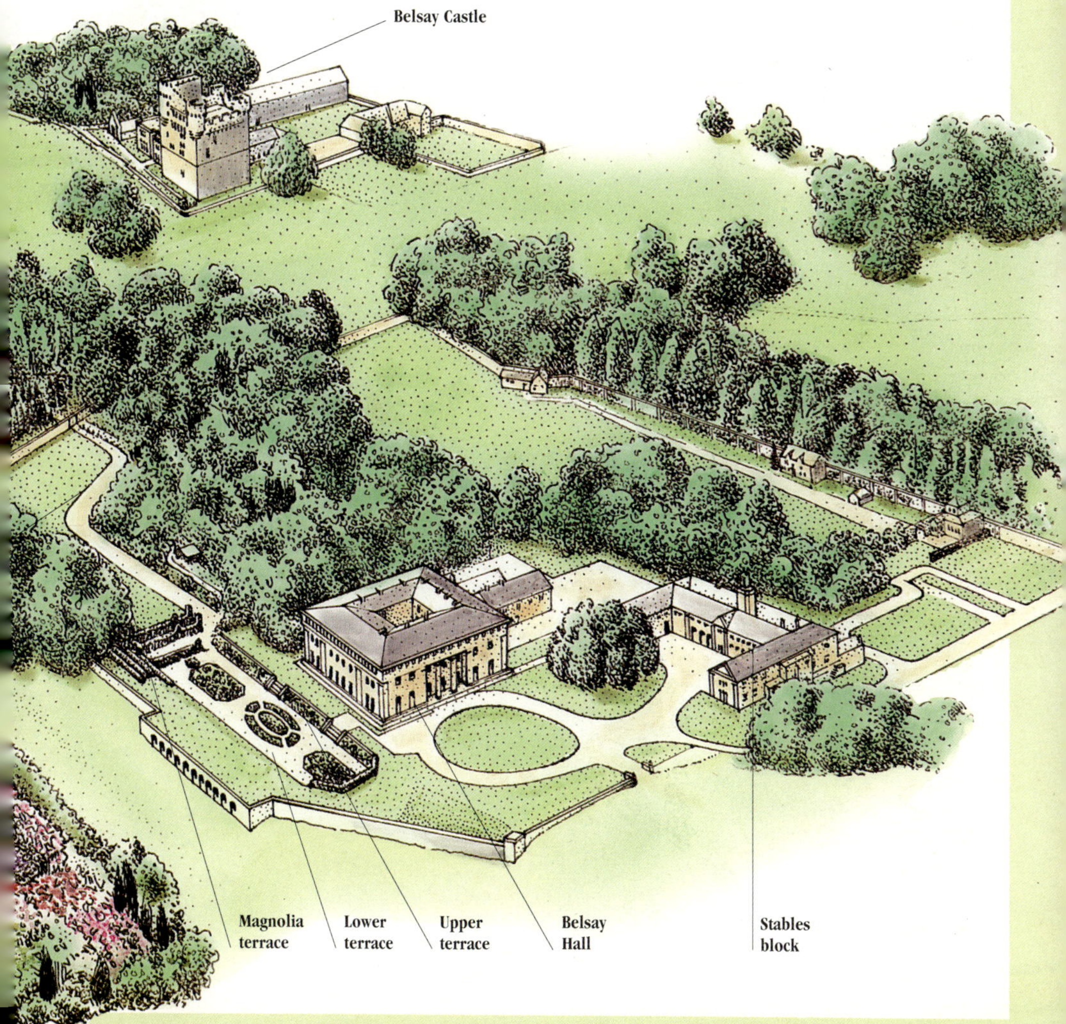

Rhododendron cinnabarinum (above) and the quarry garden in spring (left)

The south side of Belsay Hall

The castle preceded the house. Originally built in the 14th century, its L-shaped plan provided special protection to the entrance staircase and it was crowned with a prominent roof display of defensive towers and battlements.

A new range was attached to the castle in 1614. Its large windows and a classically-inspired entrance doorcase show how the need for defence in the borders had diminished.

Belsay Castle in 1728 (right), from an engraving by Samuel and Nathaniel Buck

Sir Charles Monck built the Hall to his own designs after studying ancient Greek architecture. It resembles a Greek temple, raised on a podium with giant columns at the entrance and pilasters on the walls. The interior is equally impressive, dominated by the central hall with its two-storey colonnade. Inside and out, Belsay Hall has a severity that is softened by its garden setting.

A game of croquet at Belsay

The castle was abandoned by the family in 1817 when the new Hall was built.

Belsay has much to offer: the splendour of the ancient castle, a house of key importance in the Greek Revival of the 19th century, and the glorious gardens. Plants propagated from Belsay's gardens

Belsay Castle today (above)

Medieval face above the latrine

are on sale in summer months, allowing visitors to take a small part of Belsay's beauty home with them.

From May 1996 the 'Living at Belsay' exhibition will bring the hall alive by presenting a contemporary approach to furnishing an historic house. There will be a unique combination of modern furniture, wall hangings, curtains, lighting, glassware and ceramics.

Open *1 April–31 Oct: daily, 10am–6pm (6pm/dusk in Oct). 1 Nov–31 March: daily, 10am–4pm (closed 24–26 Dec, 1 Jan).* ***Entry*** *£3.00/£2.30/ £1.50. 'Living at Belsay' (4 May–26 Oct); £3.60/ £2.80/£1.80 (inclusive of Hall, Castle and Gardens)*

✆ *01661 881636*

(grounds only; toilets) *('Belsay Hall Tearoom'; normally open summer only)*

In Belsay, 14m NW of Newcastle on A696. (OS Map 88; ref NZ 088785.)

Vasey's/Snaith's 808 from Newcastle (Tel: 01670 533128); Northumbria 508 from BR Newcastle (summer Suns only); National Express 375, 394 Newcastle–Edinburgh to within 1m. (Tel: any National Express agent).

Morpeth 10m.

The pure Greek classicism of the present Hall (left) and the less restrained entrance of its Stuart predecessor (above)

Bishop Auckland Deer House

See Auckland Castle Deer House.

Black Middens Bastle House

NORTHUMBERLAND
(220, 17H)

A 16th-century two-storey defended farmhouse, set in splendid walking country.

Open *Any reasonable time.*
Entry *Free.*

200yds N of minor road 7m NW of Bellingham; access also along minor road from A68. (OS Map 80; ref NY 774900.)

Bow Bridge

Barrow-in-Furness,
CUMBRIA (218, 14F)

Late medieval stone bridge across Mill Beck, carrying a route to nearby Furness Abbey.

Open *Any reasonable time.*
Entry *Free.*

½m N of Barrow-in-Furness, on minor road off A590 near Furness Abbey. (OS Map 96; ref SD 224715.)

Stagecoach Cumberland 6/A Barrow-in-Furness–Dalton, to within ¾m (Tel: 01946 63222).

Barrow-in-Furness 1½m.

Bowes Castle

COUNTY DURHAM (218, 15H)

Massive ruins of Henry II's tower keep, three storeys high

Brinkburn Priory

and set within the earthworks of a Roman fort.

Open *Any reasonable time.*
Entry *Free.*

In Bowes Village just off A66, 4m W of Barnard Castle. (OS Map 92; ref NY 992135.)

OK X74 Darlington–Carlisle, Primrose X69 from Newcastle, Barnard Coaches 72 from Barnard Castle. (Tel: 0191 383 3337).

Brinkburn Priory

NORTHUMBERLAND
(220, 17J)

This late 12th-century church is a fine example of early Gothic architecture, almost perfectly preserved, and is set in a lovely spot beside the River Coquet.

Open *1 April–30 Sept: daily, 12pm–5pm.*
Entry *£1.40/£1.10/70p.*
01665 570628.

(short walk from P)

4½m SE of Rothbury off B6344. (OS Map 81; ref NZ 116984.)

Northumbria 516 Morpeth–Rothbury to within ½m (Tel: 0191 232 4211).

Acklington 10m.

Brodsworth Hall

SOUTH YORKSHIRE (214, 12K)

See pp 8–15 for full details.

Brough Castle

CUMBRIA (218/220, 15H)

Ancient site dating from Roman times. The 12th-century keep replaced an earlier stronghold destroyed by the Scots in 1174. It

was restored by Lady Anne Clifford in the 17th century.

Open *Any reasonable time.*
Entry *Free.*

8m SE of Appleby S of A66. (OS Map 91; ref NY 791141.)
From BR Kirkby Stephen–Brough (Tel: 01228 812812).
Kirkby Stephen 6m.

Brougham Castle

CUMBRIA (218/220, 15G)

These impressive ruins on the banks of the River Eamont include an early 13th-century keep and later buildings. Its one-time owner Lady Anne Clifford restored the castle in the 17th century. There is an exhibition of Roman tombstones from the nearby fort.

Open *1 April–31 Oct: daily, 10am–6pm (6pm/dusk in Oct).*
Entry *£1.50/£1.10/80p.*

Brougham Castle

01768 862488
(excluding keep)
1½m SE of Penrith on minor road off A66. (OS Map 90; ref NY 537290.)
Penrith 2m.

Burton Agnes Manor House

HUMBERSIDE (219, 14L)

Rare example of a Norman house, altered and encased in brick in the 17th and 18th centuries.

Open *Any reasonable time. (The adjoining Burton Agnes Hall and Gardens are privately owned and occupied, and not managed by English Heritage.)*
Entry *Free.*

In Burton Agnes village, 5m SW of Bridlington on A166. (OS Map 101; ref TA 103633.)
E Yorkshire 744 BR York–Bridlington (Tel: 01482 27146).
Nafferton 5m.

The Countess Pillar (left) at Brougham Castle(see also p. 159)

Byland Abbey

NORTH YORKSHIRE (219, 14K)

A hauntingly lovely ruin set in peaceful meadows in the shadow of the Hambleton Hills. It illustrates the later development of Cistercian

Byland Abbey: the arch at the West front

churches, including the beautiful floor tiles.

Open *1 April–31 Oct: daily, 10am–6pm (6pm/dusk in Oct). Closed for lunch 1–2pm.*
Entry *£1.40/£1.10/70p.*
01347 868614
(including toilets)

2m S of A170 between Thirsk and Helmsley, near Coxwold village. (OS Map 100; ref SE 549789.)

Carlisle Castle

Sitting proudly on the highest point above the River Eden, Carlisle Castle has guarded the western end of the Anglo-Scottish border for over nine centuries. It was first built after William II relieved Carlisle of two centuries of Scottish domination in 1092. Since then it has often been the scene of turbulent conflict between the two nations, being fought over fairly constantly until the union of the crowns in 1603. It then fell into Scottish hands again during the Civil War and the Jacobite Rising 100 years later.

Henry I, who built the stone keep at Carlisle

Today, Carlisle Castle offers the visitor many insights into its violent past, including the legendary 'licking stones' in its dungeon, where parched Jacobite prisoners found enough moisture to stay alive, only to be barbarically executed on Gallow's Hill. The castle is now host to a new exhibition about Bonnie Prince Charlie and the Jacobite Rising of 1745; and the views from the massive keep are magnificent, stretching from the Lakes to the Pennines, from the Solway Firth to the Grampians.

Carlisle Castle's military heritage stretches back to the forging of the English and Scottish nations. Briefly the seat of Royal government while Parliament met at Carlisle in 1306–7, it has played host to kings down the centuries, been attacked by both Robert the Bruce and Bonnie Prince Charlie, and acted as a prison for Mary Queen of Scots following her abdication in 1568.

The imposing Norman keep and curtain wall date from 1157, when Carlisle and its castle were handed back to Henry II by the Scots. The keep remains the nucleus of the castle to this day, while almost every other part has been remodelled, repaired or rebuilt.

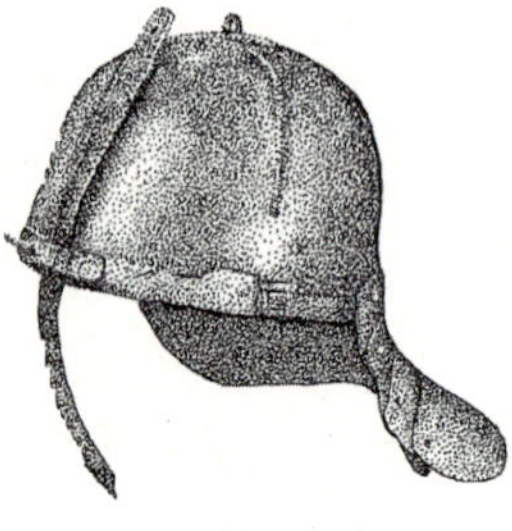

A helmet (above) from the Civil War.

The outer gatehouse (right), built about 1167, altered 1378–83

The outer gatehouse (left) with the Warden's appartments furnished in 14th-century style (above)

Throughout its long history, Carlisle has never lost its purpose as a fortress and today it remains the headquarters of the King's Own Royal Border Regiment and houses the Regimental Museum.

Graffiti by medieval prisoners

Free Children's Activity Sheet available.
Fine views from the keep and rampart walk.
***Open** 1 April–31 Oct: daily, 9.30am–6pm (6pm/dusk in Oct). 1 Nov–31 March: daily, 10am–4pm (closed 24–26 Dec, 1 Jan).*
***Entry** £2.50/£1.90/£1.30.*
01228 591922
(disabled only). Car parking in nearby city car parks (signposted) (except interiors of buildings) Guided tours available at a small extra charge. Tours are daily, June–Oct; weekends in May. Please telephone for times.
In Carlisle.
(OS Map 85; ref NY 397563.)
From surrounding areas (Tel: 01228 812812).
Carlisle ½m.

Tudor buttresses (right) strengthening the east curtain wall

Carlisle Castle

CUMBRIA (218/212, 16G)

See pp 156–7 for full details.

Castlerigg Stone Circle

CUMBRIA (218/220, 15F)

Castlerigg Stone Circle

Possibly one of the earliest Neolithic stone circles in Britain, its 33 stones stand in a beautiful setting.

Open *Any reasonable time. (Site managed by the National Trust.)*
Entry *Free.*

1½m E of Keswick. (OS Map 90; ref NY 293236.)
Stagecoach Cumberland X5 BR Penrith–Workington, to within ½m (Tel: 01946 63222).
Penrith 16m.

Chester Castle: Agricola Tower and Castle Walls

CHESHIRE (217/218, 11G)

Set in the angle of the city walls, this 12th-century tower contains a fine vaulted chapel.

Open *Castle walls open any reasonable time; cell block open 1 April–30 Sept: daily, 10am–6pm. 1 Oct–31 March: daily, 10am–4pm (closed 24–26 Dec, 1 Jan).*
Entry *Free.*
(parts)
Access via Assizes Court car park on Grosvenor St. (OS Map 117; ref SJ 405658.)
From surrounding areas (Tel: 01244 602666).
Chester 1m.

Chester Roman Amphitheatre

CHESHIRE (217/218, 11G)

The largest Roman amphitheatre in Britain, partially excavated. Used for entertainment and military training by the 20th Legion, based at the fortress of Deva.

Open *Any reasonable time.*
Entry *Free.*
(no access to amphitheatre floor)
On Vicars Lane beyond Newgate, Chester. (OS Map 117; ref SJ 404660.)
From surrounding areas (Tel: 01244 602666).
Chester ¾m.

Clifford's Tower

NORTH YORKSHIRE (219, 13K)

See pp 160–1 for full details.

Clifton Hall

CUMBRIA (218/220, 15G)

The surviving tower block of a 15th-century manor house.

Open *Any reasonable time (closed 24–26 Dec, 1 Jan).*
Entry *Free.*

In Clifton next to Clifton Hall Farm, 2m S of Penrith on A6. (OS Map 90; ref NY 530271.)
Penrith 2½m.

Conisbrough Castle

SOUTH YORKSHIRE (214/219, 12K)

The spectacular white circular keep of a 12th-century castle.

It is the oldest circular keep in England and one of the finest medieval buildings. An exciting audio-visual presentation evokes a dramatic episode in the castle's history. There is also a visitor centre and exhibition.

Open *1 April–30 Sept: daily, 10am–5pm (6pm weekends and Bank Holidays). 1 Oct–31 March: daily, 10am–4pm (5pm weekends, closed 24, 25 Dec, 1 Jan). (Castle managed by the Ivanhoe Trust.)*

Entry *£2.50/£1.50/£1.00/£6.00, family ticket/£3.00 (evening tours. Concessionary admission rates to English Heritage members and group bookings of over 25 people. (Castle managed by the Ivanhoe Trust.)*

01709 863329

(limited access)

NE of Conisbrough town centre off A630, 4½m SW of Doncaster. (OS Map 111; ref SK 515989.)

From surrounding areas (Tel: 0114 276 8688).

Conisbrough ½m.

Conisbrough Castle

Countess Pillar

Brougham, CUMBRIA

(218/220, 15G)

An unusual monument, bearing sundials and family crests, erected in 1656 by Lady Anne Clifford to commemorate her parting with her mother in 1616.

Open *Any reasonable time.*

Entry *Free.*

1m SE of Brougham on A66. (OS Map 90; ref NY 546289.)

Penrith 2½m.

Derwentcote Steel Furnace

COUNTY DURHAM

(218/220, 16J)

Built in the 18th century, the earliest and most complete authentic steel-making furnace to have survived. Closed in the 1870s, it fell into disrepair before being restored and opened to the public.

Open *1 April–30 Sept: 1st & 3rd Sunday of every month, 1pm–5pm.*

Entry *Free.*

01207 562573

10m SW of Newcastle on A694 between Rowland's Gill and Hamsterley. (OS Map 88; ref NZ 131566.)

Northern 745 Newcastle-upon-Tyne–Consett (Tel: 0191 232 5325).

Blaydon 7m.

Clifford's Tower

Standing high on its mound in the city of York, Clifford's Tower is one of the few vestiges of the pair of castles built by William the Conqueror after his victory in 1066. William urgently needed to establish his control in the northern counties, where the local people had even welcomed a Danish force in 1069; in the ensuing struggle the city was set alight and the Norman garrisons overwhelmed.

Part of a Viking sword found in York

York's castles were the stepping stones for the Normans to terrorise the North. They both had wooden keeps, with Clifford's Tower being rebuilt in stone in the 13th century. York was often the seat of government in the 13th and 14th centuries, so the castle would have been magnificently appointed.

Today, the tower stands as a proud symbol of the might of the medieval English kings.

The mound on which Clifford's Tower sits was constructed in 1069–70 from ingenious layers of gravel, clay, stone and timber to overcome the problems of waterlogged land. The original wooden keep was burnt down in 1190, when members of the Jewish community were sheltering there from a violent mob. Many of the Jews took their own lives; others died in the flames they lit; and those who finally surrendered were massacred.

The present tower, a rare and imaginative design of a quatrefoil of interlocking circles, was started in the mid-13th century by Henry III, but not completed until the early 14th century. It is thought to take its name from Roger Clifford, leader of the Lancastrian force defeated at Boroughbridge in 1322, who was hanged in chains from the keep.

The tower survived severe floods and fire during the following three centuries, and even an attempt by one of its gaolers, when it was used as a prison in the late 16th century, to demolish the tower and sell off the stone.

The south face and entrance of Clifford's Tower

A reconstruction of how Clifford's Tower may have looked in the late 13th century

An 1807 engraving of Clifford's Tower

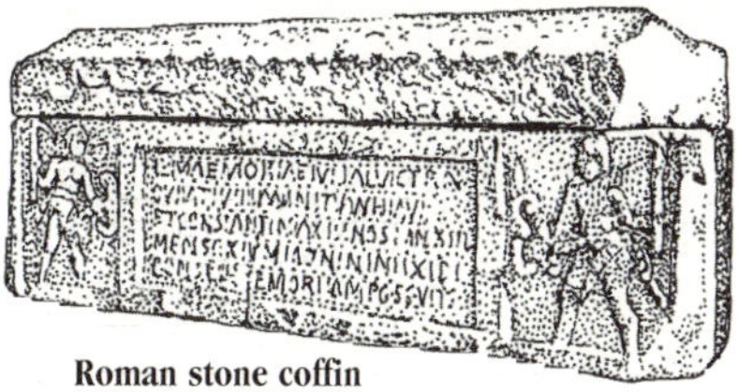

Roman stone coffin from the York Castle site

The castle survived the first Civil War intact, being first garrisoned by Royalists and then falling into Parliamentary hands after the Battle of Marston Moor in 1644. The rightful owners claimed it back following the war, but it was only handed over after it had been partially destroyed by a fire, probably started deliberately, in 1648. It has remained a shell to this day, looking down from its steep mound and offering magnificent views of the city of York spread out below.

Plan of Clifford's Tower showing its innovative geometrical shape

Family Discovery Pack and Children's Activity Sheet available.
Tactile model with Braille text.
Open *1 April–31 Oct: daily, 9.30am–6pm (6pm/dusk in Oct). 1 Oct–31 March: daily, 10am–4pm (closed 24–26 Dec, 1 Jan.)*
Entry *£1.60/£1.20/80p*
01904 646940
(city council; charge payable)
In Tower St.
(OS Map 105; ref SE 605515.)
From surrounding areas (Tel: 01904 624161).
York 1m.

The River Ouse (below) divided the sites of York's two castles

Dunstanburgh Castle

NORTHUMBERLAND

(220, 18J)

An easy coastal walk leads to the eerie skeleton of this wonderful 14th-century castle, which is sited on a basalt crag more than 30 metres (100 feet) high. Dunstanburgh is noted for its seabirds, wildlife and flowers. The surviving ruins include the large gatehouse, which later became the keep, and curtain walls.

Open *1 April–31 Oct: daily, 10am–6pm (6pm/dusk in Oct). 1 Nov–31 March: Wed–Sun, 10am–4pm (closed 24–26 Dec, 1 Jan). Closed 1–2pm in winter.*

Dunstanburgh Castle

Entry *£1.50/£1.10/80p. National Trust members admitted free. (Site owned by the National Trust, maintained and managed by English Heritage.)*

01665 576231

(in Craster village – charge payable)

8m NE of Alnwick, on footpaths from Craster or Embleton. (OS Map 75; ref NU 258220.)

Northumbria 501 Alnwick–Berwick-upon-Tweed (passes close to BR Berwick-upon-Tweed) with connections from Newcastle (passing Tyne & Wear Metro Haymarket), alight Craster, 1½m (Tel: 01670 533128).

Chathill 7m, Alnmouth 8m.

Easby Abbey

Easby Abbey

NORTH YORKSHIRE

(218/220, 15J)

Substantial remains of the medieval abbey buildings stand in a beautiful setting by the River Swale near Richmond. The abbey can be reached by a pleasant riverside walk from Richmond Castle.

Open *Any reasonable time.*

Entry *Free.*

1m SE of Richmond off B6271.

(OS Map 92; ref NZ 185003.)
United X27/8, 27/B, 28/A BR Darlington–Richmond (passes close to BR Darlington) thence 1½m (Tel: 01325 468771).

Edlingham Castle

NORTHUMBERLAND

(220, 18J)

Set in a beautiful valley, this complex ruin has defensive features spanning the 13th–15th centuries.

Open *Any reasonable time.*
Entry *Free.*

At E end of Edlingham village, on minor road off B6341 6m SW of Alnwick (OS Map 81; ref NU 115092).
Alnmouth 9m.

Egglestone Abbey

COUNTY DURHAM

(218/220, 15J)

Picturesque remains of a 12th-century abbey. Substantial parts of the church and abbey buildings remain.

Open *Any reasonable time.*
Entry *Free.*

1m S of Barnard Castle on minor road off B6277. (OS Map 92; ref NZ 062151.)
United 75/A; X75 Darlington–Barnard Castle (passes close to BR Darlington), thence 1½m, or 79 Richmond–Barnard Castle, thence ½m (Tel: 01325 468771).

Etal Castle

NORTHUMBERLAND

(220, 19H)

A 14th-century border castle located in the picturesque village of Etal. There is a major award-winning exhibition about the castle, border warfare and the Battle of Flodden, which took place nearby in 1513.

Etal Castle: the Gatehouse and Keep (below) and the exhibition (right)

A personal stereo tour guides you through this dramatic exhibition.

Open *1 April–31 Oct: daily, 10am–6pm (6pm/dusk in Oct).*
Entry *£2.30/£1.70/£1.20.*
01890 820332
(in village)
In Etal village, 10m SW of Berwick. (OS Map 75; ref NT 925394.)
Peter Pork 267 Berwick-upon-Tweed–Wooler (Tel: 01670 533128).
Berwick-upon-Tweed 10½m.

Finchale Priory

COUNTY DURHAM

(219/220, 16J)

These beautiful priory ruins, dating from the 13th century, are in a wooded setting beside the River Wear.

Open *1 April–30 Sept: daily, 12–5pm (closed 24–26 Dec, 1 Jan).*
Entry *£1.00/80p/50p.*
0191 386 3828
(on south side of river, charge payable)
3m NE of Durham, on minor road off A167. (OS Map 88; ref NZ 29471.)
Gardiners 737 Durham–Chester-le-Street (passes close to BR Durham) (Tel: 01388 814417).
Durham 5m.

Furness Abbey

CUMBRIA (218, 14F)

Arch at Furness Abbey

In a peaceful valley, the red sandstone remains of a wealthy abbey founded in 1123 by Stephen, later King of England. There is an exhibition and a museum containing fine stone carvings.

Open *1 April–31 Oct: daily, 10am–6pm (6pm/dusk in Oct). 1 Nov–31 March: Wed–Sun, 10am–4pm (closed 24–26 Dec, 1 Jan). Closed 1–2pm in winter.*

Entry *£2.30/£1.70/£1.20.*

☎ 01229 823420

1½m N of Barrow-in-Furness, on minor road off A590. (OS Map 96; ref SD 218717.)

Stagecoach Cumberland 6/A Barrow-in-Furness–Dalton, to within ½m (Tel: 01946 63222).

Barrow-in-Furness 2m.

Gainsthorpe Medieval Village

HUMBERSIDE (214/219, 12L)

Originally discovered and still best seen from the air, this hidden village comprises earthworks of peasant houses, gardens and streets.

Open *Any reasonable time.*

Entry *Free.*

On minor road W of A15 S of Hibaldstow 5m SW of Brigg (no directional signs). (OS Map 112; ref SK 955012.)

Kirton Lindsey 3m.

Gisborough Priory

CLEVELAND (219/220, 15K)

An Augustinian priory. The remains also include the gatehouse and the east end of an early 14th-century church.

Open *1 April–30 Sept: daily, 10am–5pm. 1 Oct–31 March: Tues–Sun, 10am–4pm (closed 24 Dec–1 Jan).*

Entry *80p/60p/40p. (Site managed by Langbaurgh Borough Council.)*

☎ 01287 633801

(in town)

In Guisborough town, next to parish church.

Gisborough Priory

(OS Map 94; ref NZ 618163.)
Tees X56, 93, 256/8 from Middlesbrough (passing close to BR Middlesbrough) (Tel: 01642 210131).
Marske 4½m.

Goodshaw Chapel

LANCASHIRE (218, 13H)
A recently restored 18th-century Baptist chapel with all its furnishings complete.

***Open** Keykeeper. Tel: 0191 261 1585 for details.*
***Entry** Free.*

In Crawshawbooth, 2m N of Rawtenstall, in Goodshaw Avenue off A682. (OS Map 103; ref SD 815263.)
Rossendale/Stagecoach Ribble 273 Burnley–Bolton; Stagecoach Ribble X43, 743 Burnley–Manchester. All pass BR Burnley Manchester Road (Tel: 01257 241693).
Burnley Manchester Road 4½m.

Hadrian's Wall

(166–167)
See pp 166–177 for full details and for details on the following sites on Hadrian's Wall.

Banks East Turret

Benwell Roman Temple

Benwell Vallum Crossing

Birdoswald Fort, Wall and Turret

Black Carts Turret

Brunton Turret

Cawfields Roman Wall and Milecastle

Chesters Bridge, Chesters Fort and Museum (Cilurnum)

Corbridge Roman Site (Corstopitum)

Denton Hall Turret and West Denton

Harrow's Scar

Heddon-On-The-Wall

Housesteads Roman Fort (Vercovicium)

Leahill Turret

Pike Hill Signal Tower

Piper Sike Turret

Planetrees Roman Wall

Poltross Burn

Sewingshields Wall, Turrets and Milecastle

Temple of Mithras

Vindolanda Fort and Roman Milestone

Walltown Crags Wall and Turret

Willowford Wall, Turrets and Bridge

Winshields Wall and Milecastle

Hardknott Roman Fort

CUMBRIA (218/220, 15F)
One of the most dramatic Roman sites in Britain, with stunning views across the Lakeland fells. This fort, built between AD120 and 138, controlled the road from Ravenglass to Ambleside. There are visible remains of granaries, the head-quarters building and the commandant's house, with a bath house and parade ground outside the fort.

***Open** Any reasonable time. Access may be hazardous in winter. (Site managed by the National Trust.)*

P

9m NE of Ravenglass, at W end of Hardknott Pass. (OS Map 96; ref NY 218015.)
Eskdale (Dalegarth) (Ravenglass & Eskdale Railway) 3m.

Hadrian's Wall

Stretching across northern England from the Solway Firth in the west to the Tyne in the east, Hadrian's Wall divided the 'civilized' world of the Romans, from the 'savages' beyond. Emperor Hadrian, who came to Britain in 122, was unusual in that he believed consolidation to be more glorious than new conquest. The Wall was the physical manifestation of his strategy, a defence barrier linking the existing system of forts and watchtowers along the Stanegate road. Fortified lines once marked many of the Roman Empire's boundaries – along the Rhine and the Danube, on North Africa's desert edge, and in the Middle East. These, along with Hadrian's Wall and the Antonine Wall in Britain, were the outposts of the empire. Of them all, Hadrian's Wall, a World Heritage Site, is by far the best-preserved and being there still invokes a sense of standing on the edge of the world.

Head of Hadrian, emperor from AD117 to 138

The original wall was built from AD122–23. From coast to coast 73 miles (80 Roman miles), it was punctuated by small forts a mile apart ('milecastles') with turrets positioned between them. In front of the wall was a deep ditch running in parallel, and behind it, a great earthwork or Vallum stretching along its entire length.

Looking west along the wall

Building tools found at Corbridge (below and right)

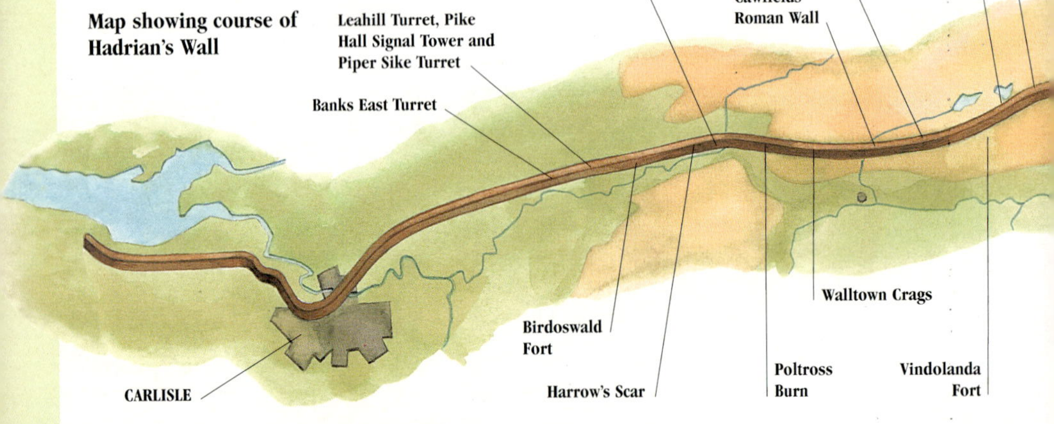

Map showing course of Hadrian's Wall

Illustration of a typical milecastle

➲ *West of Hexham, the wall runs roughly parallel to the A69 Carlisle–Newcastle-Upon-Tyne road, lying between 1–4 miles North of it, close to the B6318.* 🚌 *Northumbria/CMS 685 Newcastle–Carlisle. Closer access to wall available on special buses (Waugh's 890 & Stagecoach Cumberland 692) from May to Oct linking Hexham, Haltwhistle and Carlisle train stations and covering section from Brunton Turret to Walltown Crags Turret on Hail-and-Ride basis.* 🚂 *Carlisle railway line has stations at Hexham, Haydon Bridge, Bardon Mill, Haltwhistle and Brampton. For all Public transport information tel. 01670 533128.*

Re-enactment of legionnaries on the wall

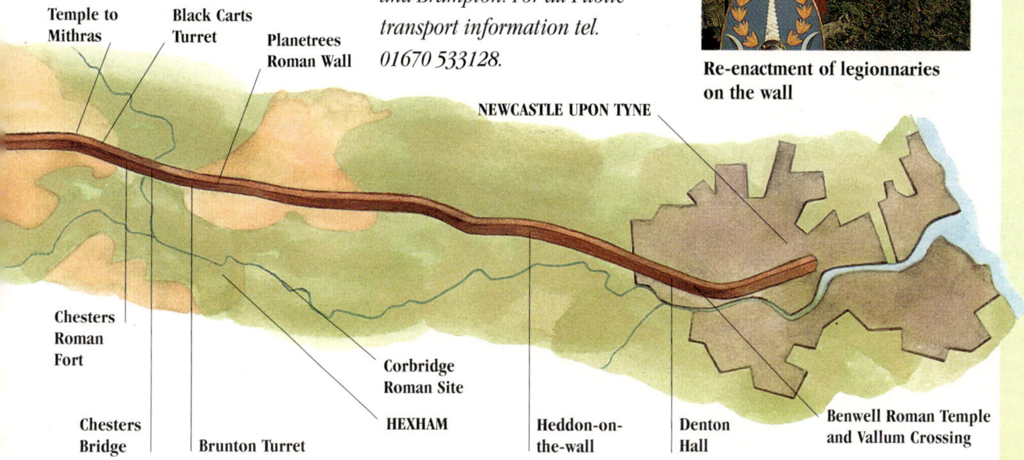

Banks East Turret

Well-preserved turret with adjoining stretches of wall and fine views.

Open *Any reasonable time.*
Entry *Free.*

On minor road E of Banks village, 3½m NE of Brampton. (OS Map 86; ref NY 575647.)
see p. 167.

Benwell Roman Temple

Remains of small temple, surrounded by modern housing.

Open *Any reasonable time.*
Entry *Free.*

Immediately S off A69 at Benwell in Broomridge Ave. (OS Map 88; ref NZ 217646.)
Frequent from centre of Newcastle (Tel 0191 232 5325).
Newcastle 2m.

Benwell Vallum Crossing

The sole remaining example of an original stone-built causeway across the ditch of the Vallum earthwork that ran parallel to the wall.

Open *Any reasonable time.*
Entry *Free.*

Immediately S off A69 at Benwell in Broomridge Ave. (OS Map 88; ref NZ 217646.)
Frequent from centre of Newcastle (Tel 0191 232 5325).
Newcastle 2m.

Centurion stone at Birdoswald

Birdoswald Fort

Almost on the edge of the Irthing escarpment, there is visible evidence of the granaries, the west gate and, most importantly, the east gate, which is among the best-preserved on the wall.

Open *1 April–31 Oct: daily 10am–5.30pm. Winter season, by arrangement only.*
Entry *£1.95/£1.45/ £1.00.*

(Site managed by Cumbria County Council.)

016977 47602

2¾m W of Greenhead, on minor road off B6318.
(OS Map 86; ref NY 615663).
see p. 167.

Black Carts Turret

A 460 metre (500 yard) length of wall and turret foundations, with magnificent views to the north

Open *Any reasonable time.*
Entry *Free.*

Black Carts Turret

2m W of Chollerford on B6318.
(OS Map 87; ref NY 884712.)
see p. 167.

Earring and statue of Fortuna found at Birdoswald

Brunton Turret

Well-preserved 2.5 metre (8 foot) high turret with a 20 metre (70 yard) stretch of wall.

Open *Any reasonable time.*
Entry *Free.*

¼m S of Low Brunton on A6079.
(OS Map 87; ref NY 922698.)
Waugh's 890; also Tyne Valley 880/2 from BR Hexham (Tel: 01670 533128).
Hexham 4m.

Cawfields Milecastle

Brunton Turret

Cawfields Roman Wall

A concentration of Roman sites – camps, turrets, a fortlet, and Milecastle 42 – along with a particularly fine, consolidated stretch of the Wall, and one of the best-preserved sections of the Vallum earthwork and ditch.

Open *Any reasonable time.*
Entry *Free.*

1 ¼m N of Haltwhistle off B 6318.
(OS Map 87; ref NY 716667.)
see p. 167.

Chesters Bridge

Fragments of the bridge that carried Hadrian's Wall across the North Tyne are visible on each bank. The most impressive remains are on the east side, across from Chesters Fort, where a short stretch of the Wall itself leads from the broad splay of the bridge's east abutment, and ends at a gatehouse tower.

Open *Any reasonable time.*
Entry *Free.*

¼m S of Low Brunton on A6079.
(OS Map 87; ref NY 922698.)
Waugh's 890; also Tyne Valley 880/2 from BR Hexham (Tel: 01670 533128).
Hexham 4m.

Chesters Bridge abutment

Chesters Roman Fort

Throughout the Empire, Roman forts were built to a very similar pattern. Chesters, located between the 27th and 28th milecastles, is one of the best-preserved examples. Laid out in a rectangle but with rounded corners, it had two gates on the shorter sides, with a main road running between them, and two gates in each of the longer sides.

Bath-house statue of Neptune

Chesters from the north

An artist's reconstruction of Chesters Roman Fort (below)

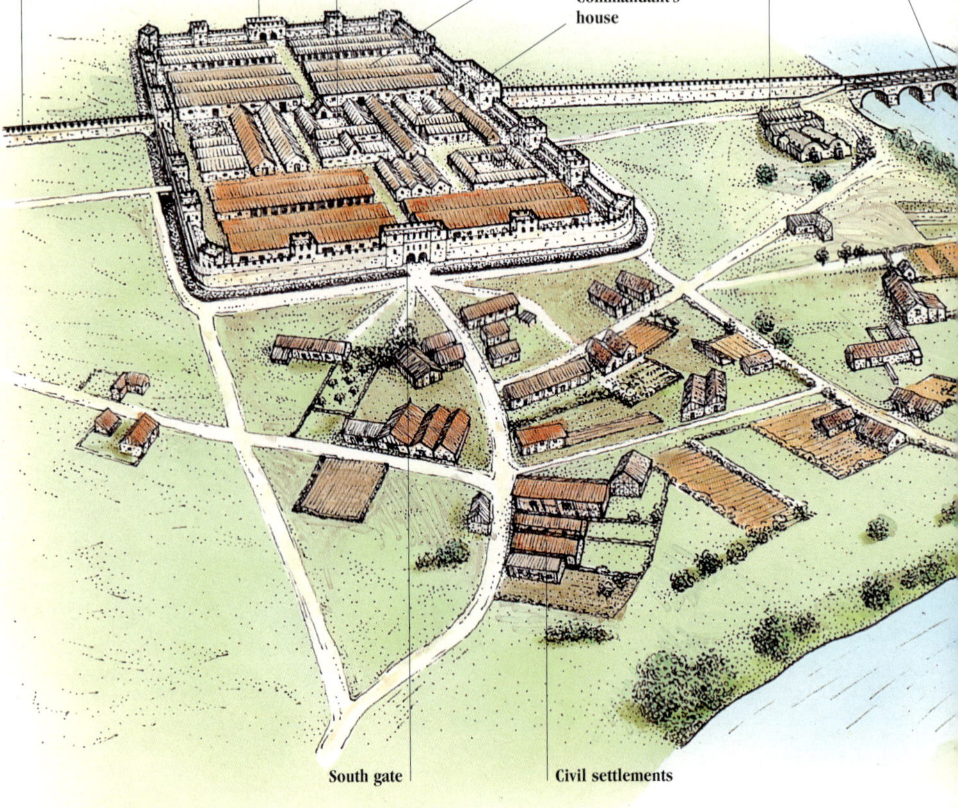

The administrative buildings were placed in the centre, including the headquarters of the legion or garrison and the commanding officer's house. The complete plan is not exposed at Chesters, but many parts are visible above ground: the four principal gates, the headquarters building, commandant's house and barracks for the troops. The wall's line ran through the fort and down to cross the River Tyne. The finely preserved bath-house is sited between the fort and the river. Originally an aqueduct brought water from the river to serve both fort and baths. Large changing rooms led to a welcoming sequence of hot, steam, warm (and cold) baths. An altar to the goddess Fortuna (Luck), found in the bath-house, suggests that gambling and bathing co-existed.

The goddess Juno Dolichena standing on a heifer

So much is known about this early fort because of the pioneering archaeological work of John Clayton, who inherited the local estate in 1832. The museum, built in 1896 soon after his death, houses many important finds from the site, and still contains its original displays.

A glass flask from the bath-house

River Tyne

Abutment of the bridge at Chesters

***Open** 1 April–31 Oct (6pm/dusk in Oct): daily, 9.30am–6pm. 1 Oct–31 March: daily, 10am–4pm (closed 24–26 Dec, 1 Jan).*
***Entry** £2.50/£1.90/£1.30*
01434 681379
(not managed by English heritage).
1½m W of Chollerford on B6318.
(OS Map 87; ref NY 913701.)
Waugh's 890. See p. 167, also Tyne Valley 880/2 from BR Hexham to within ½m (Tel: 01670 533128).
Hexham 5½m.

Corbridge Roman Site

Originally the site of a fort on the former patrol road, Corbridge evolved into a principal town of the Roman era, flourishing until the 5th century. The large granaries, with their ingenious ventilation system, are among its most impressive remains.

The Corbridge Lion

Altar to Jupiter and other gods

Activity book for children available.

Open *1 April–31 Oct: daily, 10am–6pm (6pm/dusk in Oct). 1 Nov–31 March: Wed–Sun, 10am–4pm (closed 24–26 Dec, 1 Jan). Closed 1–2pm in winter.*

Entry *£2.50/£1.90/£1.30.*

01434 632349

(also available for the partially sighted)

½m NW of Corbridge on minor road signposted Corbridge Roman Site.

(OS Map 87; ref NY 983649.)

Northumbria 602, 685 Newcastle-upon-Tyne–Hexham to within ½m (Tel: 01670 533128).

Corbridge 1¼m

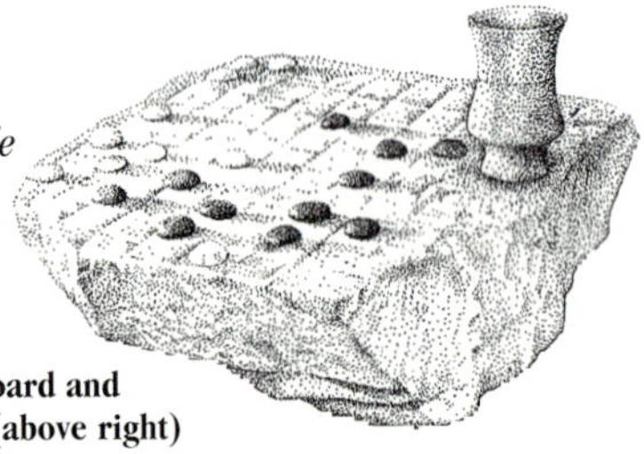

Gaming board and counters (above right)

An artist's impression of Corbridge Roman Site (below)

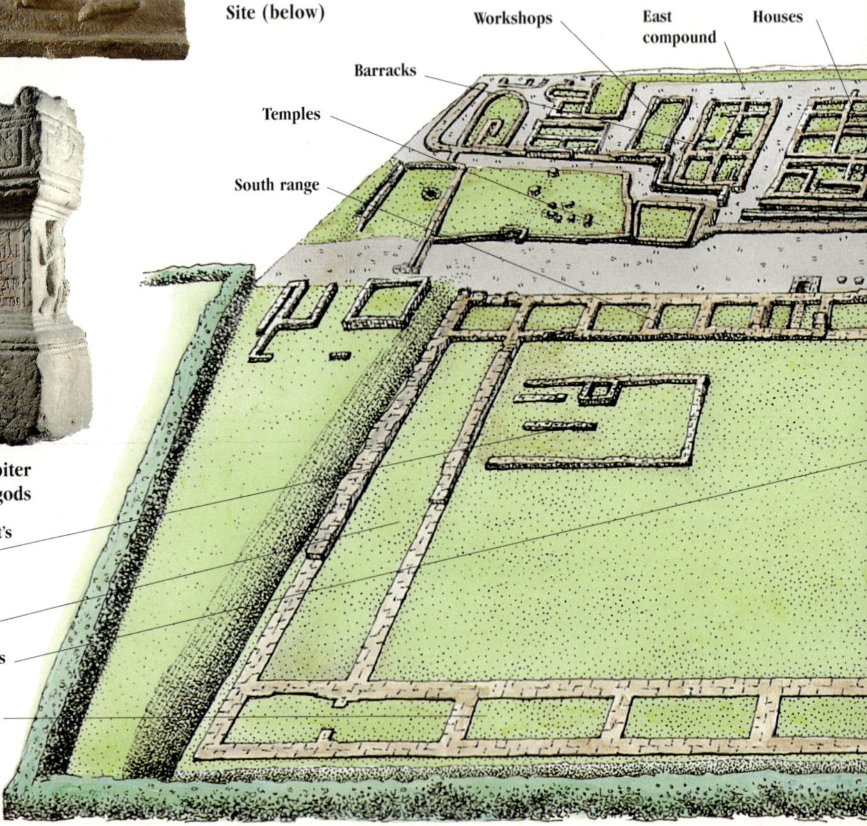

Denton Hall Turret
Foundations and 65 metre (70 yard) section of wall. The turret retains the base of the platform on which rested the ladder to the upper floor.

Open *Any reasonable time.*
Entry *Free.*
4m W of Newcastle city centre on A69.
(OS Map 88; ref NZ 195656.)
Frequent from centre of Newcastle (Tel: 0191 232 5325).
Blaydon 2m.

Harrow's Scar Milecastle
Remains linked to Birdoswald Fort by probably the most instructive mile section on the whole length of Hadrian's Wall.

Open *Any reasonable time.*
(Site managed by Cumbria County Council.)
Entry *Free.*
¼m E of Birdoswald, on minor road off B6318.
(OS Map 86; ref NY 621664.)
see p. 167.

Heddon-on-the-Wall
A fine stretch of the wall up to three metres (ten feet) thick, with the remains of a medieval kiln near the west end.

Open *Any reasonable time.*
Entry *Free.*
Immediately E of Heddon village, S of A69.
(OS Map 88; ref NZ 136669.)
Blue Bus 83, OK 684, Northumbria 685 from Newcastle-upon-Tyne (Tel: 0191 232 5325).
Wylam 3m.

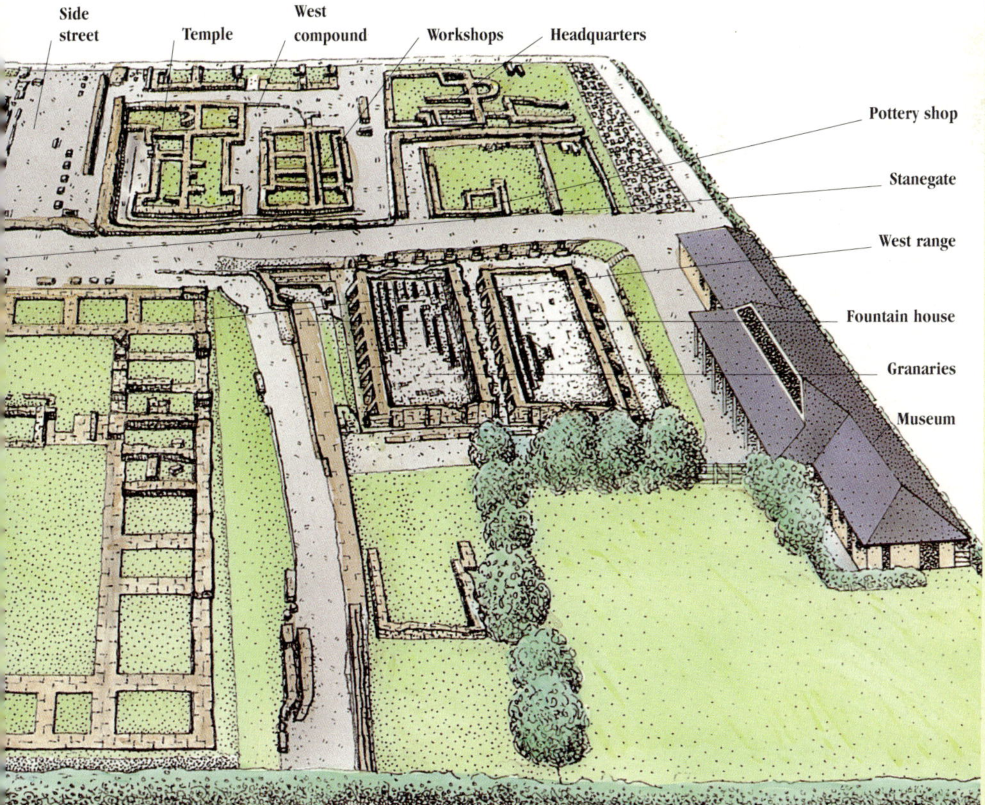

Housesteads Roman Fort

Housesteads occupies a commanding position on the basalt cliffs of the Whin Sill.

Sculpture of Victory which once adorned the east gate at Housesteads and is now in Chesters Museum

The latrines today (above) and an artist's reconstruction of how they would have looked (right)

One of the twelve permanent forts built by Hadrian *c.* 124, between milecastles 36 and 37, Housesteads is the most complete example of a Roman fort to be seen in Britain. Its visible remains include four gates, with towers at intervals between, and their curtain walls, as well as examples of the principal types of buildings within an auxiliary fort: military headquarters: commandant's house, barracks, granaries, a hospital and latrines. There are also remains of the civilian settlement that clustered at Housesteads' gates, while standing sections of Hadrian's Wall run to the east.

From the archaeological record of Housesteads, we can glimpse at the type of people who lived at the edge of the Empire.

A view of Housesteads from the south, with the civil settlement outside the fort walls in the foreground

Reconstruction drawing of Housesteads, looking north-east to Sewingshields Crags

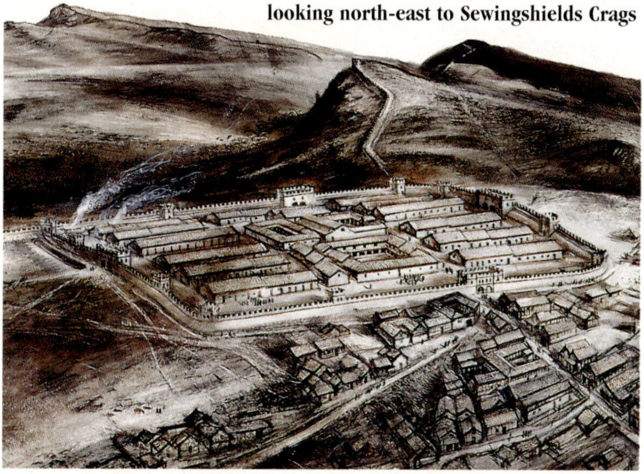

We know that cavalry from Frisia, in what is now in the north-eastern Netherlands, were stationed here in the third century – the pottery found at the site, mainly flat-bottomed dishes and larger cooking pots, is Frisian in origin. A child's shoe was also found in the wet ground alongside. Deities represented in carvings from a shrine wear the hooded cape raingear, byrrus Britannicus, that was one of the famed exports of Roman Britain and an important garment for life on Hadrian's Wall.

To the east of Housesteads, Knag Burn Gate, constructed in the third century, was an alternative way through the wall when the north gate in the fort itself fell out of use. It is one of only two isolated gates – all the rest are found at forts and milecastles. This gate and some of the wall have been partially reconstructed, and much has been consolidated, to give one of the most coherent pictures of the Romans and their great works in Britain.

Activity book for children available.

Open *1 April–31 Oct: daily, 10am–6pm (6pm/dusk in Oct). 1 Nov–31 March: daily, 10am– 4pm (closed 24–26 Dec, 1 Jan).*

Entry *£2.50/£1.90/£1.30. National Trust members admitted free. (Site owned by the National Trust, and maintained and managed by English Heritage.)*

01434 344363

(both on main road, ½m walk to S) (car park at site; enquire at information centre on main road)

2¾m NE of Bardon Mill on B6318.

(OS Map 87; ref NY 790687.)

see p. 167.

Third-century hooded deities found in a shrine at Housesteads (left)

Looking towards Housesteads along the Wall (right)

Leahill Turret and Piper Sike Turret
Turrets in the section of wall west of Birdoswald, originally constucted for the turf wall.

Open *Any reasonable time.*
Entry *Free.*

On minor road 2m W of Birdoswald Fort.
(OS Map 86; ref NY 585653.)
see p. 167

Pike Hill Signal Tower
Remains of a signal tower joined to the wall at an angle of 45 degrees.

Open *Any reasonable time.*
Entry *Free.*

On minor road E of Banks village.
(OS Map 86; ref NY 597648.)
see p. 167

Planetrees Roman Wall
A 15-metre (50-foot) length of narrow wall on broad foundations, showing extensive rebuilding in Roman times

Open *Any reasonable time.*
Entry *Free.*

Planetrees Roman Wall

On minor road E of Banks village.
(OS Map 86; ref NY 597648.)
see p. 167.

Poltross Burn Milecastle
One of the best-preserved milecastles, with part of a flight of steps to the top of the wall and the remains of the gates, enclosing walls and barrack blocks.

Open *Any reasonable time.*
Entry *Free.*
(near Station Hotel)
Immediately SW of Gilsland village by old railway station.
(OS Map 86; ref NY 634662.)
see p. 167

Temple of Mithras, Carrawburgh
Remains of a third-century temple and facsimiles of altars found during excavations.

Open *Any reasonable time.*
Entry *Free.*

3¾m W of Chollerford on B6318.
(OS Map 87; ref NY 869713.)
see p. 167.

Vindolanda Fort
A fort and well-excavated civil settlement. A museum there contains unusual artefacts of everyday Roman life.

Poltross Burn Milecastle

Open *April and Sept: daily, 10am–5.30pm. May and June: daily, 10am–6pm. July and Aug: daily, 10am–6.30pm. March and Oct: daily, 10am–5pm. Nov–Feb: daily, 10am–4pm (closed 25 Dec) (usually site open at reduced charge and museum closed during this period). Site owned and managed by Vindolanda Trust*

Sewingshields Wall
Largely unexcavated section of wall. Remains of Sewingshields Milecastle and Turret and Grindon and Coesike Turrets.

Open *Any reasonable time.*
Entry *Free.*

N of B6318, 1½m E of Housesteads Fort.
(OS Map 87; ref NY 813702.)
see p. 167

Bronze terrier found at Coventina's Well near the Temple of Mithras

Entry *£3.50/£2.75/£2.25.*
(10% discount for English Heritage members and groups of 15 or more.)
☎01434 344277
Ⓜ 🚻 🅿
➲ *1¼m SE of Twice Brewed, on minor road off B6318.*
(OS Map 87; ref NY 771664.)
🚌 🚂 *see p. 167.*

Walltown Crags
One of the best-preserved sections of the wall, snaking over the crags to the turret on its summit.
Open *Any reasonable time.*
Entry *Free.*
🅿*(nearby)*
➲*1m NE of Greenhead off B6318.*
(OS Map 87; ref NY 674664.)
🚌 🚂 *see p. 167.*

Willowford Wall, Turrets and Bridge
One thousand yards of wall, including two turrets, leading to bridge abutment remains.

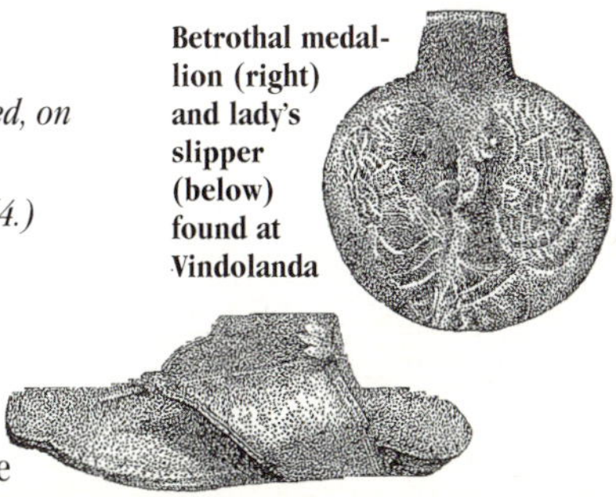

Betrothal medallion (right) and lady's slipper (below) found at Vindolanda

Open *Any reasonable time. (Access to bridge controlled by Willowford Farm; small charge levied.)*
Entry *Free but see above.*
➲ *W of minor road ¾m W of Gilsland.*
(OS Map 86; ref NY 629664.)
🚌 🚂 *see p. 167.*

Winshields Wall
Very rugged section of the wall, including the highest point at Winshields Crag.

Open *Any reasonable time.*
Entry *Free.*
➲ *W of Steel Rigg car park, on minor road off B6318. (OS Map 87; ref NY 745676.)*
🚌 🚂 *see p. 167.*

Vindolanda Fort

Helmsley Castle
NORTH YORKSHIRE
(219, 14K)
This 12th-century castle lies close to the market square, with a view of the town. Spectacular earthworks surround a great ruined Norman keep. There is an exhibition and tableau on the history of the castle in Elizabethan buildings.

Open *1 April–31 Oct: daily, 10am–6pm (6pm/dusk in Oct). 1 Nov–31 March: Wed–Sun, 10am–4pm (closed 24–26 Dec, 1 Jan). Closed 1–2pm in winter.*
Entry *£2.00/£1.50/£1.00.*
01439 770442
(large car park north of castle; charge payable) (in car park and in town centre)
Near town centre. (OS Map 100; ref SE 611836.)
Scarborough & District 128 from BR Scarborough (Tel: 01723 375463); Stephensons from BR York (Tel: 01347 838990).

Helmsley Castle

Howden Minster
HUMBERSIDE (219, 13L)
A large, cathedral-like church dating from the 14th century, which belonged to the Bishop of Durham. The ruined chancel and octagonal chapter house are in the care of English Heritage, and managed by Howden Minster Parochial Church Council. Chancel and chapter house may be viewed from the outside only.

Open *Any reasonable time (closed 24–26 Dec, 1 Jan).*
Entry *Free.*
(street parking nearby)
In Howden, 23m W of Kingston Upon Hull, 25m SE of York, near junction of A63 & A614. (OS Map 106; ref SE 748283.)
East Yorkshire 155 Goole–Hull (Tel: 01432 27146).
Howden 1½m.

Hylton Castle
TYNE & WEAR (219/220, 16J)
A 15th-century keep-gatehouse, with a fine display of medieval heraldry adorning the facades.

Kirkham Priory Gatehouse

Open *Any reasonable time (access to grounds only). (Site managed by Sunderland City Council.)*
Entry *Free.*
(grounds only)
3¾m W of Sunderland. (OS Map 88; ref NZ 358588.)
From surrounding areas (Tel: 0191 232 5325).
Seaburn 2½m.

Kirkham Priory
NORTH YORKSHIRE
(219, 14K)
The ruins of this Augustinian priory, including a magnificent carved gatehouse, are set in a peaceful and secluded valley by the River Derwent.

Open *1 April–30 Sept: daily, 12pm–5pm.*
Entry *£1.40/£1.10/70p.*
✆ 01653 618768

5m SW of Malton on minor road off A64.
(OS Map 100; ref SE 735657.)
Yorkshire Coastliner 840/2/3 Leeds–Scarborough (passes BR York and Malton) to within ¾m (Tel: 01653 692556).
Malton 6m.

Lanercost Priory

CUMBRIA
(220, 17G)

Augustinian priory founded *c*.1166. The church's nave contrasts with the ruined chancel, transepts and priory buildings.

Open *1 April–31 Oct: daily, 10am–6pm (6pm/dusk in Oct). (Parish church not managed by English Heritage.)*
Entry *£1.00/80p/50p.*
✆ 016977 3030

Off minor road S of Lanercost, 2m NE of Brampton.
(OS Map 86; ref NY 556637.)
Stagecoach Cumberland/Northumbria 685 Carlisle–Newcastle-upon-Tyne to within 1½m (Tel:01946 63222).
Brampton 3m.

Lindisfarne Priory

NORTHUMBERLAND
(220, 19J)
See pp 180–1 for full details.

Marmion Tower

NORTH YORKSHIRE
(219, 14J)
A medieval gatehouse with a fine oriel window.

Open *Any reasonable time (closed 24–26 Dec, 1 Jan).*
Entry *Free.*

N of Ripon on A6108 in West Tanfield.
(OS Map 99; ref SE 267787.)
Thirsk 10m.

Mayburgh Earthwork

CUMBRIA (218/220, 16G)
An impressive prehistoric circular earthwork, with banks up to 4.5 metres (15 feet) high, which enclose a central area of one and a half acres containing a single large stone.

Open *Any reasonable time.*
Entry *Free.*

At Eamont Bridge, 1m S of Penrith off A6.
(OS Map 90; ref NY 519285.)
Penrith 1½m.

Lanercost Priory: the undercroft (left) and tomb of Elizabeth Dacre Howard (above)

LINDISFARNE PRIORY

One of the holiest sites of Anglo-Saxon England, Lindisfarne was renowned as the original burial place of St Cuthbert, and for being founded by St Aidan, who came from Iona, the centre of Christianity in Scotland.

The island of Lindisfarne, with its wealthy monastery, was easy prey for Viking raiders from the end of the 8th century. Only in the 12th century did monks from Durham, Cuthbert's final resting place, re-establish a religious house on Lindisfarne, now more commonly known as Holy Island. The small priory was a victim of the dissolution of monastic houses in 1537 and seems to have become disused by the early 18th century.

Priory pottery design

Lindisfarne, with its ancient associations, is still a holy site and place of pilgrimage. Today, going to Lindisfarne requires prior knowledge of the tide tables (see ➲ opposite). At high tide the causeway linking Holy Island to the Northumberland coast is submerged under water and the island is cut off from the mainland.

St Aidan founded Lindisfarne in 635. Austerity was the watchword of the community – a few monks and a simple wooden church. It was, however, to become a shrine when the corpse of the former bishop St Cuthbert was dug up 11 years after his burial in 698 and found undecayed. Cuthbert was an exceedingly holy man who earlier withdrew to be a hermit on the lonely Farne Islands and later returned there to die. His relics survive in Durham Cathedral, taken there after the monks fled the plundering Vikings at the end of the 8th century. Lindisfarne was a treasure house of jewels and manuscripts, including incomparable illuminated Gospels (now in

The priory ruins with Lindisfarne Castle in the distance

A modern sculpture of St Aidan, founder of Lindisfarne (above)

Grave-marker (*c.* 900) with a procession of armed soldiers

The priory's 'Rainbow Arch' (top) and Norman arcading (above)

A modern version of Lindisfarne's Madonna and Child

the British Library. Today, in the award-winning museum, Anglo-Saxon carvings are displayed in a lively, atmospheric exhibition. The dramatic ruins of the medieval priory express its lasting power and beauty.

Free Children's Activity Sheet available.

Open *1 April–31 Oct: daily, 10am–6pm (6pm/dusk in Oct). 1 Oct–31 March: daily, 10am–4pm (closed 24–26 Dec, 1 Jan.)*

Entry *£2.50/£1.90/£1.30*

01289 389200

On Holy Island, only reached at low tide across causeway (tide tables at each end). (OS Map 75; ref NU 126418.)

Northumbria 477 from Berwick-upon-Tweed (passes close to BR Berwick-upon-Tweed). Times vary with tides (Tel: 01670 533128).

Berwick-upon-Tweed 14m via causeway.

Lindisfarne Museum (below)

Middleham Castle

NORTH YORKSHIRE

(218, 14J)

This childhood home of Richard III stands controlling the river that winds through Wensleydale. There is a massive 12th-century keep with splendid views of the surrounding countryside from the battlements.

Open *1 April–31 Oct: daily, 10am–6pm (6pm/dusk in Oct). 1 Nov–31 March: Wed–Sun, 10am–4pm (closed 24–26 Dec, 1 Jan). Closed 1–2pm in winter.*

Entry *£1.60/£1.20/80p.*

01969 623899

(except tower)

(in town centre)

At Middleham, 2m S of Leyburn on A6108.

(OS Map 99; ref SE 128875.)

Middleham Castle (below) and a re-enactment there (below right)

Monk Bretton Priory

SOUTH YORKSHIRE

(214/219, 12K)

Ruins of a Cluniac monastery founded in 1153. There are extensive remains of the fully restored 14th-century gatehouse.

Open *Any reasonable time.*

Entry *Free.*

1m E of Barnsley town centre off A633.

(OS Map 111; ref SE 373065.)

from surrounding areas (Tel: 0114 276 8688).

Barnsley 2½m.

Mount Grace Priory aerial view

Mount Grace Priory

NORTH YORKSHIRE

(219/220, 15K)

The only well-preserved Carthusian monastery in England, founded in 1398 and beautifully situated in attractive woodland. Each of the monks had his own two-storey cell, one of which has been fully restored and now contains hand-carved replica cabinets, beds and chests. There are also extensive remains of the cloister, church and outer court,

an award-winning exhibition and gardens, including a monks' herb garden.

Picnic spot of exceptional beauty and nature trail. Free Children's Activity Sheet available.

Open *1 April–31 Oct: daily, 10am–6pm (6pm/dusk in Oct). Last admission 5.30pm. 1 Nov–31 March: Wed–Sun, 10am–4pm. Last admission 3.30pm. Closed 1–2pm in winter.*
Entry *£2.40/£1.80/£1.20. National Trust members admitted free. (Site owned by the National Trust, maintained and managed by English Heritage.)*
✆ 01609 883494
12m N of Thirsk, 7m NE of Northallerton on A19. (OS Map 99; ref SE 453982.)
United/Tees 90/A Northallerton–Middlesbrough (passes close to BR Northallerton) to within ½m (Tel: 01642 210131).
Northallerton 6m.

Mount Grace Priory

Norham Castle

NORTHUMBERLAND
(220, 19H)

Set on a promontory in a curve of the River Tweed, this was one of the strongest of the border castles, built *c.*1160.

Open *1 April–30 Sept: daily, 10am–6pm. 1 Oct–31 March: daily, 10am–4pm (closed 24–26 Dec, 1 Jan).*
Entry *Free.*
(excluding keep)
(on sale at Sheppard's Newsagents, Norham, Etal Castle, Etal and Berwick Barracks).
Norham village, 6½m SW of Berwick-upon-Tweed on minor road off B6470 (from A698). (OS Map 75; ref NT 907476.)
Swan/Northumbria/ Lowland 23 BR Berwick-upon-Tweed–Kelso (Tel: 01670 533128).
Berwick-upon-Tweed 7½m.

Penrith Castle

CUMBRIA (218/220, 16G)

A 14th-century castle, set in a park on the edge of the town.

Open *Park: summer, 7.30am–9pm; winter, 7.30am–4.30pm).*
Entry *Free.*
Opposite Penrith railway station. (OS Map 90; ref NY 513299.)
Penrith.

Pickering Castle

NORTH YORKSHIRE

(219, 14L)

A splendid motte and bailey castle, once a royal ranch. It is well preserved, with much of the original walls, towers and keep, and spectacular views over the surrounding countryside. There is an exhibition on the castle's history.

Free Children's Activity Sheet available.

Open *1 April–31 Oct: daily, 10am–6pm (6pm/dusk in Oct). 1 Nov–31 March: Wed–Sun, 10am–4pm (closed 24–26 Dec, 1 Jan). Closed 1–2pm in winter.*

Entry *£2.00/£1.50/£1.00.*

01751 474989

(except motte)

In Pickering 15m SW of Scarborough.

(OS Map 100; ref SE 800845.)

Yorkshire Coastliner 840/2 from BR Malton (Tel: 01653 692556). Scarborough & District 128 from BR Scarborough (Tel: 01723 37563).

Malton 9m; Pickering (N York Moors Rly) ¼m.

Piel Castle

CUMBRIA (218, 14F)

The ruins of a 14th-century castle, accessible by boat from Roa Island, with the massive keep, inner and outer baileys, and curtain walls and towers.

Open *Any reasonable time. Access by small boat from Roa Island during summer, subject to tides and weather. For information tel. 01229 833609 or 870156.*

Entry *Free.*

On Piel Island, 3¼m SE of Barrow.

(OS Map 96; ref SD 233636.)

Stagecoach Cumberland 11/2 Barrow-in-Furness–Roa Island (Tel: 01946 63222).

Barrow-in-Furness 4m to Roa Island.

Piercebridge Roman Bridge

NORTH YORKSHIRE

(218/220, 15J)

The remains of the stone piers and abutment of a Roman timber bridge over the River Tees.

Open *Any reasonable time.*

Entry *Free.*

At Piercebridge, 4m W of Darlington on B6275.

(OS Map 93; ref NZ 214154.)

United 75/A, X75 BR Darlington–Barnard Castle (passes close to BR Darlington) (Tel: 01325 468771).

Darlington 5m.

Pickering Castle: Colemans Tower, the Motte and Keep (below) and an aerial view (right)

Richmond Castle (left) and a Civil War re-enactment there (above)

Prudhoe Castle

NORTHUMBERLAND
(218/220, 16J)
Extensive remains of

Prudhoe Castle Gatehouse

12th-century castle, with gatehouse, curtain wall and keep, overlooking the River Tyne. There is an exhibition and video presentation.

Picnic spot, brass rubbing.

Open *1 April–30 Sept: daily, 12pm–5pm.*
Entry *£1.60/£1.20/80p.*
01661 833459

In Prudhoe, on minor road off A695. (OS Map 88; ref NZ 092634.)
From surrounding areas (Tel: 01670 533128).
Prudhoe ¼m.

Ravenglass Roman Bath House

CUMBRIA (218, 15F)
The walls of the bathhouse are among the most complete Roman remains in Britain.

Open *Any reasonable time.*
Entry *Free.*

¼m E of Ravenglass, off minor road leading to A595. (OS Map 96; ref NY 088961.)
Ravenglass, adjacent.

Richmond Castle

NORTH YORKSHIRE
(218/220, 15J)
Medieval fortress, with fine 12th-century keep and 11th-century remains of curtain wall and domestic buildings. There are magnificent views from the keep.

Free Children's Activity Sheet available.
Open *1 April–31 Oct: daily, 10am–6pm (6pm/dusk in Oct). 1 Nov–31 March: daily, 10am–4pm (closed 24–26 Dec, 1 Jan). Closed 1–2pm in winter.*
Entry *£1.80/£1.40/90p.*
01748 822493

In Richmond. (OS Map 92; ref NZ 174006.)
United X27/8, 27/B, 28/A Darlington–Richmond (passes close to BR Darlington) (Tel: 01325 468771).

Richmond Castle curtain wall

Rievaulx Abbey

NORTH YORKSHIRE
(219, 14K)
See pp 188–91 for full details.

Roche Abbey

SOUTH YORKSHIRE
(214/219, 11K)
A Cistercian monastery, founded in 1147. Excavation has revealed the complete layout of the abbey.

Open *1 April–31 Oct: daily, 10am–6pm (6pm/dusk in Oct). Closed 1–2pm.*
Entry *£1.40/£1.10/70p.*
01709 812739
1½m S of Maltby off A634. (OS Map 111; ref SK 544898.)
Main Line 100–2, Northern Bus 122 Rotherham–Maltby, thence 1½m (Tel: 0114 276 8688).
Conisbrough 7m.

St Mary's Church

Studley Royal, NORTH YORKSHIRE (219, 14J)
Magnificent Victorian church, designed by William Burges in the 1870s, with a highly decorated interior. Coloured marble, stained glass, gilded and painted figures and a splendid organ remain in their original glory.

Open *1 April–30 Sept: daily, 1–5pm. (English Heritage site managed by the National Trust as part of Studley Royal estate.)*
Entry *Free.*
01765 608888
(free at visitor centre)
2½m W of Ripon off B6265, in grounds of Studley Royal estate. (OS Map 99; ref SE 278703.)
Keighley & District 801/2 Bradford–Ripon (connections from BR Harrogate), Sun, June–Aug only (Tel: 01535 603284); otherwise United 145 from Ripon (with connections from BR Harrogate), Thurs and Sat only (Tel: 01325 468771).

St. Mary's Church

Roche Abbey

St Paul's Monastery and Bede's World Museum

Jarrow, TYNE & WEAR
(220, 16J)
The home of the Venerable Bede, partly surviving as the chancel of the parish church. The monastery has become one of the best-understood Anglo-Saxon monastic sites. The museum tells the story of St Paul's Monastery and displays excavated finds. There is an Anglo-Saxon

St. Paul's Monastery

landscape with fields, crops, animals and timber buildings on land next to the museum. Phase One of the new museum building is now open.

Open *Monastery ruins any reasonable time. Museum 1 April–31 Oct: Tues–Sat and Bank Holidays, 10am–5.30pm. Sun 2.30–5.30pm; 1 Nov–31 March: Tues–Sat 11am–4.30pm, Sun 2.30–5.30pm (closed Christmas–New Year).*
Entry *£2.50/£1.25/£1.25, family ticket £6.00, UB40 family ticket £4.00. Free to monastery ruins.*
0191 489 2106
(monastery only; only guide dogs allowed to museum)
In Jarrow, on minor road N of A185.
(OS Map 88; ref NZ 339652.)
VFM 527 Newcastle-upon-Tyne–South Shields.
Metro: Bede ¾m, Jarrow ¾m.

St Peter's Church

Barton-upon-Humber, HUMBERSIDE (219, 12L)
A fine 15th-century former parish church, with an Anglo-Saxon tower and baptistry.

Open *Daily, 2–4pm (closed 24–26 Dec, 1 Jan).*
Entry *Free.*
01652 632516
In Barton-upon-Humber.
(OS Map 112; ref TA 034220.)
Road Car/E Yorks/ Applebys/Hornsby 350 Hull–Scunthorpe (Tel: 01482 884036).
Barton-upon-Humber ½m.

Salley Abbey

LANCASHIRE (218, 13H)
The remains of a Cistercian abbey founded in 1147.

Open *Any reasonable time. (Site managed by Lancashire Heritage Trust.)*
Entry *Free.*
At Sawley 3½m, N of Clitheroe off A59.
(OS Map 103; ref SD 776464.)
Clitheroe 4m.

Sandbach Crosses

CHESHIRE (217/218, 11H)
Rare Saxon stone crosses, carved with animals, dragons and biblical scenes, in the centre of the market square.

Open *Any reasonable time.*
Entry *Free.*
Market square, Sandbach.
(OS Map 118; ref SJ 758608.)
North Western K33/7 from BR Sandbach (Tel: 01244 602666).
Sandbach 1½m.

Sandbach Crosses from the 9th Century

Rievaulx Abbey

'Everywhere peace, everywhere serenity, and a marvellous freedom from the tumult of the world'. Those words could easily be taken to describe Rievaulx today, one of the most atmospheric of all the ruined medieval abbeys of the North. In fact, they were written over eight centuries ago by St Aelred, the monastery's third abbot. A long line of Cistercian monks lived in the beautiful River Rye valley from the 12th century until the 16th. The Cistercians, with their ascetic lifestyle and capacity for hard work, wanted to be isolated from the world. Although much of what was built by the monks is destroyed or ruined, most of the spectacular presbytery, the great eastern part of the abbey church, stands virtually to its full height. Built in the 13th century to contain the shrine of St Aelred (to whom an exhibition is now devoted), its soaring beauty conveys a sense of the glory and splendours that Rievaulx once possessed.

A three-faced corbel from the abbey ruins

Rievaulx was founded directly by the great and holy St Bernard of Clairvaux, as part of the missionary effort to bring Christianity to western Europe. Twelve Clairvaux monks came to Rievaulx in 1132, and from these modest beginnings sprang one of the wealthiest monasteries of medieval England and the first Cistercian monastery in the North.

The incomparable setting of Rievaulx Abbey (left)

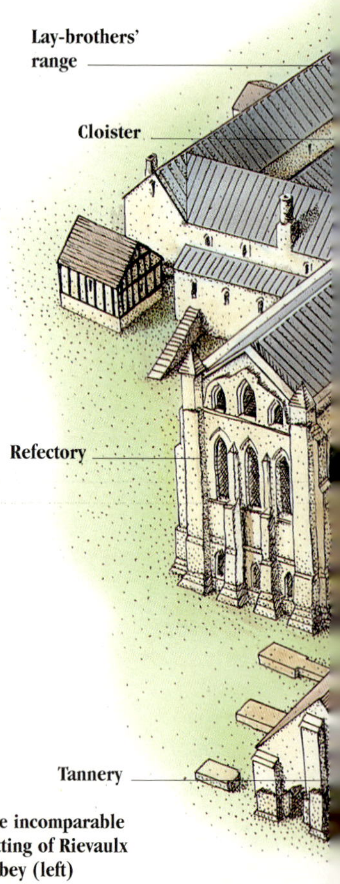

A reconstruction of how Rievaulx Abbey might have appeared at the end of the 15th century

A view through the arcades of the abbey church

In the Middle Ages, wealthy families vied with each other in founding churches. Rievaulx enjoyed the protection and endowment of Walter Espec, who provided much of the abbey's land. The monks of Byland Abbey, over the river, cooperated with the Cistercians in agreeing to divert the course of the River Rye. You can still make out traces of the old river, and the channels dug by the monks.

A medieval carving depicting the abbey's mill (above)

The ruins in 1841 drawn by William Richardson

A steady stream of monks came to Aelred, author and preacher, who was regarded then, and since, as a wise and saintly man. After his death in 1167 the monks sought his canonisation and, in the 1220s, rebuilt the east part of their church in a much more elaborate style for his tomb. Rievaulx was still a vibrant community when Henry VIII dissolved it in 1538. Its new owner, Thomas Manners, first Earl of Rutland, swiftly began the systematic destruction of the buildings. What he left was one of the most eloquent of all monastic sites, free 'from the tumult of the world', as Aelred once said.

Ruins of the monastic buildings

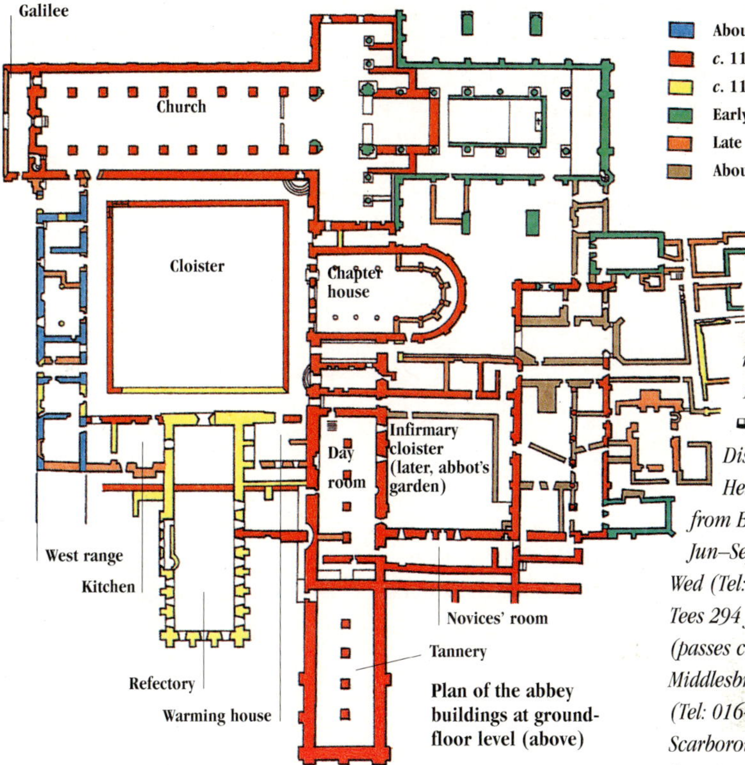

Plan of the abbey buildings at ground-floor level (above)

Family Discovery Pack available.

***Open** 1 April–31 Oct: daily, 10am–6pm (6pm/dusk in Oct). 1 Nov–31 March: daily, 10am–4pm (closed 24–26 Dec, 1 Jan).*

***Entry** £2.50/£1.90/£1.30.*

01439 798228

(also available for the partially sighted, those with learning difficulties and in French, German and Japanese.

In Rievaulx, 2¼m W of Helmsley on minor road off B1257. (OS Map 100; ref; SE 577849.)

Scarborough & District Moorsbus from Helmsley (connections from BR Scarborough) Jun–Sept; Sun. Aug; Tue and Wed (Tel: 01723 375463); Tees 294 from Middlesbrough (passes close to BR Middlesbrough), Fri only (Tel: 01642 210131); or Scarborough & District 128 from Scarborough (Tel: 01723 375463), Stephensons 57 from BR York (Tel: 01347 838990), alighting Helmsley, thence 2½m.

Medieval floor tile patterns

A corner of the cloister arcade reconstructed (left)

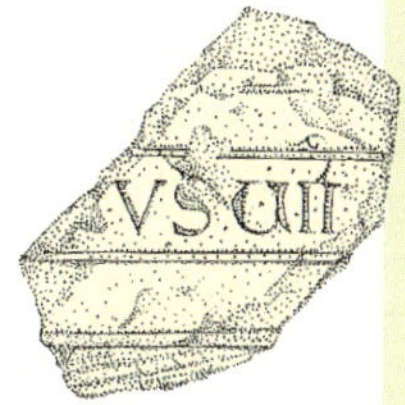

A fragment of an abbot's tomb (above)

Scarborough Castle and a decorated 16th-century slipware plate found there

Scarborough Castle

NORTH YORKSHIRE

(219, 14L)

There are spectacular coastal views from the walls of this enormous 12th-century castle. The buttressed castle walls stretch out along the cliff edge and the remains of the great rectangular stone keep still stand to over three storeys high. There is also the site of a 4th-century Roman signal station. The castle was often attacked, but despite being blasted by cannons of the Civil War and bombarded during World War I, it is still a spectacular place to visit.

Free Children's Activity Sheet available.

Open *1 April–31 Oct: daily, 10am–6pm (6pm/dusk in Oct). 1 Nov–31 March: Wed–Sun, 10am–4pm (closed 24–26 Dec, 1 Jan). Closed 1–2pm in winter.*

Entry *£1.80/£1.40/90p.*

01723 372451

(except keep)

Castle Rd, E of town centre. (OS Map 101; ref TA 050893.)

From surrounding areas (Tel: 01723 375463).

Scarborough 1m.

Shap Abbey

CUMBRIA (218/220, 15G)

The striking tower and other remains of this Premonstratensian abbey stand in a remote and isolated location.

Open *Any reasonable time.*

Entry *Free.*

1½m W of Shap on bank of River Lowther. (OS Map 90; ref NY 548153.)

Stagecoach Cumberland 107 Penrith–Shap, to within 1½m (Tel: 01946 63222).

Penrith 10m.

Skipsea Castle

HUMBERSIDE (219, 13M)

The remaining earthworks of a Norman motte and bailey castle.

Open *Any reasonable time.*

Entry *Free.*

8m S of Bridlington, W of Skipsea village. (OS Map 107; ref TA 163551.)

Bridlington 9m.

Spofforth Castle

NORTH YORKSHIRE

(219, 13J)

This manor house has some fascinating features including an undercroft built into the rock. It was once owned by the Percy family.

Open *1 April–30 Sept: daily, 10am–6pm. 1 Oct–31 March: daily, 10am–4pm (closed 24–26 Dec, 1 Jan). Keykeeper.*

Entry *Free.*

3½m SE of Harrogate, on minor road off A661 at Spofforth. (OS Map 104; ref SE 360511.)

Harrogate & District 78/A, 79 Harrogate–York (Tel: 01423 566061).

Pannal 4m.

Stanwick Iron Age Fortifications

NORTH YORKSHIRE

(218/220, 15J)

Stanwick was the tribal stronghold of the Brigantes, who built vast earthworks covering some 850 acres. Today you can see an excavated section of the ditch, cut into the rock, and the rampart.

Open *Any reasonable time.*
Entry *Free.*

➔ *On minor road off A6274 at Forcett Village. (OS Map 92; ref NZ 178124.)*
Barnard Castle Coaches 78 from Darlington (passes close to BR Darlington), Sat only (Tel: 01833 621302).
Darlington 10m.

Steeton Hall Gateway

NORTH YORKSHIRE (219, 13K)

A fine example of a small, well-preserved 14th-century gatehouse.

Open *Daily, 10am–5pm (exterior only).*
Entry *Free.*
Regional Office 0191 261 1585

➔ *4m NE of Castleford, on minor road off A162 at South Milford. (OS Map 105; ref SE 484314.)*
South Milford 1m.

Stott Park Bobbin Mill

CUMBRIA (218, 14G)

Working mill, built in 1835. It is typical of the mills in the Lake District which supplied the spinning and weaving industry in Lancashire.

See a real working Victorian mill.

Open *1 April–30 Sept: daily, 10am–6pm. Guided tours lasting 45 minutes included in admission charge, last tour 5pm. 1–31 Oct: daily, 10am–4pm, last tour 4pm. Steam engine operating Tues, Weds and Thurs.*
Entry *£2.50/£1.90/£1.30.*
015395 31087
(ground floor only)

➔ *½m N of Finsthwaite near Newby Bridge. (OS Map 96; ref SD 373883.)*
Stagecoach Cumberland 518 Ulverston–Ambleside to within 1½m (Tel: 01946 63222).
Grange-over-Sands 8m.

Stott Park Bobbin Mill

Thornton Abbey and Gatehouse

HUMBERSIDE (219, 12M)

Ruined Augustinian priory with magnificent brick gatehouse.

Open *Abbey Grounds any reasonable time. Gatehouse 1 April–30 Sept: 1st & 3rd Sun, 12–6pm. 1 Oct–31 March: 3rd Sun, 12–4pm.*
Entry *Free.*
(except interior of gatehouse and part of chapter house ruins)

➔ *18m NE of Scunthorpe on minor road N of A160; 7m SE of Humber Bridge on minor road E of A1077. (OS Map 113; ref TA 115190.)*
Thornton Abbey ¼m.

Thornton Abbey

Tynemouth Priory and Castle

TYNE & WEAR (220, 17J)

The castle walls and gatehouse enclose substantial remains of a Benedictine priory founded *c.*1090 on Saxon monastic site.

Explore underground chambers beneath the World War I gun batteries.

Open *1 April–31 Oct: daily, 10am–6pm (6pm/dusk in Oct). 1 Nov–31 March: Wed–Sun, 10am–4pm (closed 24–26 Dec, 1 Jan). Closed 1–2pm in winter. Gun battery April–Sept: Sat, Sun and Bank Holidays 10am–6pm.*

Entry *£1.50/£1.10/80p.*

0191 257 1090

(nearby; local council)

(priory)

In Tynemouth, near North Pier. (OS Map 88; ref NZ 374695.)

From surrounding areas (Tel: 0191 232 5325).

Metro: Tynemouth ½m.

Warkworth Castle

NORTHUMBERLAND (220, 18J)

The magnificent eight-towered keep on its hill above the River Coquet was the home of Harry Hotspur, the warrior immortalised in Northumbrian ballads and Shakespeare's *Henry IV*. From here, Hotspur (Sir Henry Percy) and his father, the Earl of Northumberland, dominated the Border in the 15th century and fought off the Scots on behalf of the King. They helped remove Richard II from the throne, but when his replacement, Henry IV, displeased them, Warkworth became the nerve-centre for plots to overthrow him. They failed, and both Hotspur and his father died on the battlefield.

Many chambers, passageways and dark staircases to explore. Free Children's Activity Sheet available.

Open *1 April–31 Oct: daily, 10am–6pm (6pm/dusk in Oct). 1 Nov–31 March: daily, 10am–4pm (closed 24–26 Dec, 1 Jan). Closed 1–2pm in winter.*

Entry *£2.00/£1.50/£1.00.*

01665 711423

(at castle) *(castle, excluding keep)*

In Warkworth, 7½m S of Alnwick on A1068. (OS Map 81; Castle ref NU 247057, Hermitage ref NU 242060.)

Northumbria X18 Newcastle–Alnwick (Tel: 01670 533128).

Alnmouth 3½m.

Tynemouth Castle: the Barbican.

Warkworth Hermitage

NORTHUMBERLAND (220, 18J)

Upstream from the castle by boat, this curious hermitage is cut into the rock of the river cliff.

Open *1 April–30 Sept: Wed, Sun and Bank Holidays, 11am–5pm.*

Entry *£1.00/80p/50p.*

Warton Old Rectory

LANCASHIRE (218, 14G)

Rare medieval stone house with remains of the hall, chambers and domestic offices.

Open *Any reasonable time (closed 24–26 Dec, 1 Jan).*

Entry *Free.*

At Warton, 1m N of Carnforth on minor road off A6. (OS Map 97; ref SD 499723.)

Stagecoach Ribble 55/A Lancaster–Warton (passes BR Carnforth) (Tel: 01257 241693).

Carnforth 1m.

Warkworth Castle

Wetheral Priory Gatehouse

CUMBRIA (218/220, 16G)

A Benedictine priory gatehouse.

Open *Any reasonable time (closed 24–26 Dec, 1 Jan).*

Entry *Free.*

On minor road in Wetheral village, 6m E of Carlisle on B6263. (OS Map 86; ref NY 469542.)

Stagecoach Cumberland 74/5 Carlisle–Wetherall (Tel: 01946 63222).

Wetherall ½m.

Whalley Abbey Gatehouse

LANCASHIRE (218, 13H)

The outer gatehouse of the nearby Cistercian abbey.

Open *Any reasonable time. (Site managed by Lancashire Heritage Trust.)*

Entry *Free.*

In Whalley, 6m NE of Blackburn on minor road off A59. (OS Map 103; ref SD 730360.)

Stagecoach Ribble 225 BR Blackburn–Clitheroe (Tel: 01257 241693).

Whalley ½m. Rishton 5½ m.

Wharram Percy Deserted Medieval Village

NORTH YORKSHIRE (219, 14L)

One of over 3,000 deserted villages identified from faint outlines of walls and foundations. The remains of the medieval church still stand.

Open *Any reasonable time.*

Entry *Free.*

(at Bella Farm, ¾m walk to site)

6m SE of Malton, on minor road from B1248 ½m S of Wharram le Street. (OS Map 100; ref SE 859645.)

Malton 8m.

Wheeldale Roman Road

NORTH YORKSHIRE (219, 15L)

Mile-long stretch of Roman road, still with its hardcore and drainage ditches.

Open *Any reasonable time. (Site managed by North York Moors National Park.)*

Entry *Free.*

S of Goathland, W of A169, 7m S of Whitby. (OS Map 94; ref SE 805975.)

Goathland (N York Moors Rly) 4m.

The deserted medieval village at Wharram Percy

Whitby Abbey

N. YORKSHIRE (219, 15L)

See pp 196–7 for full details.

WHITBY ABBEY

Pilgrims badge

Set high on a North Yorkshire clifftop, the remains of Whitby Abbey overlook a picturesque town and harbour with associations ranging from Victorian jewellery and whaling to Count Dracula. Whitby Abbey is a magnificent reminder of the early church's power and dedication; it contained the shrine of St Hilda, the foundress who died in 680, and it symbolized the continuing Christian tradition in the north.

Silver bronze cross

Destroyed by Viking invaders, rebuilt by Normans, embellished by later generations and dismantled under Henry VIII, the abbey is today a gaunt and moving ruin. Those who choose to approach it up the 199 steps from Whitby town also know the meaning of dedication.

St Hilda brought nuns and monks, including the poet Caedmon, to found a religious house on the coastal headland in 657. Because of her reputation, the Synod of 664 was held there and the two branches of early English Christianity, the Celtic and Roman churches, buried many differences in practice and doctrine. The matter that had principally divided them was the date of Easter and the Synod decided in favour of the Roman tradition. When the Vikings invaded Northumbria in 867, The abbey was destroyed and its wealth pillaged.

A Norman invader, Reinfrid, revived Whitby Abbey in the late 1070s; he also resettled Jarrow, home of Bede, whose writings had kept alive the memory of the early holy places, and refounded Whitby.

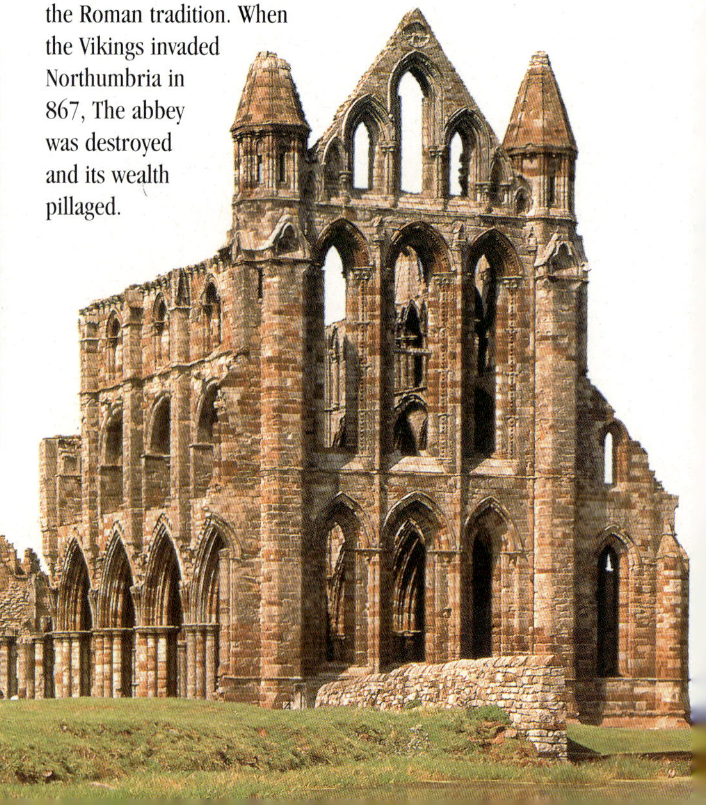

Surviving tracery (above) and the towering mass of the largely standing east end (right)

The abbey ruins in 1789

ℓ 01947 603568
(both local council; charge payable)
(We regret access unsuitable for wheelchairs.)
On cliff top E of Whitby town centre.
(OS Map 94; ref NZ 904115.)
From surrounding areas (Tel: 01947 602146).
Whitby ½m.

The Norman church proved inadequate under the pressure of pilgrims, and in the 1220s rebuilding commenced. Since its Dissolution in 1538, Whitby's dramatic location has attracted 18th-century painters and engravers. They helped begin the appreciation of the grandeur of these ruins, which has led to their continued preservation.

***The town is the setting of famous scenes from Bram Stoker's novel* Dracula.**
Activity book for children available

Open *1 April–31 Oct: daily, 10am–6pm (6pm/dusk in Oct). 1 Nov–31 March: daily, 10am–4pm (closed 24–26 Dec, 1 Jan).*
Entry *£1.60/£1.20/80p.*

Plan of existing remains at Whitby, showing the underlying 12-century apsed east end

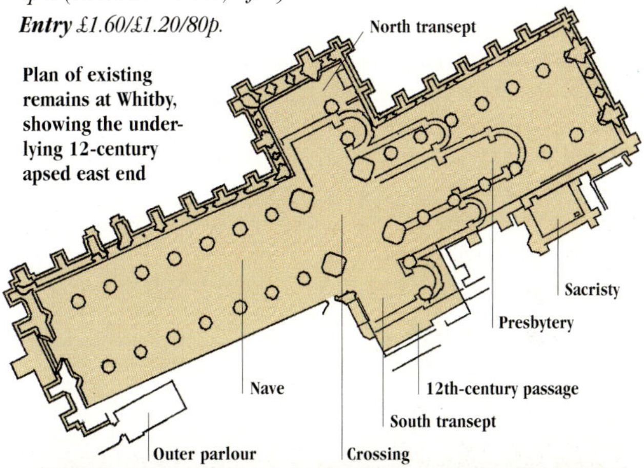

Sculpted decoration around the north transept windows (above)

The abbey and parish church, perched above the town and harbour

Other historic sites to see in England

As well as giving you free entry to our own properties, becoming a member of English Heritage opens up many other opportunities for enjoying England's past. You can enjoy the benefits of half- or reduced-price admission to numerous other historic attractions throughout the country, including for the first time the Weald and Downland Museum in the South Downs, and Pendle Heritage Centre, which lies at the start of the Pendle Way.

For further information about these sites, please contact the relevant organisations:

SUSSEX PAST Sussex Past, Bull House, 92 High Street, Lewes, East Sussex, BN7 1XH. Tel: 01273 486260.

Anne of Cleves House and Museum

LEWES (213, 3M)

This picturesque timber-framed house forms part of a range of buildings grouped round a reconstruction of a Tudor garden.

✆ 01273 474610. ➲ In Southover High Street, Lewes, off A27.

Fishbourne Roman Palace

CHICHESTER (212, 3C)

The remains of the largest Roman residence yet discovered north of the Alps, featuring some of the finest mosaics in northern Europe.

✆ 01243 785859. ➲ In Fishbourne village, 1½ miles W of Chichester, off A27/A259.

Lewes Castle

LEWES (213, 4M)

A splendid Norman castle with superb views across the Sussex countryside. The adjacent Barbican House is home to the Museum of Sussex Archaeology.

✆ 01273 486290. ➲ In Lewes town centre, off A27, A26 and A275.

Marlipins Museum

SHOREHAM (212, 3M)

Dedicated to the history of Shoreham, with its long maritime tradition, the building dates back to Norman times.

✆ 01273 462994. ➲ In town centre of Shoreham-by-Sea on A259 and off A27.

Michelham Priory

HAILSHAM (213, 3N)

An Elizabethan country house in a tranquil moated setting and spacious gardens. The house incorporates parts of the medieval priory.

✆ 01323 844224. ➲ Nr Hailsham, off A22/A27.

Priest House

WEST HOATHLY (213, 4M)

A 15th-century timber-framed house, containing a fine collection of 17th- and 18th-century furniture.

✆ 01342 810479. ➲ West Hoathly, 4 miles W of Wych Cross off A22.

Weald & Downland Open Air Museum, Singleton, Chichester, West Sussex PO18 0EU. Tel: 01243 811348

Weald & Downland Open Air Museum

SINGLETON (212, 4L)

A museum of historic buildings rescued from destruction and re-built on a beautiful 40-acre site in the South Downs.

➲ In Singleton village off A286.

FLAG FEN Flag Fen Bronze Age Excavation, Fourth Drive, Fengate, Peterborough PE1 5UR. Tel: 01733 313414.

Flag Fen Excavations

PETERBOROUGH (214, 9M)

One of Europe's most important ongoing archaeological sites. The Bronze Age museum contains the earliest wheel in England. See also 3,000-year-old timbers, a re-created fen landscape and primitive breeds of pig and sheep.

Award-winning exhibition hall and Bronze Age farm.

♿ (toilets) ➲ Signposted from A47 and A1139, 2m from Peterborough city centre.

PENDLE HERITAGE CENTRE

Pendle Heritage Centre, Park Hill, Barrowford, Nelson, Lancashire BB9 6JQ.
Tel. 01282 695366

Pendle Heritage Centre

LANCASHIRE (218, 13H)

Situated in a group of historic buildings representing several centuries of architectural styles, the Museum contains displays about the house and its families and the Pendle area.

Open *All year: daily, 10am–5pm.*

Entry *£2.75/£1.50 (50% discount to English Heritage members).*

(toilets)

In Barrowfield at junction of A682 and B6247.

9/10 from Nelson.

Nelson 1½m.

JORVIK VIKING CENTRE

Jorvik Viking Centre, Coppergate, York YO1 1NT.
Tel: 01904 643211.

Jorvik Viking Centre

YORK (219, 13K)

A time-car journey back 1,000 years to a bustling street in Jorvik – Viking age York – reconstructed on the site of extensive excavations beneath Coppergate in the heart of the city. A wharf, houses and workshops, merchants and fisherfolk, have been recreated in accurate detail complete with sounds and smells evocative of the time. Many of the magnificent objects found during the excavations are on display in an exhibition at the centre.

Open *1 April–31 Oct: daily, 9am–7pm. 1 Nov–31 March: daily, 9am–5.30pm.*

10% discount to English Heritage members. Discount not applicable on Family or PASTport tickets or other reduced admission promotions .

Jorvik Viking Centre is a project of the York Archaeological Trust.

(toilets provided)

Information Hotline 01904 643212.

In Coppergate, York city centre.

From surrounding areas (Tel. 01904 624161).

York ¾m.

ARC

The Archaeological Resource Centre (ARC), St Saviour's Church, St Saviourgate, York YO1 2NN.
Tel: 01904 654324.

The Archaeological Resource Centre (ARC)

YORK (219, 13K)

Visit the ARC and touch the past. Meet real archaeologists, learn to sort and identify finds, try out ancient crafts and use computers to learn the value of technology in uncovering the past. Hands-on archaeology for all ages.

Open *All year: Mon–Fri, 10am–4pm, Sat 1–4pm (last admission 3.30pm). Closed Suns and last 2 weeks of December.*

25% discount for English Heritage members. Discount not applicable on Family or PASTport tickets or other reduced admission promotions .

The ARC is a project of the York Archaeological Trust. *(toilets provided)*

Information Hotline 01904 643212.

In St Saviourgate, York city centre

Merchant Adventurers' Hall, Fossgate, York YO1 2XD.
Tel: 01904 654818.

Merchant Adventurers' Hall

YORK (219, 13K)

Finest remaining guild hall in Europe today, little altered since its mid-14th-century origin. It houses furniture, paintings, silver and other objects used by the merchants of York.

In York. Entrance from Piccadilly near Clifford's Tower.

The two properties below are in the care of the Ministry of Defence.

Royal Naval College

GREENWICH (213, 5M)

Conceived as a Seamen's hospital by King William and Queen Mary, and planned by Sir Christopher Wren. William and Mary's Quarters are open to the public.

On the Northern edge of Greenwich Park, 1 mile N of the A2.

Tyneham Village

DORSET (211, 3H)

Part ruin, part memorial, part museum. The village was evacuated in 1943 and used by the allied forces. The villagers never returned. The school house is now a museum, depicting life 60 years ago, and the other buildings are managed as controlled ruins.

5 miles SW of Wareham, between Corfe Castle on A351 and Lulworth Camp on B3070.

Free or half-price admission to historic sites throughout Britain

English Heritage members planning to spend some time across England's borders will benefit from our long-standing arrangement with our sister organizations in Scotland, Wales and the Isle of Man. Entry to these properties, totalling over 100 sites, is half-price in the first year of membership and free in the following years.

For further information about these sites, please contact our sister organizations:

HISTORIC SCOTLAND

Historic Scotland,
Longmore House,
Salisbury Place,
Edinburgh EH9 1SH.
Tel: 0131 668 8800.

Aberdour Castle

FIFE & CENTRAL (220, 20F)

A 14th-century tower, extended in the 16th and 17th centuries with splendid residential accommodation and a terraced garden and bowling green. There is a fine circular dovecote.

☎ 01383 860519. ➲ In Aberdour.

Arbroath Abbey

TAYSIDE (220, 21G)

The substantial ruins of a Tironensian monastery, founded by William the Lion in 1178. Parts of the abbey church and domestic buildings remain. This was the scene of the Declaration of Arbroath of 1320, which asserted Scotland's independence from England.

☎ 01241 78756. ➲ In Arbroath.

Balvenie Castle

GRAMPIAN (220, 24G)

A castle of enclosure first owned by the Comyns with a curtain wall of 13th-century date. Added to in the 15th and 16th centuries and visited by Mary Queen of Scots in 1562.

☎ 01340 820121. ➲ At Dufftown.

Bishop's and Earl's Palaces

ORKNEY (220, 29G)

The Bishop's palace is a 12th-century hall-house, later much altered, with a round tower begun by Bishop Reid in 1541. A later addition was made by the notorious Patrick Stewart, Earl of Orkney, who built the adjacent Earl's Palace between 1600 and 1607 in a splendid Renaissance style.

☎ 01856 875461. ➲ In Kirkwall.

Black House

Arnol,HIGHLANDS & WESTERN ISLES (220, 27A)

A traditional Lewis thatched house, with byre, attached barn and stackyard,complete and furnished.

☎ 01851 710395. ➲ In Arnol village, Lewis.

Blackness Castle

FIFE & CENTRAL (220, 20F)

Built in the 1440s, and massively strengthened in the 16th century as an artillery fortress, Blackness was an ammunition depot in the 1870s. It was restored by the Office of Works in the 1920s.

☎ 01506 834807. ➲ 4m N of Linlithgow, on a promontory in the Forth estuary.

Bonawe Iron Furnace

ARGYLL & BUTE & ARRAN (220, 21C)

Founded in 1753 by a Lake District partnership, this is the most complete charcoal-fuelled ironworks in Britain. Displays illustrate how iron was made here.

☎ 01866 2432. ➲ Close to the village of Taynuilt.

Bothwell Castle

SOUTH STRATHCLYDE (220, 19E)

The largest and finest 13th-century stone castle in Scotland, much fought over during the Wars of Independence. Part of the original circular keep survives, but most of the castle dates from the 14th and 15th centuries

☎ 01698 816894. ➲ In Bothwell, approached from Uddingston, off the B7071.

Broch of Gurness

ORKNEY (220, 30G)

Protected by three lines of ditch and rampart, the base of the broch is surrounded by a warren of Iron Age buildings.

☎ 01831 579478. ➲ At Aikerness, about 14m NW of Kirkwall.

Caerlaverock Castle

DUMFRIES & GALLOWAY (220, 17F)

One of the finest castles in Scotland, on a triangular site surrounded by

moats. Its special features are the twin-towered gatehouse and the Nithsdale Lodging, a Renaissance range dating from 1638.
☎ 01387 77244. ➲ 8m SE of Dumfries.

Cardoness Castle

DUMFRIES & GALLOWAY (220, 16D)
The well-preserved ruin of a tower house of 15th-century date, the ancient home of the McCullochs.
☎ 01557 814427. ➲ 1m SW of Gatehouse of Fleet.

Castle Campbell

FIFE & CENTRAL (220, 20E)
Traditionally known as the 'Castle of Gloom'. The oldest part is a well-preserved 15th-century tower, around which other buildings were constructed, including an unusual loggia.
☎ 01259 472408. ➲ At the head of Dollar Glen.

Corgarff Castle

GRAMPIAN (220, 23F)
A 16th-century tower house converted into a barracks for Hanoverian troops in 1748. Its last military use was to control the smuggling of illicit whisky between 1827 and 1831. Still complete and with star-shaped fortification.
☎ 019756 51460. ➲ 8m W of Strathdon village.

Craigmillar Castle

LOTHIAN (220, 19F)
Built round an L-plan tower house of the early 15th century, Craigmillar was much expanded in the 15th and 16th centuries. It is a handsome ruin, and includes a range of private rooms.
☎ 0131 661 4445. ➲ 2½m SE of central Edinburgh, to E of Edinburgh-Dalkeith road.

Craignethan Castle

SOUTH STRATHCLYDE (220, 19E)
The oldest part is a tower house built by Sir James Hamilton of Finnart in the 16th century, defended by an outer wall pierced by gun ports, and by a wide and deep ditch with a most unusual 'caponier' – a stone vaulted chamber for artillery.
☎ 01555 86364. ➲ 5½m NW of Lanark.

Crichton Castle

LOTHIAN (220, 19G)
A large and sophisticated castle, of which the most spectacular part is the range erected by the Earl of Bothwell between 1581 and 1591.
☎ 01875 320017. ➲ 2½m SW of Pathhead.

Crossraguel Abbey

SOUTH STRATHCLYDE (220, 18D)
The 13th-century remains, which are remarkably complete and of high quality, include the church, cloister, chapter house and much of the domestic premises.
☎ 01655 883113. ➲ 2m S of Maybole.

Dallas Dhu Distillery and Visitor Centre

GRAMPIAN (220, 25F)
A perfectly preserved time capsule of the distiller's art. Built in 1898 to supply malt whisky for Wright and Greig's 'Roderick Dhu' blend. Video presentation and a glass of whisky to end your visit.
☎ 01309 76548. ➲ About 1m S of Forres off the Grantown Road.

Dirleton Castle and Gardens

LOTHIAN (220, 20G)
The oldest part of this romantic castle dates from the 13th century. It was rebuilt in the 14th century and extended in the 16th century, when the gardens were established.
☎ 01620 850330. ➲ In the village of Dirleton.

Doune Castle

FIFE & CENTRAL (220, 20E)
A late 14th-century courtyard castle built for the Regent Albany. Its most striking feature is the combination of keep, gatehouse and hall, with its kitchen in a massive frontal block.
☎ 01786 841742. ➲ In Doune.

Dryburgh Abbey

BORDERS (220, 18G)
Both beautifully situated and of intrinsic quality, the ruins of Dryburgh Abbey are remarkably complete. Much of the work is of the 12th and 13th century. Sir Walter Scott and Field Marshal Earl Haig are buried in the abbey.
☎ 01835 822381. ➲ 5m SE of Melrose, near St Boswells.

Dumbarton Castle

SOUTH STRATHCLYDE (220, 20D)
Spectacularly sited on a volcanic rock, this was the site of the ancient capital of Strathclyde. The most interesting features are the 18th-century artillery fortifications, with 19th-century guns.
☎ 01389 32167. ➲ At Dumbarton.

Dundonald Castle

SOUTH STRATHCLYDE (220, 18D)
A fine 13th-century tower built by Robert II incorporating part of an earlier building. The king used the castle as a summer residence until his death in 1390.
☎ 01563 850201. ➲ In Dundonald, off the A759.

Dundrennan Abbey
DUMFRIES & GALLOWAY
(220, 16E)
The beautiful ruins of a Cistercian abbey founded by David I. Mary Queen of Scots spent her last night on Scottish soil here.
✆ 01557 5262. ➲ 6½m SE of Kirkcudbright.

Dunfermline Abbey and Palace
FIFE & CENTRAL (220, 20F)
Remains of a Benedictine abbey founded by Queen Margaret in the 11th century. The foundations of her church are under the superb, Romanesque nave, built in the 12th century. Robert the Bruce was buried in the choir, now the site of the present parish church.
✆ 01383 739026. ➲ In Dunfermline.

Dunstaffnage Castle and Chapel
ARGYLL & BUTE & ARRAN
(220, 21B)
A very fine 13th-century castle enclosure, built on a rock, with nearby ruins of a chapel of exceptional architectural refinement.
✆ 01631 62465. ➲ By Loch Etive, 3½m from Oban.

Edinburgh Castle
LOTHIAN (220, 20F)
The most famous of Scottish castles has a complex history. The oldest part dates from the Norman period; there is a Great Hall built by the James IV; the Half Moon battery was built by Regent Morton in the late 16th century; the Scottish National War Memorial was formed after World War I. The castle also houses the crown jewels (Honours) of Scotland, the history of which is described in a new exhibition. Also see the famous 15th-century gun, Mons Meg. Attractive restaurant with spectacular views over the city.
✆ 0131 225 9846. ➲ In the centre of Edinburgh.

Edzell Castle and Garden
TAYSIDE (220, 22G)
Very beautiful complex with a late-medieval tower house incorporated into a 16th-century courtyard mansion. The carved decoration of the garden walls is unique in Britain.
✆ 01356 648631. ➲ At Edzell, 6m N of Brechin.

Elgin Cathedral
GRAMPIAN (220, 25F)
The superb ruin of what many think was Scotland's most beautiful cathedral. Much of the work is in a rich late 13th century style, much modified after the burning of the church by the Wolf of Badenoch in 1390. The octaganol chapter house is the finest in Scotland.
✆ 01343 547171. ➲ In Elgin.

Fort George
HIGHLANDS & WESTERN ISLES
(220, 25E)
A vast site and one of the most outstanding artillery fortifications in Europe. It was planned in 1747 as a base for George II's army, and was completed in 1769. Since then it has served as a barracks. There are reconstructions of barrack rooms in different periods and a display of muskets and pikes.
✆ 01667 462777. *➲ 11m NE of Inverness, by the village of Ardersier.*

Glenluce Abbey
DUMFRIES & GALLOWAY
(220, 16C)
Cistercian abbey founded in 1192. The remains include a handsome early 16th-century chapter house.
✆ 01581 300541. ➲ 2m N of Glenluce village.

Hermitage Castle
BORDERS (220, 17G)
A vast and eerie ruin in a lonely situation, but with fabric from the 14th century. Mary Queen of Scots made her famous ride there to meet the Earl of Bothwell.
✆ 013873 76222. ➲ In Liddesdale, 5½m NE of Newcastleton, off the B6399.

Huntingtower Castle
TAYSIDE (220, 21F)
Two fine and complete towers, of the 15th and 16th centuries, now linked by a 17th-century range. There are fine painted ceilings.
✆ 01738 27231. ➲ 2m W of Perth.

Huntly Castle
GRAMPIAN (220, 24G)
A magnificent ruin consisting mainly of a palace block erected in the 16th and 17th centuries by the Gordon family.
✆ 01466 793191. ➲ In Huntly.

Inchcolm Abbey
FIFE & CENTRAL (220, 20F)
The best-preserved group of monastic buildings in Scotland, founded in about 1123, and including a 13th-century octagonal chapter house.
✆ 01383 823332. ➲ On an island on the Firth of Forth, opposite Aberdour. Ferries from South Queensferry and North Queensferry.

Inchmahome Priory
FIFE & CENTRAL (220, 20D)
A beautifully situated Augustinian monastery founded in 1238, with much of the original 13th-century building surviving.

☎ 01877 385294. ➲ On an island in the Lake of Menteith, approached by boat from Port of Menteith.

Jarlshof Prehistoric and Norse Settlement

SHETLAND (220, INSET)

An very important site with a complex of ancient settlements within three acres. The oldest is a Bronze Age village of oval stone huts. On the crest of the mound is a house built *c.* 1600. The visitor centre has new displays on Iron Age life and a history of the site.

☎ 01950 60112. ➲ At Sumburgh Head, about 22m S of Lerwick.

Jedburgh Abbey and Visitor centre

BORDERS (220, 18G)

One of the abbeys founded by David I and the Bishop of Glasgow in about 1138 for Augustinian canons. The church is mostly in Romanesque and early Gothic styles and is remarkably complete.

☎ 01835 863925. ➲ In Jedburgh.

Kildrummy Castle

GRAMPIAN (220, 24G)

Though ruined, the best example in Scotland of a 13th-century castle, with a curtain wall, four round towers, hall and chapel. The seat of the Earls of Mar, it was dismantled after the 1715 Jacobite Rising.

☎ 019755 71331. ➲ 10m W of Alford.

Kinnaird Head Lighthouse

GRAMPIAN (220, 25H)

Built in 1787 within a 16th-century tower-house, Kinnaird Head was the first lighthouse built by the Northern Lighthouse Company.

☎ 01346 511022. ➲ On a promontory in Fraserburgh.

Linlithgow Palace

LOTHIAN (220, 20E)

Magnificent ruin of a great royal palace, set in its own park. All the Stewart kings lived here, and work commissioned by James I, III, IV, V and VI can be seen. The great hall and the chapel are particularly fine.

☎ 01506 842896. ➲ In Linlithgow.

Lochleven Castle

TAYSIDE (220, 21F)

Late 14th-century tower on one side of an irregular courtyard. Mary Queen of Scots was imprisoned here in 1567 and escaped in 1568.

☎ 01786 450000. ➲ On an island in Loch Leven, accessible by boat from Kinross.

Maclellan's Castle

DUMFRIES & GALLOWAY (220, 16E)

A castellated town house built by the then provost of Kirkcudbright from 1577, with particularly good architectural details.

☎ 01557 331856. ➲ In the centre of Kirkcudbright.

Maes Howe Chambered Cairn

ORKNEY (220, 29G)

The finest megalithic tomb in the British Isles, with a large mound covering a stone-built passage and a large burial chamber with cells in the walls. Of Neolithic date, broken into during Viking times, with Viking runes carved on the walls.

☎ 01856 76606. ➲ About 9m W of Kirkwall.

Meigle Sculptured Stone Museum

TAYSIDE (220, 22F)

A magnificent collection of 25 sculptured monuments of the Celtic Christian period, one of the finest collections of Dark Age sculpture in Western Europe.

☎ 011828 64612. ➲ In Meigle.

Melrose Abbey

BORDERS (220, 19G)

Probably the most famous ruin in Scotland, founded around 1136 as a Cistercian abbey by David I, and repeatedly wrecked in the Wars of Independence. The surviving remains of the church are 15th century and of an elegance unique in Scotland. The Commendator's house contains displays relating to the abbey's history and to the Roman fort at Newstead.

☎ 01896 822562. ➲ In Melrose.

New Abbey Corn Mill

DUMFRIES & GALLOWAY (220, 17E)

A carefully renovated water-powered oatmeal mill, in working order, and demonstrated regularly to visitors in the summer.

☎ 01387 785260. ➲ In New Abbey village.

Newark Castle

SOUTH STRATHCLYDE (220, 20D)

The oldest part of the castle is a tower built soon after 1478, with a detached gatehouse. The main part was added in 1597–9 by Patrick Maxwell.

☎ 01475 741858. ➲ In Port Glasgow.

Rothesay Castle

ARGYLL & BUTE & ARRAN (220, 20C)

A remarkable 13th-century, circular castle of enclosure. A favourite residence of the Stewart kings.

☎ 01700 502691. ➲ In Rothesay, Isle of Bute.

St Andrews Castle and Visitor Centre

FIFE & CENTRAL (220, 21G)

Ruins of the castle of the Archbishops of St Andrews, dating in part from the 13th century. Features include a 'bottle dungeon', and mine and counter-mine tunnelled during the siege that followed the murder of Cardinal Beaton in 1546. Visitor Centre with shop and major exhibition depicting the history of the castle and cathedral.

✆ 01334 477196. ➲ In St Andrews.

St Andrews Cathedral

FIFE & CENTRAL (220, 21G)

Remains of the largest cathedral in Scotland, and of the priory's domestic ranges. The precinct walls are particularly well-preserved.

✆ 013334 472563. ➲ In St Andrews.

Seton Collegiate Church

LOTHIAN (220, 20G)

The chancel and apse of this lovely building date from the 15th century, and the transepts and steeple were built by the widow of Lord Seton, who was killed at Flodden in 1513.

✆ 01875 813334. ➲ 1m SE of Cockenzie off Edinburgh–North Berwick Road.

Skara Brae Prehistoric Village

ORKNEY (220, 29F)

The best-preserved group of Stone Age houses in Western Europe. The houses contain stone furniture, hearths and drains, and give a remarkable picture of life in Neolithic times.

✆ 01856 84815. ➲ 19m NW of Kirkwall.

Smailholm Tower

BORDERS (220, 19G)

A simple rectangular tower in a good state of preservation. It houses costume figures and tapestries relating to Sir Walter Scott's 'Minstrelsy of the Scottish Borders'.

✆ 01573 460365. ➲ Near Smailholm village, 6m NW of Kelso.

Spynie Palace

GRAMPIAN (220, 25F)

Residence of the Bishops of Moray from the 14th century to 1686. The site is dominated by the massive tower built by Bishop David Stewart (1461–77).

✆ 01343 546358. ➲ 2m N of Elgin, off the A941.

Stirling Castle

FIFE & CENTRAL (220, 20E)

The grandest of all Scottish castles. The Great Hall and the Gatehouse of James IV, the marvellous Palace of James V, the Chapel Royal remodelled by James VI, and the artillery fortifications of the 16th and 18th centuries, are all of outstanding interest. Restaurant and introductory display now open.

✆ 01786 447873. ➲ In Stirling.

Sweetheart Abbey

DUMFRIES & GALLOWAY (220, 17E)

Splendid ruin of a late 13th- and early 14th-century Cistercian abbey founded by Dervorgilla, Lady of Galloway.

✆ 01387 785397. ➲ In New Abbey village, 7m S of Dumfries.

Tantallon Castle

LOTHIAN (220, 20G)

Remarkable fortification with earthwork defences, and a massive 14th-century curtain wall with towers. Interpretive displays include replica guns.

✆ 01620 892727. ➲ 3m E of North Berwick.

Threave Castle

DUMFRIES & GALLOWAY (220, 17E)

Massive tower built in the late 14th century. Round its base is an artillery fortification built before 1455, when the castle was besieged by James II. It is on an island, approached by boat, followed by a long walk.

✆ 01831 168512. ➲ 3m W of Castle Douglas.

Tolquhon Castle

GRAMPIAN (220, 24H)

Built for the Forbes family, Tolquhon has an early 15th-century tower. Noted for its highly ornamented gatehouse.

✆ 01651 5286. ➲ 15m from Aberdeen off the Pitmedden–Tarves Road.

Urquhart Castle

HIGHLANDS & WESTERN ISLES (220, 24D)

Standing above Loch Ness, this was one of the largest castles in Scotland, having fallen into decay after 1689. Most of the existing buildings date from after the 16th century.

✆ 01456 450551. ➲ On Loch Ness, near Drumnadrochit.

Whithorn Priory and Museum

DUMFRIES & GALLOWAY (220, 16D)

Site of the first Christian church in Scotland, founded as 'Candida Casa' by St Ninian in the early 5th century. The priory was built over the church for Premonstratensian canons in the 12th century and became the cathedral church of Galloway. In the museum is a fine collection of early Christian stones.

✆ 01988 500700. ➲ In Whithorn.

CADW Welsh Historic Monuments, Brunel House,
2 Fitzalan Road,
Cardiff CF2 1UY.
Tel: 01222 500200.

Beaumaris Castle

GWYNEDD (216, 11D)

Begun in 1295, this unfinished castle was the last and largest of King Edward I's Welsh fortifications. Formidable defences survive, surrounded by a partly restored moat.

✆ 01248 810361. ➲ In Beaumaris, off A545.

Blaenavon Ironworks

GWENT (217, 6F)

Substantial remains of five early blast furnaces and associated workers' housing, dating in part from 1788–89.

➲ 6m N of Pontypool, off A4043.

Caerleon Roman Fortress

GWENT (217, 6F)

Site of the 50-acre Roman legionary fortress of Isca, dating from ***c.*** AD75. Impressive remains of the Fortress Baths, amphitheatre ('King Arthur's Round Table'), barracks and fortress wall.

✆ 01633 422518. ➲ B4596 to Caerleon, from M4.

Caernarfon Castle

GWYNEDD (216, 11D)

With its nine polygonal towers (including the great Eagle Tower), two gatehouses and walls of colour-banded stone, the castle was intended by King Edward I to be a royal residence and seat of government for North Wales.

✆ 01286 677617. ➲ In Caernarfon town centre.

Caerphilly Castle

MID GLAMORGAN (216, 6F)

One of the largest medieval fortresses in Britain, begun in 1268 by the Anglo-Norman Marcher lord, Gilbert de Clare. Famous for its 'leaning tower'. Impressive great hall, now used for various functions.

✆ 01222 883143. ➲ In Caerphilly town centre.

Carreg Cennen Castle

DYFED (216, 7E)

Magnificently located castle, high on a limestone precipice. Surviving remains date from the late 13th and early 14th centuries, including an underground passage and cave.

✆ 01588 822291. ➲ Near Trapp, off A484, 4m SE of Llandeilo.

Castell Coch

SOUTH GLAMORGAN (216, 6F)

Unique, late 19th century fairytale-style castle, designed for the third marquess of Bute by William Burges. Lavishly decorated and furnished in the Victorian Gothic style; a 'romantic' vision of the Middle Ages.

✆ 01222 810101. ➲ Near Tongwynlais, off A470, 5m NW of Cardiff.

Chepstow Castle

GWENT (217, 6G)

Substantial remains of one of the earliest stone-built castles in Britain and the centre of the medieval Marcher lordship of Chepstow. The castle was modified and developed in successive stages throughout the Middle Ages and again following the Civil War.

✆ 01291 624065. ➲ In Chepstow town centre, off A48 or M4.

Cilgerran Castle

DYFED (216, 7C)

Picturesque remains that date from the early 13th century.

➲ In Cilgerran, 3m S of Cardigan, off A478.

Coity Castle

MID GLAMORGAN (216, 6E)

Although originally established soon after 1100, much of the castle dates from the 14th century and later. Parts were rebuilt following the siege by Owain Glyndwr in 1404–5.

✆ 01656 652021. ➲ In Coity, 2m NE of Bridgend, off A4061.

Conwy Castle

GWYNEDD (216, 11E)

Built for King Edward I between 1283 and 1287, Master James of St George's design at Conwy remains one of the most outstanding achievements of medieval military architecture.

✆ 01492 592358. ➲ In Conwy town centre.

Criccieth Castle

GWYNEDD (216, 10D)

Perched in an imposing position, the castle is still dominated by the twin-towered gatehouse built by Prince Llywelyn ab Iorwerth ('the Great'). Later remodelled by Edward I and Edward II.

✆ 01766 522227. ➲ On coastal bluff, near Criccieth town centre.

Cymer Abbey

GWYNEDD (216, 10E)

Remains of a simple abbey church, founded in 1198 by Maredudd ap Cynan for the Cistercian order.

✆ 01341 422854. ➲ Near Llanelltyd, off A470, 1½m N of Dolgellau.

Denbigh Castle

CLWYD (216, 11F)

Begun by Henry de Lacy in 1282, with the support of King Edward I, the site is dominated by an impressive triple-towered gatehouse, the link between defended town and castle ward.

☎ 01745 813979. ➲ On hill above Denbigh town centre.

Dolbadarn Castle

GWYNEDD (216, 11D)

Probably built by Llywelyn ab Iorwerth early in the 13th century, the castle is dominated by a massive round-towered keep.

➲ ½m SE of Llanberis, on A4086.

Dolwyddelan Castle

GWYNEDD (216, 10E)

A square stone keep, dating from the 13th century, remains of this castle built by Llywelyn ab Iorwerth. The site was later remodelled by King Edward I.

☎ 01690 750366. ➲ 1m W of Dolwyddelan, on A470.

Dyfi Furnace

DYFED (216, 9E)

Restored mid-18th-century charcoal-fired blast furnace, used for smelting iron ore.

☎ 01654 781383. ➲ 6m SW of Machynlleth, on A487.

Flint Castle

CLWYD (217, 11F)

Begun in 1277, this was one of the first castles to be built in Wales by King Edward I. Its most impressive feature is a solitary round tower, isolated from the rest of the inner ward.

➲ On NE side of Flint.

Gwydir Uchaf Chapel

GWYNEDD (216, 11E)

Simple stone-built chapel built in 1673, noted for its fine painted ceiling.

➲ ½m SW of Llanrwst, off B5106.

Harlech Castle

GWYNEDD (216, 10D)

Built between 1283 and 1289 by Master James of St George for King Edward I. The castle is designed on a concentric plan. Seized by Owain Glydwr and held successfully by him for four years.

☎ 01766 780552. ➲ Harlech town centre.

Kidwelly Castle

DYFED (216, 6D)

Impressive remains of a castle established as a huge earthwork in the early 12th century. The stone castle was raised by the de Chaworths, and was much modified later by the Earls of Lancaster.

☎ 01554 890104. ➲ In centre of Kidwelly.

Lamphey Bishop's Palace

DYFED (216, 6C)

Extensive remains of a lavish country retreat used by the bishops of St Davids, with buildings dating from the 13th to 16th centuries.

☎ 01646 672224. ➲ In Lamphey, 2½m E of Pembroke, off A4139.

Laugharne Castle

DYFED (216, 6D)

Established during the 12th century, Laugharne underwent many transformations under a long series of occupiers, which included the Anglo-Norman de Brian family and, in the 16th century, Sir John Parrot

☎ 01994 427906. ➲ In Laugherne on A4066, 14m SW of Carmarthen.

Llawhaden Castle

DYFED (216, 7C)

A fortified palace at the centre of a manorial estate belonging to the bishops of St Davids. It was totally rebuilt between 1293 and 1328.

➲ In Llawhaden, off A40, 3m NW of Narbeth, 10m E of Haverfordwest.

Neath Abbey

WEST GLAMORGAN (216, 6D)

This abbey was absorbed into the Cistercian order in 1147. Fairly complete remains survive, including the 16th-century mansion raised within its precincts.

☎ 01792 812387. ➲ 1m W of Neath, off A465.

Oxwich Castle

WEST GLAMORGAN (216, 6D)

Remains of a sumptuous courtyard house built by the Mansel family during the 16th century.

☎ 01792 390359. ➲ In Oxwich, off A4118, Gower peninsula, 8m SW of Swansea.

Raglan Castle

GWENT (217, 6G)

Remains of impressive 15th-century castle built by Sir William ap Thomas and his son William Herbert, and later remodelled by William, Earl of Worcester. Despite demolition attempts during the Civil War, much survives.

☎ 01291 690228. ➲ ½m N of Raglan, 7m SW of Monmouth, off A40.

Rhuddlan Castle

CLWYD (216, 11F)

Begun in 1277, this was the second of King Edward I's great Welsh fortifications. A protected river dock forms one side of the defences of this concentrically planned castle.

☎ 01745 590777. ➲ In Rhuddlan, 3m S of Rhyl.

Rug Chapel and Llangar Church

CLWYD (216, 7B)

Built in 1637, Rug is best described as 'the painted chapel' with its glorious interior roof carried on the wings of wooden angels, which adorn the trusses. Just a mile or so from Rug you will find the former parish church of All Saints, Llangar. The wall paintings are of immense importance, dating from the 14th to 18th centuries.

☎ 01490 412025. ➲ W of Corwen, off A5(T).

St Davids Bishop's Palace

DYFED

Imposing palace within the defended perimeter of the cathedral precincts. The surviving buildings date chiefly from the 14th century, particularly the work of Bishop Henry de Gower. It is de Gower's celebrated arcaded parapet that is one of the glories of the site.

☎ 01437 720517. ➲ Near centre of St Davids.

Strata Florida Abbey

DYFED (216, 8E)

Initially founded in 1164 on a nearby site, the present buildings were erected under the patronage of the Lord Rhys. The Cistercians at Strata Florida were loyal supporters of the Welsh princes. Burial place of Dafydd ap Gwilym.

☎ 01974 831261. ➲ 1¼m SE of Pontrhydfendigaid, off B4343, 14m SE of Aberystwyth.

Talley Abbey

DYFED (216, 7D)

Founded for the Premonstratensian order by the Lord Rhys, between 1184 and 1189, parts of the abbey church survive.

➲ In Talley, on B4302, 6m N of Llandeilo.

Tintern Abbey

GWENT (217, 6G)

This beautifully located Cistercian abbey, founded in 1131 in the stunning Wye Valley, has a remarkably complete abbey church rebuilt in the later 13th century.

☎ 01291 689251. ➲ In Tintern, on A466, 5m N of Chepstow.

Tretower Castle

POWYS (217, 7F)

Motte and bailey castle established during the Norman conquest of Brycheiniog. The shell-keep was raised on the mound about 1150, and a round tower added in the early 13th century.

☎ 01874 730279. ➲ In Tretower, off A40, 3m NW of Crickhowell.

Tretower Court

POWYS (217, 7F)

Restored courtyard house with origins in the 15th century. Magnificent timberwork survives in the northern and western ranges, with later classical-style windows dating from the 1630s.

☎ 01874 730279 ➲ Tretower, off A40, 3m NW of Crickhowell.

Valle Crucis Abbey

CLWYD (217, 10F)

There are extensive remains of this Cistercian abbey founded in 1201. The church dates from the 13th century, and the east range of the cloister was remodelled around 1400.

☎ 01978 860326. ➲ 1½m NW of Llangollen, on A542.

Weobley Castle

WEST GLAMORGAN (216, 6D)

Picturesque medieval fortified manor house. There are substantial remains dating principally from the later 13th and 14th centuries.

☎ 01792 390012. ➲ 2m W of Llanrhidian, off B4271, 11m W of Swansea.

White Castle

GWENT (217, 7G)

Imposing moated remains of a 12th-century castle, probably the work of Henry II. It was substantially remodelled in the later 13th century.

☎ 01600 780380. ➲ 6m NE of Abergavenny, off B4233.

Manx National Heritage The Manx Museum, Douglas,Isle of Man IM1 3LY.
Tel: 01624 675522.

Castle Rushen

ISLE OF MAN (216, INSET)

This impressive limestone fortress is one of Britain's most complete medieval castles. The castle has its origins in the Norse period and the last Viking King, Magnus, died here in 1265. The settlement that grew up to serve the castle became the main governmental centre and island capital until the major port of Douglas took over in 1869.

01624 675522. In Castletown.

Cregneash Village Folk Museum

ISLE OF MAN (216, INSET)

Nestling under Meayll Hill, with stunning views of the Calf of Man. Cregneash is a unique illustration of 19th-century life in a Manx upland crofting community. The distinctive whitewashed and thatched buildings include a weaver's shed, a turner's workshop and a smithy.

01624 675522. Near Port St Mary, Cregneash.

Grove Museum

Ramsey, ISLE OF MAN (216, INSET)

A perfectly preserved Victorian house, the Grove Museum was developed as a summer retreat for Duncan Gibb, a shipping merchant from Liverpool. The rooms house displays of toys and costumes, whilst the outhouses hold a fascinating collection of vehicles and agricultural implements.

01624 675522. In Ramsey

Laxey Wheel

Laxey, ISLE OF MAN (216, INSET)

The great Laxey Wheel was built in 1854. Designed to pump water from the Laxey Mining Company's mines, the wheel has a diameter of 22 metres, and is the largest working watermill in the world.

01624 675522. In Laxey.

Manx Museum

Douglas, ISLE OF MAN (216, INSET)

The visitor can walk through a sequence of newly designed galleries depicting art, historic maps, natural history, prehistoric, Viking and early medieval archaeology and social history bringing the chronological story of island life up to the present day.

01624 675522. In Douglas.

Nautical Museum

Castletown, ISLE OF MAN (216, INSET)

Situated at the mouth of Castletown harbour, the museum contains an 18th-century armed yacht, 'The Peggy', built by George Quayle in 1791. It is shown in its original boathouse, where it remained undisturbed for a century after its owner's death, being rediscovered in 1935. Exhibits and photographs bring alive maritime life on the Isle.

01624 675522. In Castletown.

Old Grammar School

Castletown, ISLE OF MAN (216, INSET)

Built *c.*1200 as Castletown's first church, St Mary's chapel played an important role in the history of Manx education. A school was first recorded in the chapel in 1570. Saved from destruction by the Manx Museum in 1950, its displays recount its history and include a Victorian period school room.

01624 675522. In Castletown.

Peel Castle

ISLE OF MAN (216, INSET)

Situated on the important site of St Patrick's Isle at Peel, the castle's wall encircles the ruins of many buildings, including the 11th-century church and round tower and the 13th-century Cathedral of St German. In the 11th century the castle became the ruling seat of the Norse Kingdom of Man and the Isles. Recent archaeological excavation has uncovered artefacts from the Norse period, now on display at the Manx Museum in Douglas.

01624 675522. In Peel.

Use your membership card down under

Members of English Heritage also enjoy free entry to historic properties managed by the National Trust in Australia and the New Zealand Historic Places Trust. For further information, contact our Customer Services Department (see inside back cover), or contact the Trusts direct at the addresses opposite.

The National Trust of Australia
PO Box 1002, Civic Square,
ACT 2608, Australia

The New Zealand Historic Places Trust
Antrim House, 63 Boulcott Street, Wellington, New Zealand

A Guide to Maps

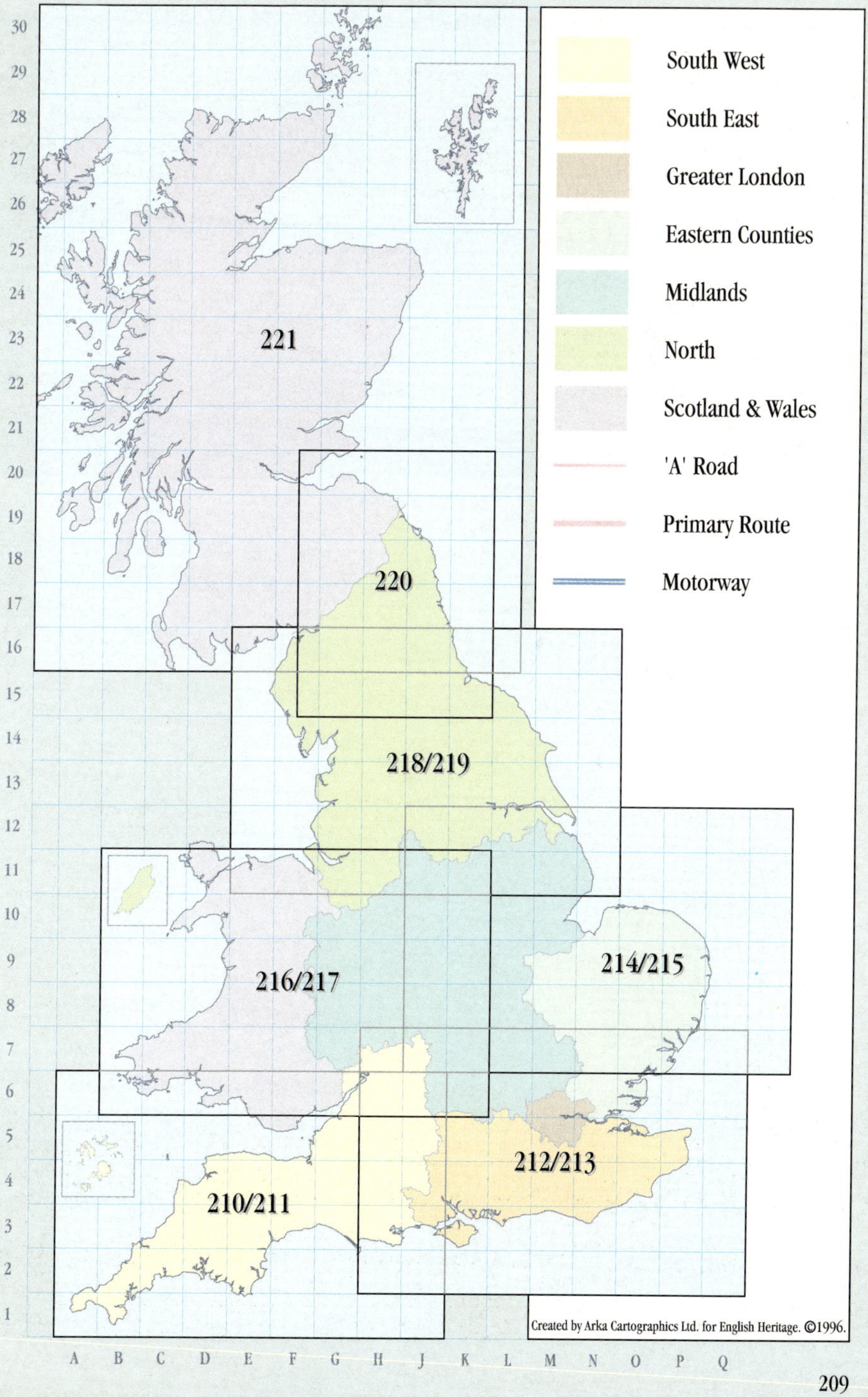

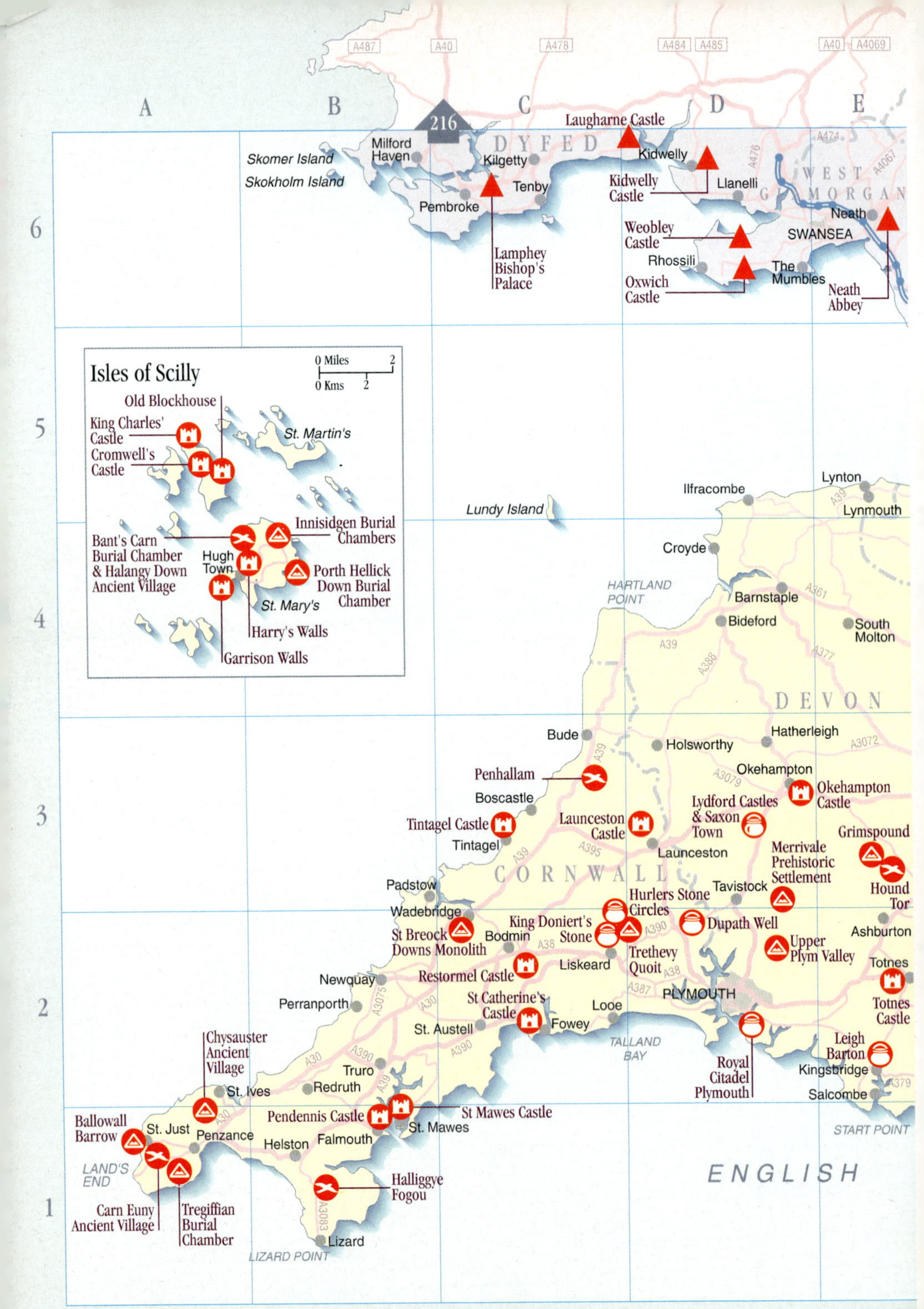
216
DYFED
WEST GLAMORGAN
Skomer Island
Skokholm Island
Milford Haven
Kilgetty
Pembroke
Tenby
Lamphey Bishop's Palace
Laugharne Castle
Kidwelly
Kidwelly Castle
Llanelli
Weobley Castle
Rhossili
Oxwich Castle
The Mumbles
SWANSEA
Neath
Neath Abbey
A487
A40
A478
A484
A485
A4069
A474
A476
A4067
Isles of Scilly
0 Miles 2
0 Kms 2
Old Blockhouse
King Charles' Castle
Cromwell's Castle
St. Martin's
Innisidgen Burial Chambers
Bant's Carn Burial Chamber & Halangy Down Ancient Village
Hugh Town
Porth Hellick Down Burial Chamber
St. Mary's
Harry's Walls
Garrison Walls
Lundy Island
Ilfracombe
Lynton
Lynmouth
Croyde
HARTLAND POINT
Barnstaple
Bideford
South Molton
DEVON
A39
A388
A361
A377
Bude
Holsworthy
Hatherleigh
A3072
Okehampton
A3079
Okehampton Castle
Penhallam
Boscastle
Tintagel Castle
Tintagel
Launceston Castle
Lydford Castles & Saxon Town
Launceston
Grimspound
Merrivale Prehistoric Settlement
Hound Tor
A395
CORNWALL
Padstow
Wadebridge
St Breock Downs Monolith
King Doniert's Stone
Hurlers Stone Circles
Tavistock
Dupath Well
Ashburton
Bodmin
A38
Trethevy Quoit
Upper Plym Valley
Liskeard
A390
Newquay
Restormel Castle
Totnes
Totnes Castle
Perranporth
A3075
A30
St Catherine's Castle
Looe
PLYMOUTH
A387
St. Austell
Fowey
TALLAND BAY
Royal Citadel Plymouth
Leigh Barton
Kingsbridge
Salcombe
A379
Chysauster Ancient Village
St. Ives
Truro
Redruth
Pendennis Castle
St Mawes Castle
St. Mawes
Ballowall Barrow
St. Just
Penzance
Helston
Falmouth
LAND'S END
Carn Euny Ancient Village
Tregiffian Burial Chamber
Halliggye Fogou
A3083
Lizard
LIZARD POINT
START POINT
ENGLISH
A B C D E
1 2 3 4 5 6

Raglan Castle
Monmouth
217
GLOUCESTER
CHELTENHAM
Great Witcombe Roman Villa
Minster Lovell Hall and Dovecote
MID GLAM.
Blaenavon Ironworks
Raglan
Tintern Abbey
St Briavel's Castle
Offa's Dyke
Stroud
GLOUCS.
Aberdare
Uley Long Barrow
Nympsfield Long Barrow
Cirencester
Cirencester Amphitheatre
Lechlade
Caerleon Roman Fortress
Chepstow Castle
Chepstow
Kingswood Abbey Gatehouse
Wayland's Smithy
Maesteg
Caerphilly Castle
Caerphilly
Coity Castle
Castell Coch
NEWPORT
CARDIFF
Chipping Sodbury
Malmesbury
Uffington Castle, White Horse & Dragon Hill
SWINDON
Porthcawl
SOUTH GLAM.
Penarth
Barry
Avonmouth
Portishead
Temple Church
BRISTOL
Sir Bevil Grenville's Monument
Avebury Stone Circles & Museum
Windmill Hill
Silbury Hill
Avebury
Marlborough
WESTON-SUPER-MARE
AVON
BATH
West Kennet Avenue & Long Barrow
The Santuary
Chisbury Chapel
BRISTOL CHANNEL
Stanton Drew Circles & Cove
Bradford-on -Avon Tithe Barn
Farleigh Hungerford Castle
Stoney Littleton Long Barrow
Hatfield Earthworks
Ludgershall Castle & Cross
Burnham-on-Sea
Daws Castle
Bratton Camp & White Horse
Netheravon Dovecote
Minehead
Nunney Castle
Frome
Wells
Yarn Market & Butter Cross
Meare Fish House
Stonehenge
Woodhenge
Cleeve Abbey
Gallox Bridge
Glastonbury Tribunal
Glastonbury
Amesbury
Ratfyn Barrows
Bridgwater
WILTS
Old Sarum
Stockbridge
SOMERSET
Old Wardour Castle
Salisbury
Taunton
Muchelney Abbey
Ilchester
Sherborne Old Castle
Shaftesbury
Romsey
Bampton
Sherborne
SOUTHAMPTON
Yeovil
Fiddleford Manor
Knowlton Church & Earthworks
Tiverton
Ilminster
Lyndhurst
212
DORSET
Honiton
Axminster
Winterbourne Poor Lot Barrows
The Nine Stones
Wimborne Minster
Christchurch Castle & Norman House
EXETER
Blackbury Camp
Lyme Regis
Maiden Castle
BOURNEMOUTH
Bowhill
Sidmouth
Dorchester
POOLE
Christchurch
Kingston Russell Stone Circle
Jordan Hill Roman Temple
Exmouth
Abbotsbury
Lulworth Castle
Weymouth
Hurst Castle
Dawlish
Abbotsbury Abbey Remains
Swanage
Tyneham Village Chapel
Newton Abbot
St Catherine's Chapel
TORQUAY
Portland Castle
BILL OF PORTLAND
Berry Pomeroy Castle
Kirkham House
Bayard's Cove Fort
Dartmouth
Dartmouth Castle
CHANNEL
Scale
0 Miles
20
0 Kms
30
Key to Heritage Symbols
Castle/Fort
Historic House
Romantic Ruin
Humps & Bumps
Roman
Garden/Park
Industrial Monument
Pot Luck
Far From The Crowd
Great Antiquity
CADW Sites and Other Historic Sites
Created by Arka Cartographics Ltd. for English Heritage. © 1996.
E
F
G
H
J
1
2
3
4
5
6

WORCESTER
NORTHAMPTON
214
211
Great Malvern
Evesham
Towcester
Newport Pagnell
MILTON KEYNES
BEDFORD
Biggleswade
Houghton House
Wrest Park House & Gdns.
De Grey Mausoleum
Letchworth
St. Mary's Church Kempley
Moreton-in-Marsh
Banbury
Buckingham
Bletchley
Odda's Chapel
Belas Knap Long Barrow
Hailes Abbey
Rollright Stones
Deddington Castle
BUCKS
Stevenage
GLOUCESTER
Over Bridge
CHELTENHAM
Chipping Norton
Notgrove Long Barrow
Dunstable
LUTON
Blackfriars & Greyfriars
Woodstock
Minster Lovell Hall & Dovecote
North Leigh Roman Villa
Aylesbury
Berkhamstead Castle
Old Gorhambury House
Great Witcombe Roman Villa
Witney
Rycote Chapel
Tring
Berkhamsted
Roman Wall
GLOUCS.
OXFORD
HEMEL HEMPSTEAD
St. Albans
Stroud
Cirencester
Cirencester Amphitheatre
North Hinksey Conduit House
Thame
Nympsfield Long Barrow
Uley Long Barrow
Abingdon County Hall
Faringdon
Abingdon
HIGH WYCOMBE
Kingswood Abbey Gatehouse
Wayland's Smithy
OXFORD
Uffington Castle, White Horse & Dragon Hill
Didcot
Marlow
Kenwood
Chipping Sodbury
Malmesbury
SWINDON
Maidenhead
SLOUGH
Albert Memorial
Avebury Stone Circles & Museum
Windsor
Chiswick House
Sir Bevil Grenville's Monument
Windmill Hill
Silbury Hill
Marlborough
Donnington Castle
READING
Marble Hill House
Avebury
West Kennet Avenue & Long Barrow
The Santuary
Hungerford
BERKSHIRE
Coombe Conduits
Bradford-on-Avon Tithe Barn
Newbury
Chisbury Chapel
Silchester Roman City Walls & Amphitheatre
BATH
CAMBERLEY
LONDON
Stoney Littleton Long Barrow
Farleigh Hungerford Castle
WOKING
Leatherhead
Hatfield Earthworks
Ludgershall Castle & Cross
BASINGSTOKE
Bratton Camp & White Horse
GUILDFORD
Dorking
Netheravon Dovecote
Farnham Castle Keep
Frome
Farnham
SURREY
Nunney Castle
Stonehenge
Woodhenge
Andover
Waverley Abbey
HAMPSHIRE
Amesbury
Ratfyn Barrows
CRAWLEY
WILTS
Flowerdown Barrows
The Grange
Old Sarum
Horsham
Haslemere
Old Wardour Castle
Winchester
Salisbury
WEST SUSSEX
Wolvesey Castle
Sherborne Old Castle
Shaftesbury
Romsey
Petersfield
Bramber Castle
EASTLEIGH
SOUTHAMPTON
Bishop's Waltham Palace
Weald & Downland Museum
Fiddleford Manor
Medieval Merchants House
Knowlton Church & Earthworks
Netley Abbey
Titchfield Abbey
HAVANT
Boxgrove Priory
Lyndhurst
FAREHAM
Arundel
Christchurch Castle & Norman House
Porchester Castle
PORTSMOUTH
Chichester
DORSET
WORTHING
Wimborne Minster
Calshot Castle
Fishbourne Roman Palace
Littlehampton
Bognor Regis
Marlipins Museum
Lymington
BOURNEMOUTH
Cowes
Selsey
POOLE
Christchurch
Ryde
Royal Garrison Church
Dorchester
Newport
Fort Cumberland
Jordan Hill Roman Temple
Yarmouth
King James's & Landport Gates
Hurst Castle
Sandown
Lulworth Castle
Fort Brockhurst
Weymouth
Shanklin
Osborne House
Swanage
Tyneham Village Chapel
Yarmouth Castle
ISLE OF WIGHT
Portland Castle
Carisbrooke Castle
ENGLISH
Appuldurcombe House
St. Catherine's Oratory
H
J
K
L
M
7
6
5
4
3
2

M11
A11
A134
A14
A12
CAMBRIDGE
M
N
O
P
Q
215
Duxford Chapel
Haverhill
St. James's Chapel
Sudbury
IPSWICH
SUFFOLK
Audley End House & Park
ESSEX
Mistley Towers
Felixstowe
Landguard Fort
Halstead
St. Botolph's Priory
Harwich
Prior's Hall Barn
Lexden Earthworks
St. John's Abbey Gate
7
Bishop's Stortford
Braintree
COLCHESTER
Walton-on-the-Naze
Frinton-on-Sea
HERTS
Tiptree
Witham
Clacton-on-Sea
Hertford
Waltham Abbey Gatehouse & Bridge
HARLOW
Maldon
West Mersea
CHELMSFORD
Epping
Southminster
Pyx Chamber Chapter House & Abbey Museum Westminster Abbey
Hill Hall
6
Brentwood
BASILDON
Hadleigh Castle
London Wall, Tower Hill
Winchester Palace
Canvey Island
SOUTHEND-ON-SEA
Tilbury Fort
Tilbury
Reculver Towers & Roman Fort
Jewel Tower
Dartford
Rochester Castle
Sheerness
Faversham Stone Chapel
Ranger's House
Milton Chantry
MARGATE
Eltham Palace
Eynsford Castle
Temple Manor
Broadstairs
Upnor Castle
Kit's Coty House
GILLINGHAM
Whitstable
St. Augustine's Cross
Lullingstone Roman Villa
Sittingbourne
Faversham
Richborough Roman Amphitheatre & Richborough Castle
5
MAIDSTONE
Maison Dieu
Canterbury
Conduit House
Sandwich
REIGATE
Sevenoaks
St. Leonard's Tower
Deal Castle
Deal
Old Soar Manor
Sutton Valence Castle
KENT
St. Augustine's Abbey
Walmer Castle & Gardens
East Grinstead
Royal Tunbridge Wells
Western Heights
Ashford
St. John's Commandery
Dover Castle
Dover
Bayham Abbey
Knight's Templar Church
Priest House
Tenterden
Hythe
Folkestone
Dymchurch Martello Tower
Haywards Heath
EAST SUSSEX
Horne's Place Chapel, Appledore
Dymchurch
4
Uckfield
New Romney
Battle Abbey
Rye
Lydd
Lewes Castle & Museum of Sussex Archaeology
Battle
Lewes
Hailsham
HASTINGS
Camber Castle
Anne of Cleves House
Michelham Priory
Bexhill
Pevensey
BRIGHTON
Pevensey Castle
Newhaven
EASTBOURNE
Key to Heritage Symbols
Castle/Fort
Historic House
Romantic Ruin
Humps & Bumps
Roman
Garden/Park
Industrial Monument
Pot Luck
Far From The Crowd
Great Antiquity
Other Historic Sites
3
CHANNEL
0 Miles
20
Scale
0 Kms
30
2
Created by Arka Cartographics Ltd. for English Heritage. © 1996.
M
N
O
P
Q

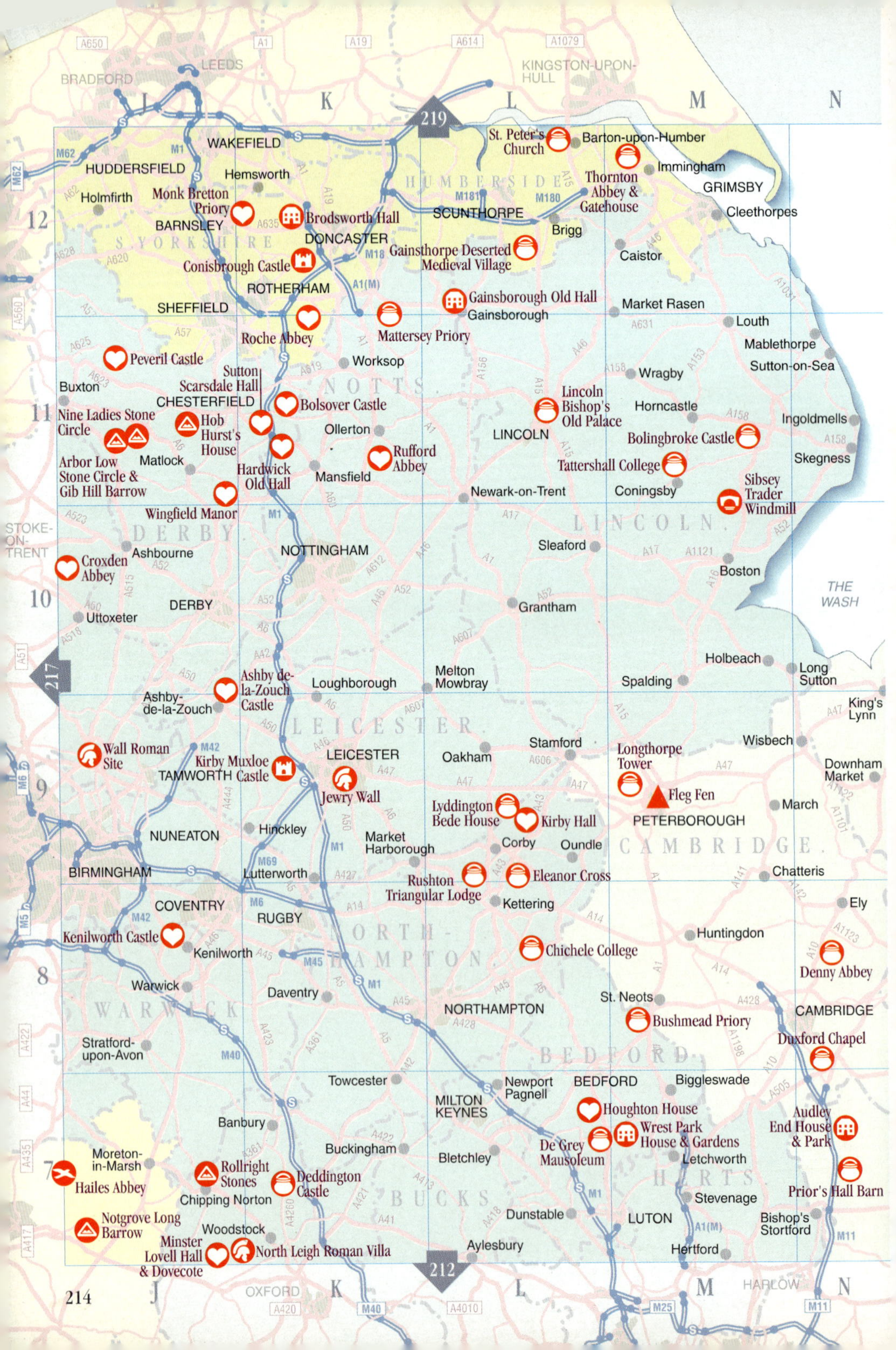
219
217
212
J
K
L
M
N
12
11
10
9
8
7
LEEDS
BRADFORD
KINGSTON-UPON-HULL
WAKEFIELD
HUDDERSFIELD
Hemsworth
Holmfirth
Monk Bretton Priory
BARNSLEY
Brodsworth Hall
S. YORKSHIRE
DONCASTER
Conisbrough Castle
ROTHERHAM
SHEFFIELD
Roche Abbey
HUMBERSIDE
St. Peter's Church
Barton-upon-Humber
Immingham
Thornton Abbey & Gatehouse
GRIMSBY
Cleethorpes
SCUNTHORPE
Brigg
Gainsthorpe Deserted Medieval Village
Caistor
Gainsborough Old Hall
Gainsborough
Market Rasen
Louth
Mablethorpe
Sutton-on-Sea
Mattersey Priory
Peveril Castle
Worksop
Buxton
Sutton Scarsdale Hall
CHESTERFIELD
NOTTS.
Wragby
Lincoln Bishop's Old Palace
Horncastle
Ingoldmells
Nine Ladies Stone Circle
Hob Hurst's House
Bolsover Castle
Ollerton
LINCOLN
Bolingbroke Castle
Skegness
Arbor Low Stone Circle & Gib Hill Barrow
Matlock
Hardwick Old Hall
Mansfield
Rufford Abbey
Tattershall College
Coningsby
Sibsey Trader Windmill
Wingfield Manor
Newark-on-Trent
LINCOLN.
STOKE-ON-TRENT
DERBY.
NOTTINGHAM
Sleaford
Croxden Abbey
Ashbourne
Boston
THE WASH
DERBY
Uttoxeter
Grantham
Holbeach
Long Sutton
Ashby de-la-Zouch Castle
Loughborough
Melton Mowbray
Spalding
King's Lynn
Ashby-de-la-Zouch
LEICESTER.
Stamford
Wisbech
Wall Roman Site
Kirby Muxloe Castle
TAMWORTH
LEICESTER
Oakham
Longthorpe Tower
Downham Market
Jewry Wall
Fleg Fen
Lyddington Bede House
Kirby Hall
March
PETERBOROUGH
NUNEATON
Hinckley
Market Harborough
Corby
Oundle
CAMBRIDGE.
BIRMINGHAM
Lutterworth
Rushton Triangular Lodge
Eleanor Cross
Chatteris
COVENTRY
RUGBY
Kettering
Ely
NORTH-HAMPTON.
Huntingdon
Kenilworth Castle
Kenilworth
Chichele College
Denny Abbey
Warwick
Daventry
St. Neots
WARWICK.
NORTHAMPTON
CAMBRIDGE
Bushmead Priory
Stratford-upon-Avon
Duxford Chapel
BEDFORD.
Towcester
Newport Pagnell
BEDFORD
Biggleswade
MILTON KEYNES
Houghton House
Audley End House & Park
Banbury
Wrest Park House & Gardens
De Grey Mausoleum
Letchworth
Moreton-in-Marsh
Buckingham
Bletchley
Hailes Abbey
Rollright Stones
Deddington Castle
HERTS.
Prior's Hall Barn
Chipping Norton
BUCKS.
Stevenage
Notgrove Long Barrow
Dunstable
LUTON
Bishop's Stortford
Woodstock
Aylesbury
Minster Lovell Hall & Dovecote
North Leigh Roman Villa
Hertford
OXFORD
HARLOW
A650
A1
A19
A614
A1079
M62
M1
M18
M180
M181
A1(M)
M42
M6
M69
M45
M5
M40
M11
M25
A420
A4010

N
O
P
Q
R
Scale 0 Miles 20
0 Kms 30
12
11
10
9
8
7
NORTH SEA
Creake Abbey
Blakeney Guildhall
Wells-next-the-Sea
Hunstanton
Sheringham
Cromer
Holt
Binham Wayside Cross
Binham Priory
Baconsthorpe Castle
Castle Rising Castle
Fakenham
Aylsham
North Walsham
Castle Acre Bailey Gate
Castle Acre Castle
Castle Acre Priory
North Elmham Chapel
Hemsby
East Dereham
Cow Tower
Caister Roman Site
Great Yarmouth
Swaffham
NORWICH
Berney Arms Windmill
Old Merchant's House, Row 111 Houses & Greyfriars Cloisters
NORFOLK
Wymondham
Loddon
Burgh Castle
St. Olave's Priory
Attleborough
LOWESTOFT
Grime's Graves
Weeting Castle
Thetford Warren Lodge
Bungay
Beccles
Brandon
Thetford
Kessingland
Diss
Thetford Priory
Church of the Holy Sepulchre
Isleham Priory Church
Halesworth
Southwold
Framlingham Castle
Newmarket
Bury St. Edmunds
Saxted Green Post Mill
Leiston Abbey
Bury St. Edmunds Abbey
Moulton Packhorse Bridge
Stowmarket
Aldeburgh
SUFFOLK
Woodbridge
Orford Castle
Orford
Haverhill
St. James's Chapel
IPSWICH
Sudbury
ESSEX
Mistley Towers
Felixstowe
Halstead
St. Botolph's Priory
Landguard Fort
Harwich
Lexden Earthworks
St. John's Abbey Gate
Braintree
COLCHESTER
Walton-on-the-Naze
Frinton-on-Sea
Tiptree
Witham
West Mersea
Clacton-on-Sea
CHELMSFORD
213
Key to Heritage Symbols
Castle/Fort
Historic House
Romantic Ruin
Humps & Bumps
Roman
Garden/Park
Industrial Monument
Pot Luck
Far From The Crowd
Great Antiquity
Other Historic Sites
Created by Arka Cartographics Ltd. for English Heritage. © 1996.

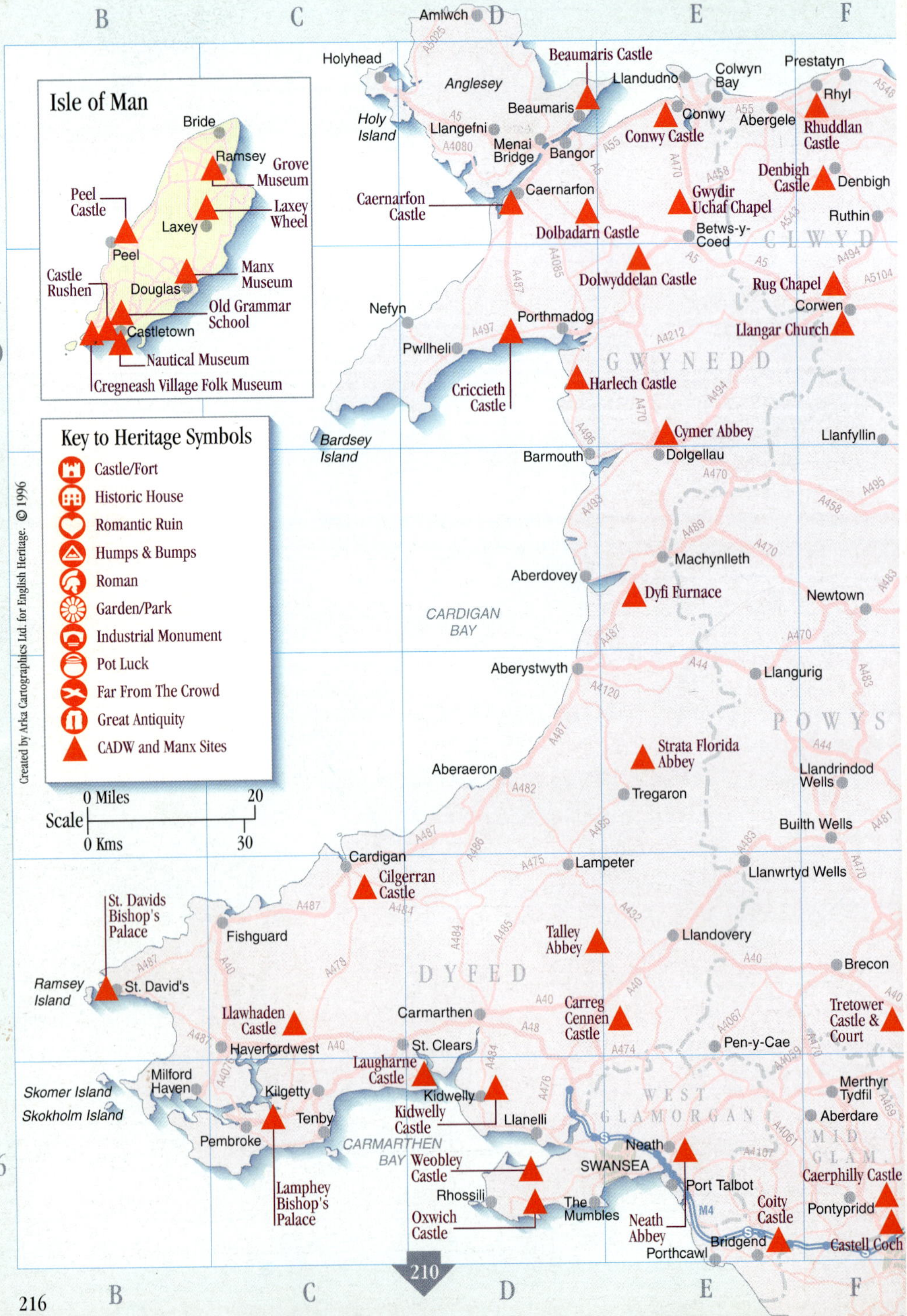
Isle of Man
Bride
Ramsey
Grove Museum
Peel Castle
Laxey
Laxey Wheel
Peel
Castle Rushen
Douglas
Manx Museum
Old Grammar School
Castletown
Nautical Museum
Cregneash Village Folk Museum
Key to Heritage Symbols
Castle/Fort
Historic House
Romantic Ruin
Humps & Bumps
Roman
Garden/Park
Industrial Monument
Pot Luck
Far From The Crowd
Great Antiquity
CADW and Manx Sites
Scale
0 Miles
20
0 Kms
30
Created by Arka Cartographics Ltd. for English Heritage. © 1996
B
C
D
E
F
11
10
9
8
7
6
Amlwch
Holyhead
Anglesey
Holy Island
Beaumaris Castle
Llandudno
Colwyn Bay
Prestatyn
Rhyl
Beaumaris
Conwy
Abergele
Rhuddlan Castle
Llangefni
Menai Bridge
Bangor
Conwy Castle
Denbigh Castle
Denbigh
Caernarfon
Caernarfon Castle
Gwydir Uchaf Chapel
Ruthin
Dolbadarn Castle
Betws-y-Coed
CLWYD
Dolwyddelan Castle
Rug Chapel
Corwen
Nefyn
Porthmadog
Llangar Church
Pwllheli
GWYNEDD
Criccieth Castle
Harlech Castle
Cymer Abbey
Llanfyllin
Bardsey Island
Barmouth
Dolgellau
Machynlleth
Aberdovey
Dyfi Furnace
Newtown
CARDIGAN BAY
Aberystwyth
Llangurig
POWYS
Strata Florida Abbey
Aberaeron
Llandrindod Wells
Tregaron
Builth Wells
Cardigan
Lampeter
Llanwrtyd Wells
Cilgerran Castle
St. Davids Bishop's Palace
Fishguard
Talley Abbey
Llandovery
Brecon
DYFED
Ramsey Island
St. David's
Carreg Cennen Castle
Tretower Castle & Court
Llawhaden Castle
Carmarthen
Haverfordwest
St. Clears
Pen-y-Cae
Milford Haven
Laugharne Castle
Merthyr Tydfil
Skomer Island
Kilgetty
Kidwelly
Skokholm Island
Tenby
Kidwelly Castle
Llanelli
WEST GLAMORGAN
Aberdare
Pembroke
CARMARTHEN BAY
Neath
Weobley Castle
SWANSEA
MID GLAM.
Caerphilly Castle
Lamphey Bishop's Palace
Rhossili
Port Talbot
The Mumbles
Coity Castle
Pontypridd
Oxwich Castle
Neath Abbey
Bridgend
Castell Coch
Porthcawl
M4
A5
A55
A470
A487
A40
A44
A483

210

218
211
214
F
G
H
J
K
11
10
9
8
7
6
BOOTLE
KIRKBY
LIVERPOOL
WARRINGTON
OLDHAM
SALFORD
MANCHESTER
BARNSLEY
DONCASTER
ROTHERHAM
BIRKENHEAD
WIDNES
RUNCORN
ELLESMERE PORT
CHESHIRE
Baguley Hall
Knutsford
SHEFFIELD
Roche Abbey
Mattersey Priory
Peveril Castle
Worksop
Sutton Scarsdale Hall
Flint Castle
Flint
Neston
Northwich
Macclesfield
Buxton
CHESTERFIELD
Bolsover Castle
CHESTER
Nine Ladies Stone Circle
Hob Hurst's House
Ollerton
Chester Roman Amphitheatre
Chester Castle
Winsford
Sandbach
Congleton
Arbor Low Stone Circle & Gib Hill Barrow
Mansfield
Mold
Beeston Castle
Sandbach Crosses
Matlock
Hardwick Old Hall
Rufford Abbey
Gresford
Crewe
Leek
Wingfield Manor
Wrexham
Nantwich
NEWCASTLE-UNDER-LYME
STOKE-ON-TRENT
Ashbourne
NOTTS
Valle Crucis Abbey
Croxden Abbey
NOTTINGHAM
Llangollen
Whitchurch
DERBY
Old Oswestry Hill Fort
Market Drayton
Stone
Uttoxeter
Oswestry
STAFFS
Moreton Corbet Castle
Ashby de-la-Zouch Castle
Melton Mowbray
STAFFORD
Ashby-de-la-Zouch
Loughborough
Haughmond Abbey
Lilleshall Abbey
SHREWSBURY
White Ladies Priory
TELFORD
CANNOCK
Wroxeter Roman City
Buildwas Abbey
Boscobel House & the Royal Oak
Wall Roman Site
LEICESTER
Welshpool
Kirby Muxloe Castle
Cantlop Bridge
Iron Bridge
WOLVERHAMPTON
TAMWORTH
Jewry Wall
Acton Burnell Castle
Mitchell's Fold Stone Circle
Church Stretton
Wenlock Priory
WALSALL
Langley Chapel
M42
NUNEATON
Hinckley
Bridgnorth
WEST MIDLANDS
Market Harborough
SHROPSHIRE
Halesowen Abbey
BIRMINGHAM
Lutterworth
Clun Castle
Stokesay Castle
COVENTRY
RUGBY
KIDDERMINSTER
Ludlow
Kenilworth Castle
Kenilworth
Wigmore Castle
Mortimer's Cross Water Mill
Edvin Loach Old Church
Witley Court
Warwick
Daventry
Leominster
WORCESTER
NORTHAMPTON
Bromyard
WARWICK
HEREFORD & WORCESTER
Leigh Court Barn
Stratford-upon-Avon
Great Malvern
Towcester
Arthur's Stone
Hereford
Evesham
Hay-on-Wye
Rotherwas Chapel
Ledbury
Banbury
Moreton-in-Marsh
Buckingham
Longtown Castle
St. Mary's Church Kempley
Odda's Chapel
Belas Knap Long Barrow
Hailes Abbey
Rollright Stones
Deddington Castle
Ross-on-Wye
Chipping Norton
Tretower
White Castle
Goodrich Castle
Over Bridge
CHELTENHAM
Notgrove Long Barrow
Woodstock
Abergavenny
Raglan Castle
GLOUCESTER
Minster Lovell Hall and Dovecote
North Leigh Roman Villa
Monmouth
Blackfriars & Greyfriars
Great Witcombe Roman Villa
Blaenavon Ironworks
Raglan
St Briavel's Castle
Stroud
Witney
Rycote Chapel
GLOUCS
OXFORD
Tintern Abbey
Offa's Dyke
Cirencester
Cirencester Amphitheatre
North Hinksey Conduit House
Thame
GWENT
Chepstow Castle
Uley Long Barrow
Nympsfield Long Barrow
Abingdon County Hall
Caerleon Roman Fortress
Chepstow
Kingswood Abbey Gatehouse
Faringdon
Abingdon
Wayland's Smithy
OXFORD
NEWPORT
(Opens 1997)
Uffington Castle, White Horse & Dragon Hill
Didcot
Chipping Sodbury
Malmesbury
SWINDON
CARDIFF
Avonmouth
BRISTOL
READING
M58
M6
M63
M1
A1(M)
M18
M56
M54
M5
M50
M40
M4
M45
M69
A616
A46
A429
A346
A34

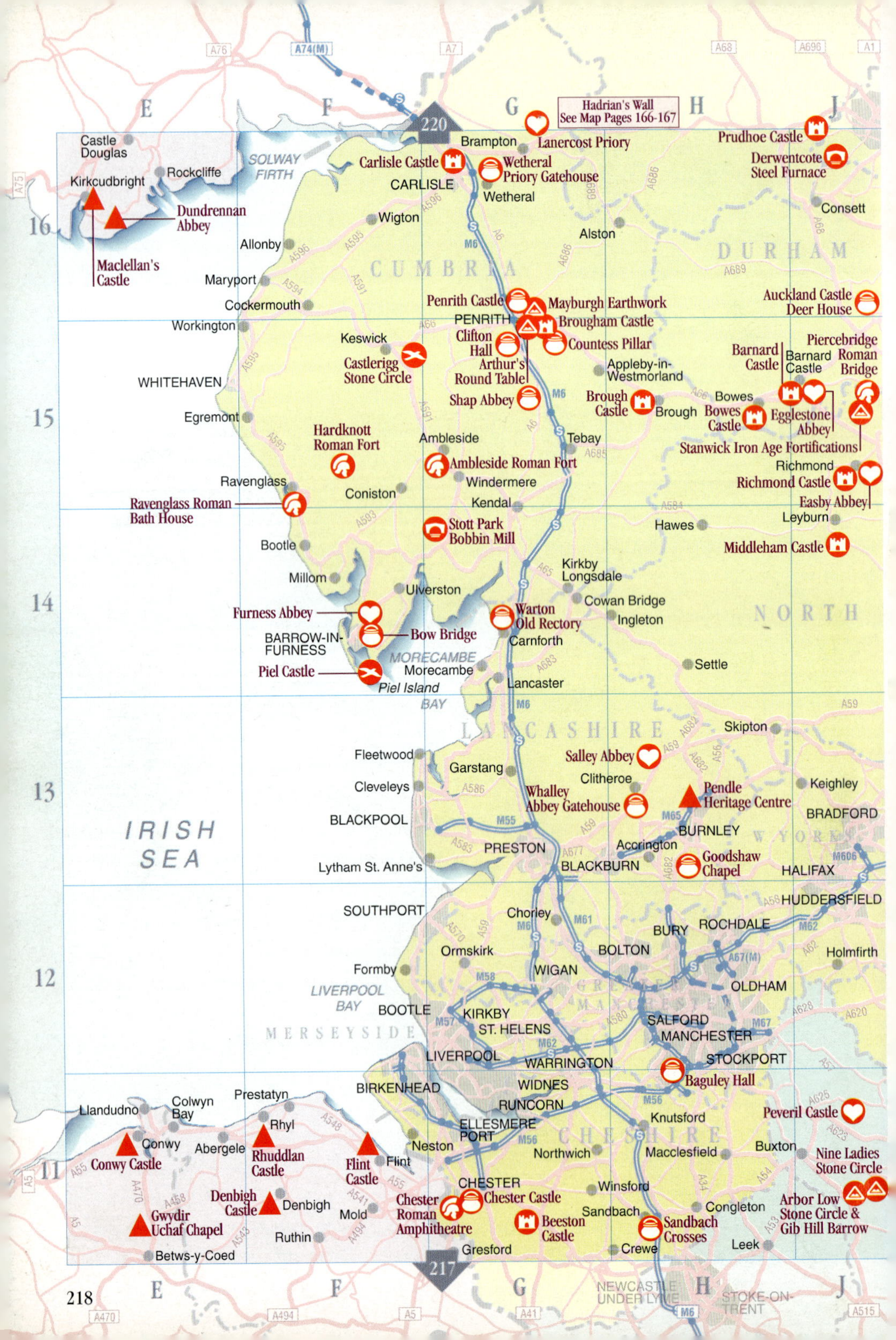
Hadrian's Wall
See Map Pages 166-167
220
217
Lanercost Priory
Brampton
Carlisle Castle
Wetheral Priory Gatehouse
CARLISLE
Wetheral
Prudhoe Castle
Derwentcote Steel Furnace
Consett
Castle Douglas
Kirkcudbright
Rockcliffe
SOLWAY FIRTH
Dundrennan Abbey
Maclellan's Castle
Wigton
Allonby
Maryport
Cockermouth
Workington
Alston
CUMBRIA
DURHAM
Penrith Castle
Mayburgh Earthwork
PENRITH
Brougham Castle
Clifton Hall
Countess Pillar
Arthur's Round Table
Keswick
Castlerigg Stone Circle
WHITEHAVEN
Appleby-in-Westmoreland
Auckland Castle Deer House
Piercebridge Roman Bridge
Barnard Castle
Barnard Castle
Shap Abbey
Brough Castle
Brough
Bowes
Bowes Castle
Egglestone Abbey
Stanwick Iron Age Fortifications
Egremont
Hardknott Roman Fort
Ambleside
Ambleside Roman Fort
Tebay
Windermere
Richmond
Richmond Castle
Easby Abbey
Ravenglass
Ravenglass Roman Bath House
Coniston
Kendal
Stott Park Bobbin Mill
Hawes
Leyburn
Middleham Castle
Bootle
Millom
Kirkby Longsdale
Ulverston
Cowan Bridge
Ingleton
Furness Abbey
Warton Old Rectory
NORTH
BARROW-IN-FURNESS
Bow Bridge
MORECAMBE BAY
Carnforth
Morecambe
Piel Castle
Piel Island
Settle
Lancaster
LANCASHIRE
Skipton
Fleetwood
Salley Abbey
Garstang
Clitheroe
Cleveleys
Pendle Heritage Centre
Keighley
Whalley Abbey Gatehouse
BLACKPOOL
BRADFORD
BURNLEY
IRISH SEA
PRESTON
Accrington
Lytham St. Anne's
BLACKBURN
Goodshaw Chapel
HALIFAX
SOUTHPORT
HUDDERSFIELD
Chorley
BURY
ROCHDALE
Ormskirk
BOLTON
Holmfirth
Formby
WIGAN
OLDHAM
LIVERPOOL BAY
BOOTLE
KIRKBY
ST. HELENS
SALFORD
MANCHESTER
MERSEYSIDE
GREATER MANCHESTER
LIVERPOOL
WARRINGTON
STOCKPORT
BIRKENHEAD
WIDNES
Baguley Hall
RUNCORN
Llandudno
Colwyn Bay
Prestatyn
Rhyl
Knutsford
Peveril Castle
ELLESMERE PORT
CHESHIRE
Conwy
Abergele
Neston
Buxton
Nine Ladies Stone Circle
Conwy Castle
Rhuddlan Castle
Flint Castle
Flint
Northwich
Macclesfield
CHESTER
Winsford
Denbigh Castle
Denbigh
Chester Roman Amphitheatre
Chester Castle
Arbor Low Stone Circle & Gib Hill Barrow
Gwydir Uchaf Chapel
Mold
Sandbach
Congleton
Beeston Castle
Sandbach Crosses
Ruthin
Leek
Gresford
Crewe
Betws-y-Coed
NEWCASTLE UNDER LYME
STOKE-ON-TRENT
E
F
G
H
J
16
15
14
13
12
11

Key to Heritage Symbols
Castle/Fort
Historic House
Romantic Ruin
Humps & Bumps
Roman
Garden/Park
Industrial Monument
Pot Luck
Far From The Crowd
Great Antiquity
CADW Sites and Other Historic Sites
Created by Arka Cartographics Ltd. for English Heritage. © 1996.
Scale
0 Miles
20
0 Kms
30
J
K
L
M
N
16
15
14
13
12
11
NORTH SEA
TYNE & WEAR
CLEVELAND
YORKSHIRE
HUMBERSIDE
S. YORKS
NOTTS
LINCOLN
St. Paul's Monastery & Bede's World Museum
NEWCASTLE UPON TYNE
Hylton Castle
SUNDERLAND
Bessie Surtees House
Finchale Priory
DURHAM
Peterlee
A1(M)
A19
Spennymoor
HARTLEPOOL
Newton Aycliffe
Billingham
Redcar
STOCKTON-ON-TEES
Brotton
MIDDLESBROUGH
Gisborough Priory
DARLINGTON
Great Ayton
A174
A171
Whitby
Whitby Abbey
A172
A19
A167
Mount Grace Priory
Wheeldale Roman Road
Catterick
Northallerton
A169
Scarborough Castle
SCARBOROUGH
Rievaulx Abbey
Helmsley Castle
Pickering Castle
A170
Thirsk
Pickering
A61
Byland Abbey
Filey
Marmion Tower
A64
A165
Ripon
Norton
B1257
St. Mary's Church, Studley Royal
Aldborough Roman Town
Kirkham Priory
Wharram Percy Church & Deserted Medieval Village
Burton Agnes Manor House
A166
Bridlington
A1
Knaresborough
Merchant's Adventurer's Hall
Driffield
Skipsea Castle
HARROGATE
YORK
Clifford's Tower
Spofforth Castle
The ARC
Wetherby
Pocklington
A163
A1079
A165
Hornsea
Jorvik Viking Centre
Tadcaster
A58
Market Weighton
Beverley
A64
LEEDS
A163
M621
Steeton Hall Gateway
A63
Selby
Howden Minster
M62
A15
KINGSTON UPON HULL
Withernsea
Goole
Barton-upon-Humber
M1
WAKEFIELD
St. Peter's Church
Thornton Abbey & Gatehouse
Immingham
Hemsworth
Monk Bretton Priory
A19
M181
SCUNTHORPE
A180
GRIMSBY
BARNSLEY
A635
Brodsworth Hall
Brigg
Cleethorpes
DONCASTER
M180
A46
M18
Gainsthorpe Deserted Medieval Village
Caistor
Conisbrough Castle
ROTHERHAM
A1(M)
SHEFFIELD
Gainsborough Old Hall
Gainsborough
Market Rasen
A1031
A57
Roche Abbey
Mattersey Priory
A631
Louth
Mablethorpe
Sutton-on-Sea
Worksop
A619
A156
A15
A46
A158
A153
Wragby
Sutton Scarsdale Hall
CHESTERFIELD
Bolsover Castle
Lincoln Bishop's Old Palace
Horncastle
A158
Hob Hurst's House
Ollerton
LINCOLN
Bolingbroke Castle
Ingoldmells
A6
M1
A1
A15
A158
Skegness
Hardwick Old Hall
Rufford Abbey
Tattershall College
Matlock
Mansfield
Sibsey Trader Windmill
Coningsby
A52
Wingfield Manor
Newark-on-Trent
A17
214
NOTTINGHAM
M1
A46
A1
A15
A16

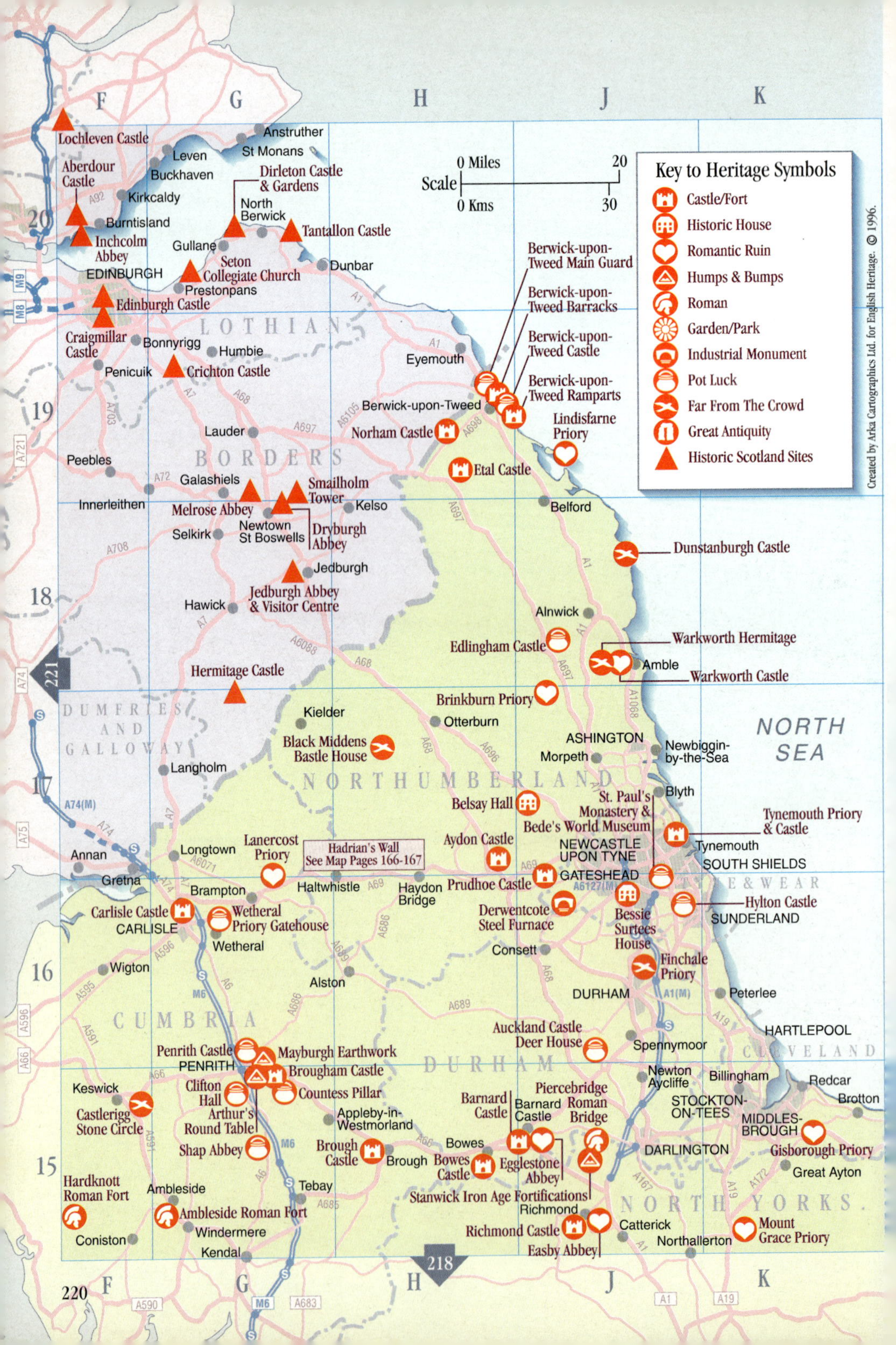
Key to Heritage Symbols
Castle/Fort
Historic House
Romantic Ruin
Humps & Bumps
Roman
Garden/Park
Industrial Monument
Pot Luck
Far From The Crowd
Great Antiquity
Historic Scotland Sites
Scale
0 Miles
20
0 Kms
30
Created by Arka Cartographics Ltd. for English Heritage. © 1996.
F
G
H
J
K
20
19
18
17
16
15
Lochleven Castle
Aberdour Castle
Anstruther
St Monans
Leven
Buckhaven
Kirkcaldy
Burntisland
Inchcolm Abbey
EDINBURGH
Edinburgh Castle
Craigmillar Castle
Dirleton Castle & Gardens
North Berwick
Tantallon Castle
Gullane
Seton Collegiate Church
Prestonpans
Dunbar
LOTHIAN
Bonnyrigg
Humbie
Penicuik
Crichton Castle
Eyemouth
Berwick-upon-Tweed Main Guard
Berwick-upon-Tweed Barracks
Berwick-upon-Tweed Castle
Berwick-upon-Tweed Ramparts
Berwick-upon-Tweed
Norham Castle
Lindisfarne Priory
Lauder
Peebles
BORDERS
Etal Castle
Galashiels
Smailholm Tower
Innerleithen
Melrose Abbey
Kelso
Belford
Newtown St Boswells
Dryburgh Abbey
Selkirk
Dunstanburgh Castle
Jedburgh
Jedburgh Abbey & Visitor Centre
Hawick
Alnwick
Edlingham Castle
Warkworth Hermitage
Amble
Warkworth Castle
Hermitage Castle
221
Brinkburn Priory
DUMFRIES AND GALLOWAY
Kielder
Otterburn
NORTH SEA
ASHINGTON
Black Middens Bastle House
Morpeth
Newbiggin-by-the-Sea
Langholm
NORTHUMBERLAND
Blyth
St. Paul's Monastery & Bede's World Museum
Belsay Hall
Tynemouth Priory & Castle
Aydon Castle
NEWCASTLE UPON TYNE
Tynemouth
Lanercost Priory
Hadrian's Wall See Map Pages 166-167
SOUTH SHIELDS
Longtown
Annan
Gretna
GATESHEAD
Prudhoe Castle
TYNE & WEAR
Brampton
Haltwhistle
Haydon Bridge
Hylton Castle
Carlisle Castle
Wetheral Priory Gatehouse
Derwentcote Steel Furnace
Bessie Surtees House
SUNDERLAND
CARLISLE
Wetheral
Consett
Finchale Priory
Wigton
Alston
DURHAM
Peterlee
CUMBRIA
HARTLEPOOL
Auckland Castle Deer House
Spennymoor
CLEVELAND
Penrith Castle
Mayburgh Earthwork
PENRITH
DURHAM
Brougham Castle
Newton Aycliffe
Billingham
Redcar
Keswick
Clifton Hall
Countess Pillar
Piercebridge Roman Bridge
Barnard Castle
Barnard Castle
STOCKTON-ON-TEES
Brotton
Castlerigg Stone Circle
Arthur's Round Table
Appleby-in-Westmorland
MIDDLESBROUGH
Shap Abbey
Brough Castle
Bowes
DARLINGTON
Gisborough Priory
Brough
Bowes Castle
Egglestone Abbey
Great Ayton
Hardknott Roman Fort
Ambleside
Tebay
Stanwick Iron Age Fortifications
NORTH YORKS.
Richmond
Ambleside Roman Fort
Catterick
Mount Grace Priory
Windermere
Richmond Castle
Northallerton
Coniston
Easby Abbey
Kendal
218
A1
A92
A7
A68
A697
A698
A6105
A703
A721
A72
A708
A6088
A74
A74(M)
A75
A6071
A69
A6127(M)
A1068
A696
A686
A689
A596
A595
A591
A66
A6
M6
A1(M)
A19
A167
A172
A685
A590
A683
M8
M9

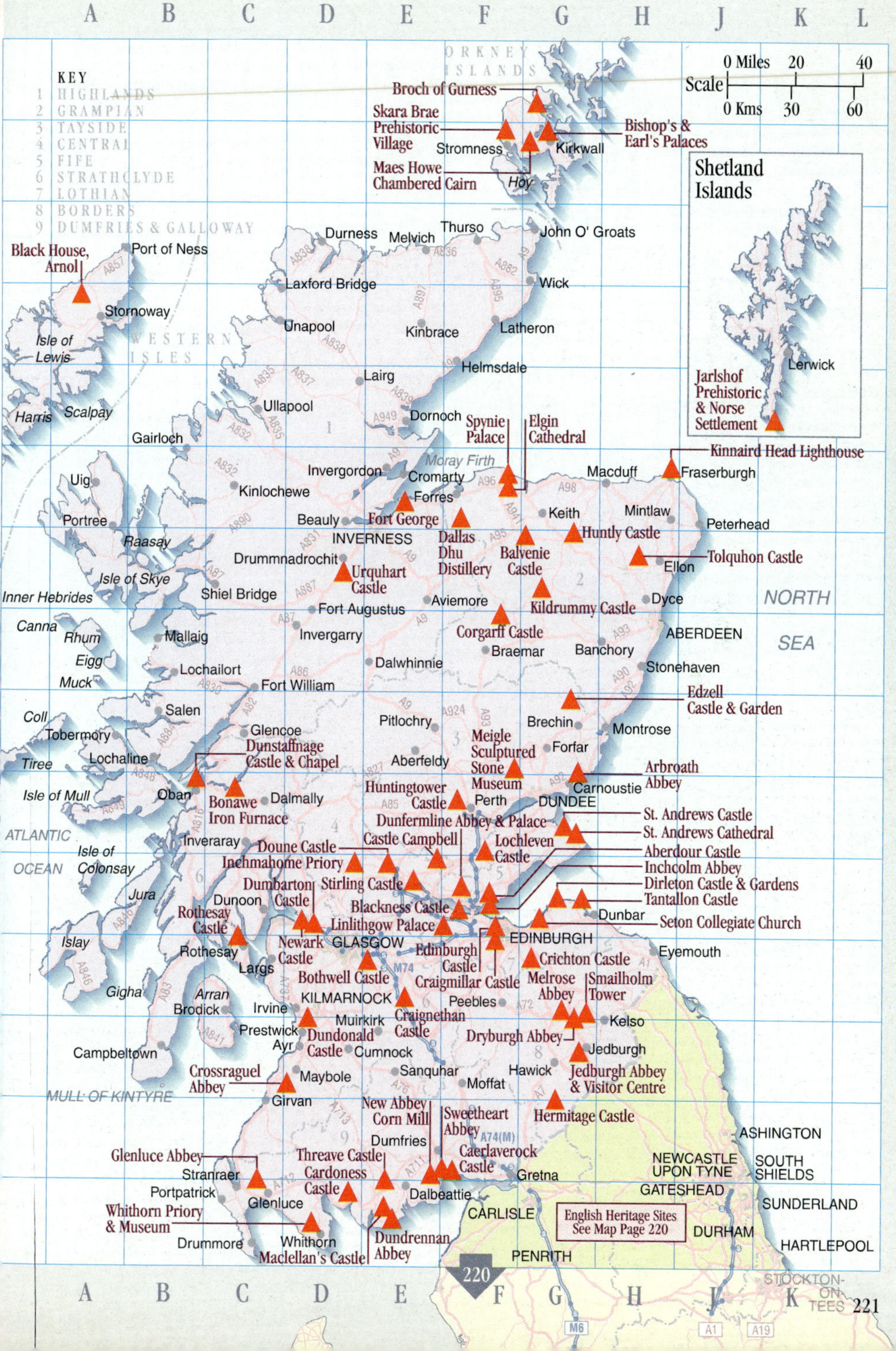

KEY
1 HIGHLANDS
2 GRAMPIAN
3 TAYSIDE
4 CENTRAL
5 FIFE
6 STRATHCLYDE
7 LOTHIAN
8 BORDERS
9 DUMFRIES & GALLOWAY
Scale
0 Miles 20 40
0 Kms 30 60
ORKNEY ISLANDS
Broch of Gurness
Skara Brae Prehistoric Village
Bishop's & Earl's Palaces
Stromness
Kirkwall
Maes Howe Chambered Cairn
Hoy
Shetland Islands
Lerwick
Jarlshof Prehistoric & Norse Settlement
Durness
Melvich
Thurso
John O' Groats
Black House, Arnol
Port of Ness
Laxford Bridge
Wick
Stornoway
Unapool
Kinbrace
Latheron
Isle of Lewis
WESTERN ISLES
Helmsdale
Lairg
Harris
Scalpay
Ullapool
Dornoch
Spynie Palace
Elgin Cathedral
Gairloch
Moray Firth
Kinnaird Head Lighthouse
Invergordon
Cromarty
Macduff
Fraserburgh
Uig
Kinlochewe
Forres
Keith
Mintlaw
Portree
Beauly
Fort George
Dallas Dhu Distillery
Huntly Castle
Peterhead
Raasay
INVERNESS
Balvenie Castle
Tolquhon Castle
Drumnadrochit
Ellon
Isle of Skye
Urquhart Castle
Kildrummy Castle
Dyce
Inner Hebrides
Shiel Bridge
Fort Augustus
Aviemore
NORTH SEA
Canna
Rhum
Mallaig
Invergarry
Corgarff Castle
ABERDEEN
Eigg
Braemar
Banchory
Muck
Lochailort
Dalwhinnie
Stonehaven
Fort William
Edzell Castle & Garden
Salen
Pitlochry
Brechin
Coll
Tobermory
Glencoe
Meigle Sculptured Stone Museum
Montrose
Tiree
Lochaline
Dunstaffnage Castle & Chapel
Aberfeldy
Forfar
Arbroath Abbey
Isle of Mull
Oban
Bonawe Iron Furnace
Dalmally
Huntingtower Castle
Carnoustie
Perth
DUNDEE
St. Andrews Castle
St. Andrews Cathedral
ATLANTIC OCEAN
Dunfermline Abbey & Palace
Isle of Colonsay
Inveraray
Doune Castle
Castle Campbell
Lochleven Castle
Aberdour Castle
Inchmahome Priory
Inchcolm Abbey
Jura
Dumbarton Castle
Stirling Castle
Dirleton Castle & Gardens
Dunoon
Tantallon Castle
Rothesay Castle
Blackness Castle
Dunbar
Linlithgow Palace
Seton Collegiate Church
Islay
Rothesay
Newark Castle
GLASGOW
EDINBURGH
Largs
Edinburgh Castle
Crichton Castle
Eyemouth
Bothwell Castle
Craigmillar Castle
Melrose Abbey
Smailholm Tower
Gigha
Arran
KILMARNOCK
Peebles
Brodick
Irvine
Craignethan Castle
Kelso
Prestwick
Muirkirk
Dryburgh Abbey
Ayr
Dundonald Castle
Cumnock
Jedburgh
Campbeltown
Crossraguel Abbey
Sanquhar
Hawick
Jedburgh Abbey & Visitor Centre
Maybole
Moffat
MULL OF KINTYRE
Girvan
New Abbey Corn Mill
Sweetheart Abbey
Hermitage Castle
ASHINGTON
Dumfries
Caerlaverock Castle
Glenluce Abbey
Threave Castle
NEWCASTLE UPON TYNE
SOUTH SHIELDS
Stranraer
Cardoness Castle
Gretna
Portpatrick
Glenluce
Dalbeattie
GATESHEAD
Whithorn Priory & Museum
CARLISLE
English Heritage Sites See Map Page 220
SUNDERLAND
Drummore
Whithorn
Dundrennan Abbey
DURHAM
HARTLEPOOL
Maclellan's Castle
PENRITH
220
STOCKTON-ON-TEES
M6
A1
A19

Index

Scotland

Index

Wales

Isle of Man

Acknowledgements

Thanks are due to the following for permission to reproduce illustrations:

Salisbury and South Wiltshire Museum: 34 centre and bottom, 48 top.
By Courtesy of The National Portrait Gallery, London: 38 centre, 101 top left.
Wiltshire Archaelogical & Natural History Society (Devizes Museum): 44 top, centre.
West Air Photography: 49 top left.
Wiltshire Archaelogical & Natural History Society: 49 centre left.
Michael Holford: 56 top, 60/61 bottom.
British Library, London/Bridgeman Art Library, London: 59 top inset, 61 top right, 156 top.
Carisbrooke Castle Museum: 64 bottom left and inset, 66 bottom.
The Hulton Deutsch Collection: 73 centre, 160 top.
Dover Museum: 75 top left.
Dover Museum (Ivan Lapper): 74 top.
Copyright British Museum: 81 bottom right, 83 centre, 194 centre right, 166 top.
The Royal Collection © Her Majesty The Queen: 90 top inset left and right.
The Royal Archives © Her Majesty The Queen: 91 bottom.
William Tomkins: 110 top.
Mansell Collection: 134 centre
Terry Ball: 160 bottom.
Carlisle City Museum and Art Gallery: 168 bottom left and inset.
Alan Sorrell: 175 top.

The following original artworks have been based on illustrations from;

Salisbury and South Wiltshire Museum: 34, top.
Sarson and Bryan: 39, top right.
Ray Martin: 52 top.
Miles Daniel: 152 top right.
Carlisle Museum and Art Gallery: 156, bottom left.
Radio Times Hulton Picture Library: 161 centre left.
Vindolanda Trust: 177 centre
Judith Dobie: 191 bottom right.
Karen Guffogg: 191 bottom left.